CW01670489

Buildings Reimagined

A DIALOGUE BETWEEN OLD AND NEW

Buildings Reimagined

A DIALOGUE BETWEEN OLD AND NEW

images
Publishing

CONTENTS

PREFACE

Buildings Reimagined: A Dialogue Between Old and New builds on an increasing body of work that engages with the still emerging practice of building transformation or adaptive reuse. It is an exploration of imaginatively designed interventions that give new life to existing buildings, thereby ensuring their survival and continued usefulness.

The book is a curated collection of contemporary examples of building transformations or adaptations across five continents. While the original buildings are in some cases more than 300 years old, the transformations were completed from 2013 to 2018. Some of the original buildings were designed by revered architects, such as Antoni Gaudí, and some of the new interventions were designed by well-known contemporary practices that include Zaha Hadid Architects and Heatherwick Studio. Some buildings are of an iconic nature, drawing tourists and international attention, while others are more understated and simply embedded in their surrounding built fabric.

These projects were designed using a variety of approaches, but as a collection there are five strategies that emerged as a way of identifying the key design driver of each intervention: architecture as furniture, renovation and insertion, structural modification, external juxtaposition, and reconstruction and expansion. These strategies may serve as a way of understanding and talking about building transformation or adaptive reuse projects and could form a thematic basis for strengthening the conceptual clarity of future interventions in existing buildings.

The strategies and case studies aim to show different ways of generating a conversation between past and present and achieving a balance between memory and imagination. They are about deciding what to value and what to contribute in order to allow for an meaningful dialogue between old and new.

Michael Louw is the director of CMAI Architects and senior lecturer at the University of Cape Town School of Architecture, Planning & Geomatics. His research interests include architectural history and temporality, technology, craft, and design-build practices. Michael co-convenes a design research studio in the master of architecture and honors programs called Adapt! which focuses on adaptive reuse.

Stella Papanicolaou is a senior lecturer at the University of Cape Town School of Architecture, Planning & Geomatics. She teaches history and theory of architecture to undergraduate students and co-convenes Adapt! in the bachelors, masters and honors programs of architecture.

INTRODUCTION

In the twentieth century, during the emergence of the modernist architecture movement, the idea of preserving historical buildings as heritage became more prevalent. The two fields however remained, on the whole and with few exceptions, quite separate. New "modern" buildings were designed by "masters" with a focus on functionality, the future, and often a utopian vision. On the other hand, projects involving historical buildings required the architect to be more humble, scholarly, rigorous, and unquestioning in the assumed requirement to preserve the material of the historical building as artefact.

The field of heritage conservation emerged into a specialization within the discipline of architecture. The architect involved with conservation had less need to be creative, but rather had to be meticulous and loyal to the evidence that told a story of the past. The architectural interventions, if any, were almost always subservient to the historical building. If the historical building was not worthy of such veneration, the option would be to demolish it to make way for a new and better design.

It is predominantly during the recent decades that working with existing buildings has emerged as a potential site for the creative production of architecture, where the focus of the design need not choose between favoring the past or the future, but can strike a mutual relationship between the two. There may be a number of reasons for this shift of interest, including changing ideas in the fields of heritage conservation and sustainability. These stand out as key drivers in the motivation to adapt buildings from the past rather than to conserve or demolish.

There has been a shift in the way in which we understand history. The idea that one should break from tradition, as the modernists believed, no longer holds sway and there is a growing tendency to find continuity between our current condition and the past. Previously, history and tradition were considered separate from our everyday lives. Historical objects were seen as something we should keep in museums, and historical buildings similarly became museums. Ideas from the modern movement stipulated that people's everyday lives should be forward-looking, and design was about being new and more progressive than the past. At the same time, the past was sentimentally considered as being idyllic and anything modern would detract from the authenticity of that often idealized world. Conservation was there to protect and preserve the original perfection of the untainted past.

Today, a growing global understanding of how the past contributes to contemporary culture has led to a more nuanced approach to heritage that allows design to engage it more directly. On the other extreme of heritage conservation, a new approach has emerged that considers the social practices of communities within a given site as heritage, rather than the material fabric itself. This places a focus on the intangible and comes in direct conflict with the concept of heritage conservation and the preservation of material things. Many of the ideas that have contributed to this new approach, referred to as "living heritage," have emerged throughout the Global South where buildings maintain continuity in their function through centuries-long use by the same community.

Overlaid onto these tensions that have emerged out of the world of heritage preservation, is the growing awareness of sustainability. While many buildings or sites may not have sufficient, if any, heritage value, they may be worth keeping for sustainability reasons. This pressure has been the strongest motivator to avoid the demolition of a building with little or no heritage value. Sustainability concerns can refer to the conservation of energy and the reduction of the carbon footprint of developments. It can refer to social realities and the promotion of sustainable livelihoods, as well as to the long-term economic feasibility of a development.

The adaptation of old buildings provides an opportunity to retain traces of history while offering environments that can be cost effective, climatically moderated, and appropriate to the occupants' lifestyles. Adaptation implies the loss of something. It is what heritage conservation in the pure, modern sense works hard to prevent. For an adaptation to be viable in an old building, some of its fabric must be up for negotiation, and the relevance of the past must be weighed equally against the demands of present everyday life.

Introducing a new intervention to engage with an existing structure brings up many rich and interesting issues that the designer must grapple with. While it can offer a range of opportunities, working with an existing building will also involve a series of challenges that often present themselves during the construction phase but must be preempted during design. Furthermore, constraints are imposed on the design by present-day building legislations that in many countries have become more stringent, while the new program has its own demands that must also be met. Challenges and constraints include structural stability, safety measures, thermal and safety standards, and the suitability of old spaces for new programs, which may involve the quality of light, circulation, and new services. These challenges and constraints need to be resolved in parallel with the primary reasons that motivated the decision not to demolish the building in order to make the design viable.

The old building may be retained for a variety of reasons, each stemming from the values placed on it. Cost is often a deal-breaker for clients and using a structure or a shell that is already there and in relatively sound condition can save a considerable amount of budget that may be spent elsewhere. Cost can also be saved on the shorter construction time required in adaptations as compared with new builds.

Existing buildings have embodied energy, and choosing not to demolish may be an ethical choice to minimize the carbon footprint of the project. In some instances, client and architect may agree to look for ways to reduce the carbon footprint of a development. In other instances, it may be that building authorities will impose sustainable criteria on a development in the approval process. Either way, the decision to adapt and not demolish will contribute beneficially, in most instances, to the material sustainability of a development. Reusing an old building presents a challenge for meeting current standards for thermal control and the reduced consumption of nonrenewable resources. Some solutions will include wrapping the exterior or lining the interior surface of the external walls, which presents the challenge of losing something of the historical aesthetic. When the aesthetic of the old is deemed important, the design may introduce an intervention that pulls away from the existing surface. In some old buildings the exterior walls have better thermal qualities than a cost-effective new construction would provide.

In addition to cost implications and embodied energy, buildings always have social value. Social interest in a building may involve a few individuals and for a limited time, or it may be far-reaching, spanning over many years and involving different and opposing groups. A building may conjure up memories, represent an ideology, an achievement, or a sense of pride for a specific group of people. Alternatively, it may represent a lost craft—a way of building no longer in practice—and therefore may hold architectural and aesthetic heritage value. Whatever the reason for not demolishing a building, the designer must take into consideration who values it and why. This will impact on the treatment of the old and its dialogue with the new.

The process of identifying the value of a building is a complex one, as values will not be the same for all stakeholders. This can create tensions and become a potential catalyst for a dialogue in the design decision. In many instances the adaptation of old buildings has led to the gentrification of neighborhoods, which raises land and rental costs and results in the less privileged being driven out of neighborhoods they always knew as home. This aspect of adapting existing buildings has not been addressed in the descriptions of this collection of works and would require deeper analysis to uncover the social complexities before and during the adaptation process.

In the process of design, and in the context of the above reasons for adapting the old, the designer must identify where the value of the building lies, for example its location, materiality, volumes, iconic presence, or architectural language. The value may be physical or it may be intangible. It may be in the detail or in the urban context. It may also be a combination of these.

Often a cluster of historical buildings are valued because of the way in which they have jointly held the edges of a public space for many years, and therefore are crucial to the memories of the place and to its continued use into the future. The height of the building and its architectural language, including colors and façade treatment, may have significance in the character of the public space. If the value lies in the memories associated with a building, the designer must consider how these memories can be represented and expressed in a meaningful way.

Three actions contribute to reimagining an existing building to make it viable for the future. Apart from the retained structure and the new insertion, the design also involves erasure through some degree of demolition: what is removed (this could be entire buildings, large or minor portions of buildings, or material surfaces), what remains untouched, what is modified, and what is inserted. These are design considerations that will add to the character and determine the qualities of the final product. Very little will be removed if the architectural language of the old is valued, and in fact some elements that may have been previously lost may be reinstated. As such, the surface will be preserved. If, however, the materials, craftsmanship, or construction is of more interest—to showcase the aesthetic and tactile qualities of the original fabric of the building—then layers of plaster may be removed to expose what previously was hidden. This is also true where a portion of a building may be cut away to reveal spatial relationships previously not imagined.

The projects in this publication have been presented within five identified strategies. Each example may involve a number of these strategies, but the selection has identified the strategy that best characterizes the dominant approach in the design. Starting at the smaller scale of intervention, "architecture as furniture" has a group of projects in which the old building is valued as found, and the adaptation approach is conceptualized as a separate furniture-like intervention that is juxtaposed within the old envelope, as if it could be removed if no longer needed. Both external and internal façades are valued and preserved more or less as is. This is the strategy that more closely resembles the historical veneration of the old, but it nevertheless has the ability to transform the spaces of the old building and to favor a contemporary way of using space. The second strategy, "renovation and insertion," generally considers the external façade of the building as valuable and in need of preservation, while the interior is transformed within the available envelope provided. The interior takes on a new language that is nevertheless dependent on the character of the old that occasionally is revealed in selected moments.

"Structural modification" becomes necessary when the existing building requires structural assistance to permit an intervention to take place within it. The new structure makes it possible for an intervention either to break free of the constraints of the found envelope and to open up tight spaces within it, or simply to avoid the demolition of the old. In "external juxtaposition," the design of the new is predominantly on the exterior and adjacent to the existing building, and will draw on a range of techniques to create a dialogue with the old. "Reconstruction and expansion" is probably the most radical and intrusive of all five strategies and may include a combination of the other strategies, specifically, but not exclusively, structural modification and external juxtaposition. The intervention is bolder in its interference with the historical building and with its external appearance.

This collection of reimagined buildings reflects a specific approach towards heritage preservation with a range of strategies to achieve it through building transformation and adaptive reuse. In all the projects presented, there is an attempt to find a dialogue that equally values the old and new. They respect and reimagine the old with bold interventions that bring them meaningfully into the present. In many cases something of the old must be lost in order for it to survive, and the new must relinquish some functionality to the existing structure. This relationship between the new intervention and what has been found on site requires careful identification of the non-negotiable aspects of the old that need to be retained, but also necessitates a considered approach in the design of the new to maximize the transformative opportunities that lie in a creative engagement with the past.

STRATEGY
1

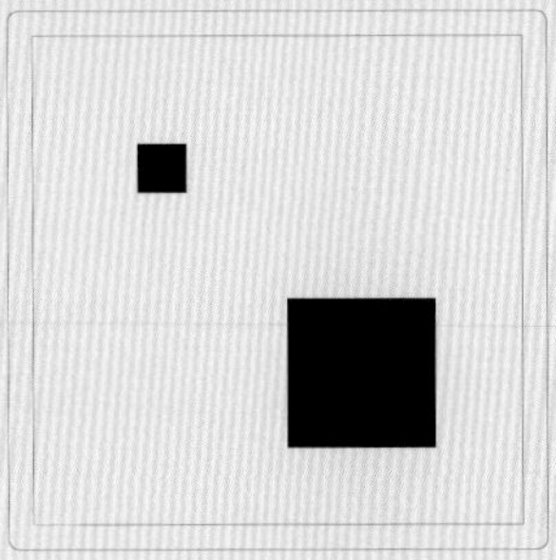

ARCHITECTURE AS FURNITURE

Architecture as furniture refers to internal juxtapositions where a light insertion is distinct from the original fabric. The existing exterior fabric remains mostly intact, and is typically left in its current state (sometimes as a ruin), renovated, or restored to its original design. The concept of architecture as furniture is that it reads as an intervention that is placed inside an existing structure and that it is essentially removable without necessarily impacting the host structure. Spatial qualities are established in the tension between the juxtaposition of old and new.

This strategy is often used when an existing building is large, has a sizeable internal volume, or offers the potential for creating or revealing a sizeable internal volume. Barns, industrial buildings, and former churches lend themselves well to this category of adaptive reuse due to their spacious interiors. This strategy can also be used when a building's existing fabric is valued for its historic importance or aesthetic qualities, and the new insertions are designed with a respectful distance from the envelope of the building.

This naturally results in three typical approaches to the existing external fabric. The first approach is where it can be retained in the state in which it was found, either because it is in good enough condition or because of its aesthetic appeal as a ruin. This requires minimal or no action to the original structure, as was the case for The Waterdog. The former chapel was retained virtually unaltered, and new office and service spaces were stacked in a box-like fashion inside the existing envelope. Inserting a series of freestanding internal functions with little intervention to the existing fabric is often the most economic option if the internal climate is manageable without having to improve the external skin. This approach is often used to create maximum contrast between the old structure and new internal interventions. The second approach is when the external fabric is renewed or restored in order to comply with current regulations in terms of insulation values, fire resistance, and waterproofing, or because of its historical value (in which case any new climatic interventions are usually concealed within the building skin). This is sometimes achieved by reusing materials from surrounding buildings of the same era, as was done at Church Hill Barn. The new insulation was inserted within the roof construction, but the internal and external appearance mimics its original state. At other times contemporary materials that are similar in appearance to the original materials can be used, or an entirely new material can be introduced in order to create a clear contrast between the old and new. The third approach is where the outer layers of the original fabric are removed in order to reveal the materials and construction techniques, as was the case for the rehabilitation of the old railway station in Burgos. Here, remedial work was required in the building skin, and the stone and brickwork were used as a mechanism to generate contrast with the new insertions. What is valued or given prominence in terms of the existing fabric does, however, raise questions about authenticity and whether an existing building's value lies in its form or in its materiality.

Buildings with large internal volumes may need incisions into the existing external skin to allow natural light to penetrate deep into otherwise dark interior spaces. This is usually done in the form of skylights, but where interventions are made in the façade and extend beyond the line of the original doors and windows, the new openings often have large planes of glass that correspond to façade features or proportions. In Church Hill Barn, the existing windows were replaced with new glazing set back from the exterior walls, while larger sections of glass were inserted within the gabled ends.

The new furniture-like insertions often have a sense of removability or reversibility. They are usually designed to contrast clearly with the existing fabric, either through their tectonic nature, materiality, texture, or color. On a pragmatic level, they often have a lightweight nature due to the limited bearing capacity of the original structure; the allowance for new components to be brought in via existing openings; to allow for dry construction; to simplify the building process; and to improve the speed of construction through prefabrication. While it may not always be easy to remove the new insertions, they nevertheless create the impression that they can be removed without adversely impacting the original fabric, which hints at the possibility for future adaptability. Sometimes the "furniture" can merge with the existing building but it retains its sense of being placed independently within the space. The mezzanine floor in DePetrus is a case in point. A new level has been inserted with an entirely different character to the former church. It still seems to have been dropped in as a loose element, although it is structurally attached to the building and will be difficult to remove. However, its clear structural articulation, material differentiation, and the way that it weaves between the columns in the space allows it to be read as furniture.

While the new insertions often create the impression that they do not touch the existing fabric, they do sometimes penetrate the original structure to reveal themselves on the outside of the building. This is either in the form of openings, or in terms of protrusions or external additions that can echo the nature of the internal insertions. The new external works also tend to contrast with the existing exterior, and can be used to mediate the scale between a large existing building mass, such as DePetrus and its surrounding context. Or they can be light, freestanding additions that signal the presence of the adapted interior and its character without overpowering the building's exterior. They also allow the historical streetscape to retain its visual continuity and coherence. While the external additions that are fixed to the existing fabric may impact future removability, like the freestanding additions they generally do create an improved connection to the building's surrounding context and facilitate improved thresholds for buildings with a changed program and public interface.

Arguably, the property that is valued the most in the strategy of architecture as furniture is the internal volume or available space of the existing building. Where there is a large vertical internal volume, as in DePetrus and The Waterdog, the new insertions are usually positioned along the perimeter or moved to one side in order to retain the sense and impact of space. Where there is a large horizontal volume, the new insertions are often arranged centrally to create a series of spaces, such as those in Cotton Lab. In some cases, former cellular divisions can be removed to generate large volumes, as was done in the old railway station in Burgos. Or strategic internal incisions can be made, to allow the new insertions to function as tools that link formerly isolated spaces. These interventions generally influence, or are influenced by, programmatic considerations: The large internal spaces or in-between spaces are usually shared spaces that are reserved for more public or social functions, while the new insertions are reserved for more private functions. The architects of Church Hill Barn describe the new room divisions in the building as "overscaled freestanding furniture," which enable the owners to use the large open-plan space for events and functions. Similarly DePetrus, The Waterdog, Burgos railway station, and Cotton Lab reserve the primary volumes for more public uses. The shared spaces generate a sense of transparency, improve visual connections between different programs, and allow for flexibility of use, which is sometimes further reinforced by versatile or moveable furniture, such as the sliding shelving systems in the library of DePetrus.

Adaptive reuse can potentially be more cost-effective in existing buildings that are in good condition and can remain largely unaltered, or where the existing condition is retained with minimal intervention. This can free up budget to be directed to the new insertions. This targeted, strategic spending means that the new insertions are often treated as finely crafted freestanding "jewels" within the larger space. This contributes to their distinctiveness from the existing structure, and it is the resulting relationship between the new insertions and original fabric that generates tension and spatial complexity. The new insertions can be similar to one another in terms of form and materiality, as was done in Church Hill Barn, The Waterdog, and the old railway station in Burgos. Or they can have very different characters to each other to signal different functions, as was done in Cotton Lab.

The relationship between the freestanding insertions and the external envelope can also be emphasized by the new insertions' service connections to the existing building. In the case of Cotton Lab, the boldly colored service ducts delicately connect the crystalline insertions to the original factory building like umbilical cords. In other cases, services might be centralized, as was done in the Burgos railway station and The Waterdog, as well as DePetrus, where they were concentrated in the new mezzanine floor to reduce the impact on the original structure. In Cotton Lab and The Waterdog the more cellular insertions can be climatized while the shared space can be naturally ventilated, which can also result in cost savings.

The strategy of architecture as furniture is usually strongly influenced by the condition

DePetrus by BURO KADE Architects ©Stijn Poelstra

of the heritage building. Besides the value placed on the internal spaces and envelope, the building's previous program, heritage value, and urban setting, amongst others factors, can influence the decision to lightly touch the original building. These relatively light insertions are often sufficient to generate new life for a building that may otherwise have decayed or fallen into ruin. This is particularly the case in DePetrus, the old railway station in Burgos, and Church Hill Barn. While the insertions can often be bold and visually striking, the projects presented are notable for the respect they show towards the existing building, but without being subservient to it.

CHURCH HILL BARN

Materials harvested from surrounding buildings enabled the restoration of the external fabric of this historic timber barn, while the concealment of insulation layers allowed the existing interior fabric to remain legible. New elements, like pieces of furniture, are delicately inserted into its large internal volumes, while the considered placement of openings provides a connection to the surrounding landscape.

Architecture:
David Nossiter Architects
Location:
Suffolk, United Kingdom
Area:
5640 square feet (524 square meters)
Completion:
2016
Photography:
Steve Lancefield

The site is situated on the Essex-Suffolk border within the landscape immortalized by painter John Constable. It was originally the home farm of the nearby estate, destroyed by fire in the 1950s. A collection of farm buildings form a courtyard, and a large barn of cathedral-like proportions is the centerpiece, offering views over the rural landscape.

The barn complex is the legacy of the model farm movement. It has a cruciform plan with a collection of smaller spaces surrounding it, which sought to provide shelter for different farming activities under the one roof. The barn is a heritage-listed structure and the contemporary refurbishment required lengthy agreements with local planning authorities.

The clients purchased the buildings in a dilapidated condition. David Nossiter had worked on a previous project with the clients and was their natural choice of architect. Having sold their property in nearby Colchester, they lived in a caravan on the site during the build.

A large component of the renovations consisted of refurbishing the roof. Roofing slates and timber materials were salvaged from the other agricultural structures on the site that were too decayed to be renovated. The roof is a "warm roof construction," with the insulation located on

Sections

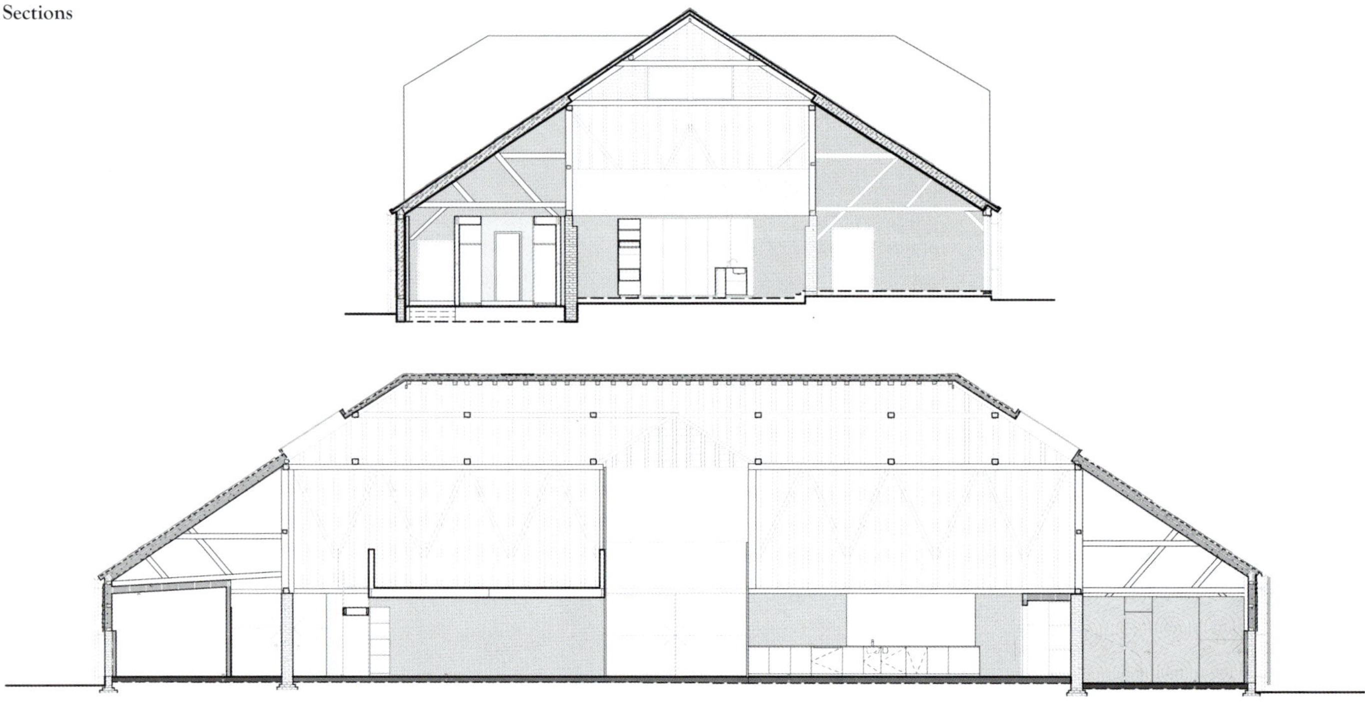

the exterior of the roof above a new timber deck. This allows the existing structure to be viewed internally while still conforming to modern standards of thermal performance.

The external walls were insulated with sheep's wool and clad with larch timber, which has been left to weather naturally. The original openings have simple fenestration with glazing set back from the external wall. Oversized bespoke glazed sliding doors fill the hipped-gable porches, allowing views from the courtyard towards open fields. Two 9.8-foot-long (3-meter-long) roof lights bring daylight deep into the interior of the 29.4-foot-high (8-meter-high) central spaces.

Spaces have been kept as open plan as possible. Overscaled freestanding furniture made with birch-faced plywood serve as partitions and screens and are strategically located to provide privacy for bathrooms and sleeping areas.

Lighting is operated using existing switch boxes—a reminder of the barn's agricultural past—and concealed within the existing structure, existing metal grilles, and new joinery.

Polished concrete flooring flows throughout with 0.4-inch (10-millimeter) floor joints aligning with the spatial demarcation. A biomass boiler is assisted by a mechanical ventilation and heat recovery system that recirculates warm air stacking in the loftier spaces.

The vast main space of the original barn has been retained as a gallery space and the owners have hosted local events, dances, and art exhibitions. Landscaping reflects the internal spaces and is kept simple with wildflower planting and brick paving salvaged from the existing barn complex.

Floor plan

DEPETRUS

A new mezzanine floor weaves its way through the structure of this former church. It is positioned around the periphery of the interior, allowing one to experience the large central volume, and its flowing forms extend outwards to create additional spaces beyond the church's original footprint. The first floor offers new and spectacular views of the church, and sliding bookshelves allow for flexibility of use.

Architecture:
BURO KADE Architects
Location:
Vught, Netherlands
Area:
32,291 square feet (3000 square meters)
Completion:
2018
Interior design:
Jan David Hanrath
Photography:
Stijn Poelstra

The self-consciousness of the Catholics in the Netherlands grew in the second half of the nineteenth century. It was the time of the Catholic revival and the period of the small barn churches was over. Around 1880, Vught was a small rural town, and the fact that a large church like DePetrus was built in such a small town was the result of two centuries of inequality and the Catholics' desire to move forward.

Built in 1884, the church has neoromantic-style elements and is considered a key work by German architect Carl Weber. It has a cross-dome plan with an aisled nave, transept arms, and interior paintings by Charles Grips. The church was given national monument status in 2001.

There was a shift toward secularization in the Netherlands in the 1960s, and the church fell into disuse by 2000. In 2005, DePetrus had to be closed due to bad maintenance. Around that same time, a foundation was formed to find a new purpose for the church. The diocese set the condition that the church must be used for a social-cultural function. The library, museum, and several community services were relocated to the church in consultation with the municipality.

The transformation process began in 2010. The objective was to turn the church into a place for working, meeting, and inspiration; a place for silence, debate, reflection, and knowledge. Transparency and connection

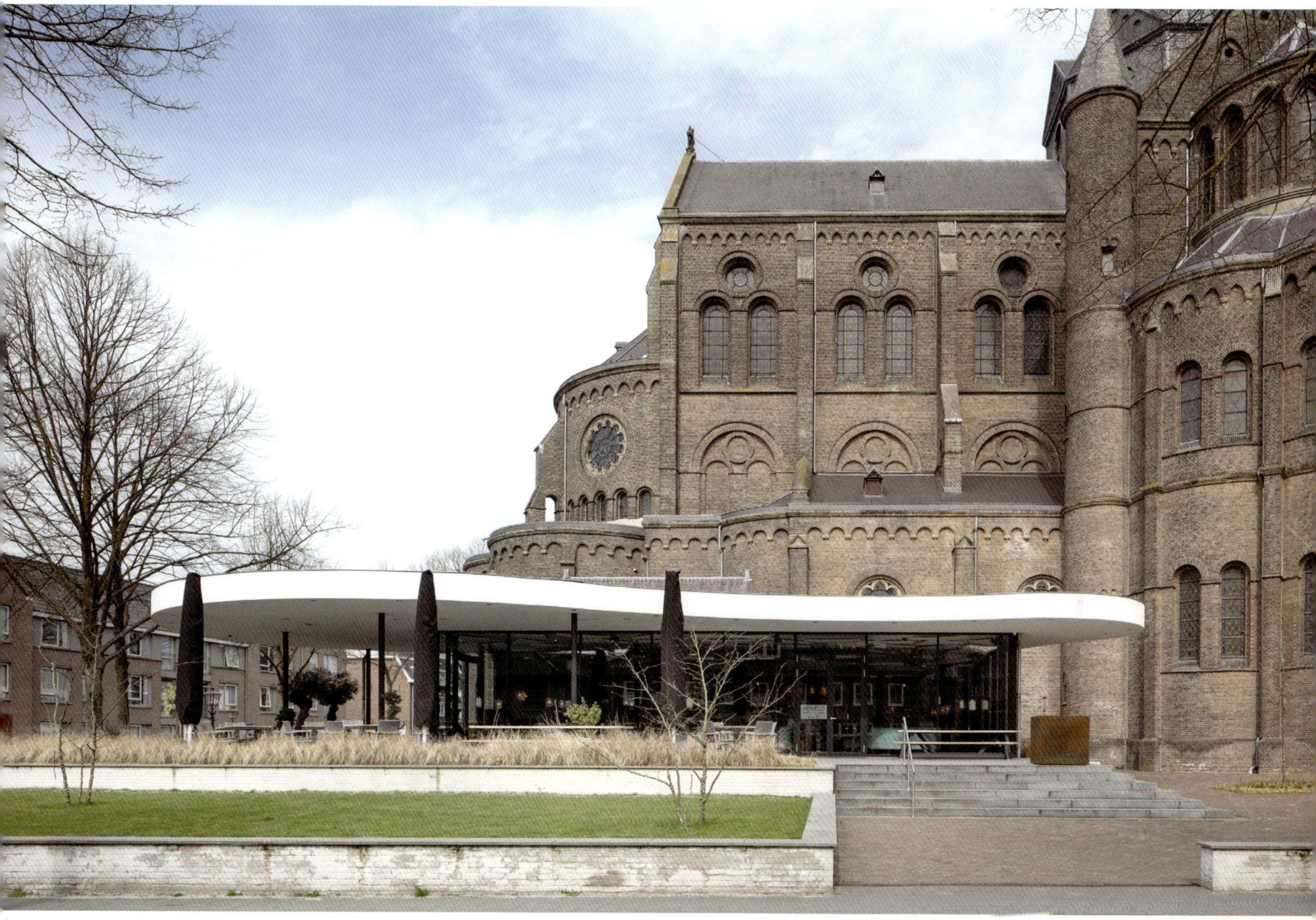

Section

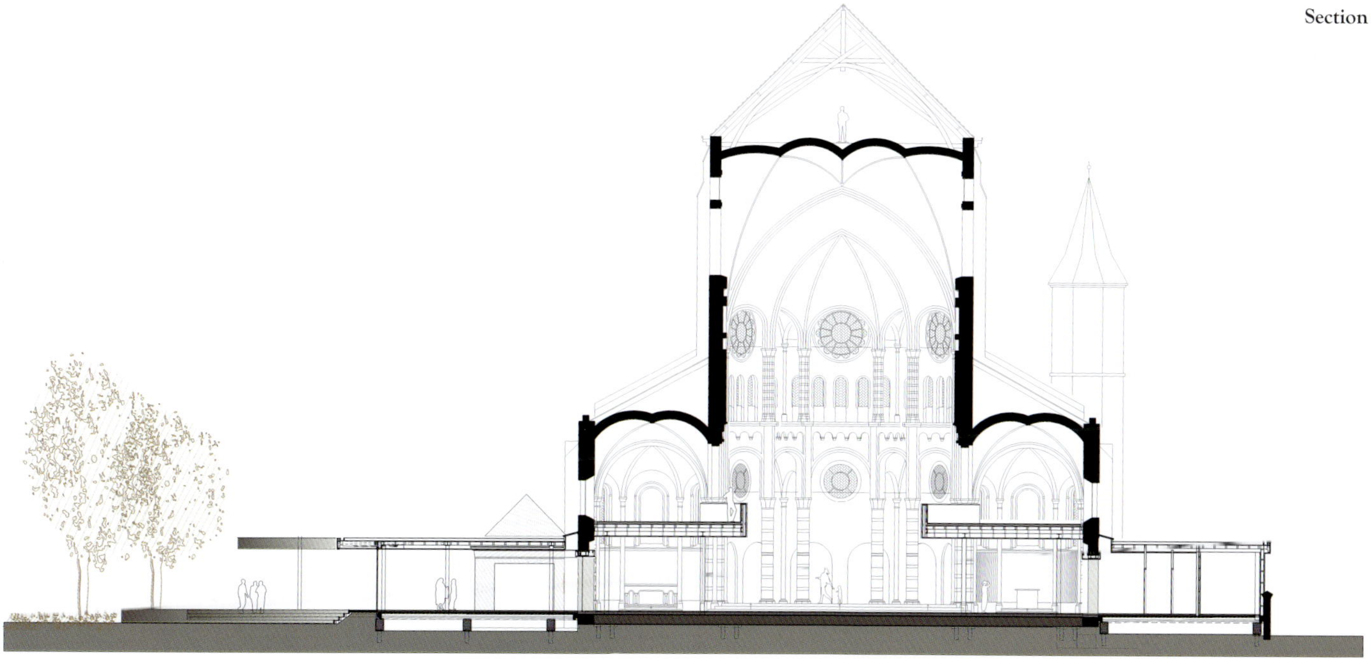

VUGHT 1629

between the different users is very important. The architecture team used the concept of shared space instead of built space to keep the church as open as possible. All users share the same visual identity. This results in a common approach, vision, and philosophy where the architecture is the connecting element.

After an extensive renovation, the church was transformed into a vibrant community center containing a library, museum, bar, and shops. The renovation focused on retaining the original layout of the church. The wide, open interior has been converted into a library with sliding bookshelves, and its attractive design and good facilities encourage people to visit.

All the functions are in the large space, which is open to the public. The mezzanine floor is a distinctive element that gives the church a new identity fitting for its new function. The 5380-square-foot (500-square-meter) floor accommodates a study area and meeting rooms. The mezzanine curves over the aisles to preserve the original spatial quality of the church.

The first floor offers new and spectacular views of the church. The bookshelves are on a rail system, so they can be moved to the aisles of the church. This allows the church floor to be used in a flexible way, providing room for small and large-scale events as well as functioning as a library.

The church space expands outside. The curvaceous mezzanine continues through to the church's exterior, where it forms the roof of four pavilions connected to the façade. There is a restaurant in the garden pavilion on the south side of the building.

VUGHT 1629

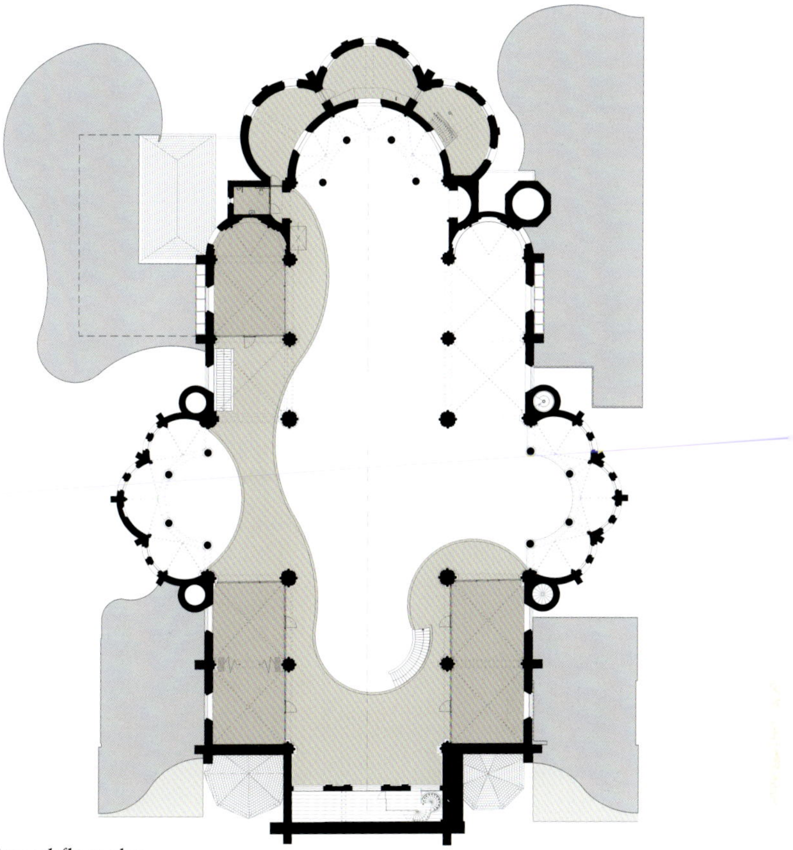

Second-floor plan

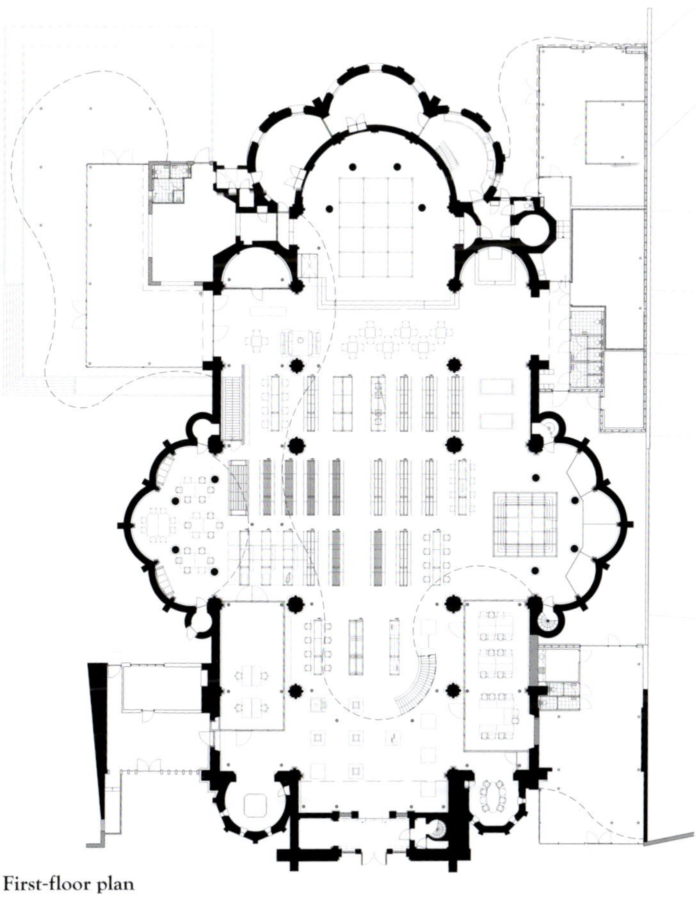

First-floor plan

BURGOS OLD RAILWAY STATION

Considered insertions and incisions adapt this former railway station for its new use as a recreational space for young people. The removal of the internal plaster reveals the building's original stone and brickwork, which creates a distinct contrast with the palette of the contemporary insertions to clearly differentiate the old and new.

Contell-Martínez Arquitectos rehabilitated an old railway station to accommodate a recreational and leisure program intended primarily for children and youth. The intervention extends, on one side, over the station square (the former Travelers Courtyard) as a pedestrian and relational space, and, on the other side, into a boulevard that is where the railways used to be. This intervention seeks to recover the essence of the building, adapting the construction to the new intended use. This is achieved by reinterpreting the space, as well as the physical and visual relationship between the parts that characterize it as an architectural piece.

A new pergola contextualizes and integrates the building. Its shape responds to the new boulevard, and it provides a transition between the scale of the building and the green area, and references the iron-and-glass marquee that protected the railways and the platforms. This pergola now serves as support for the café and it dissolves the boundaries of the building in relation to the wooded area to the west.

The building is structured along a linear axis and is divided into the children's area in the east wing, restaurant and café in the west wing, the administration area in the access space on the old mezzanine level, and a youth area on the first floor. The three towers are joined by walkways with stairs at each end.

The core of vertical communications and services is strategically built into the central body of the building, which allows the individual use of the

Architecture:
Contell-Martínez Arquitectos
Location:
Burgos, Spain
Area:
25,263 square feet (2347 square meters)
Completion:
2016
Photography:
Mariela Apollonio, Maria Dolores Contell and Juan Miguel Martínez

Sections

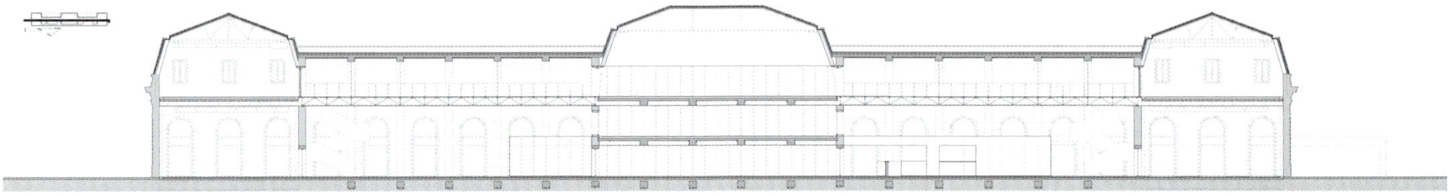

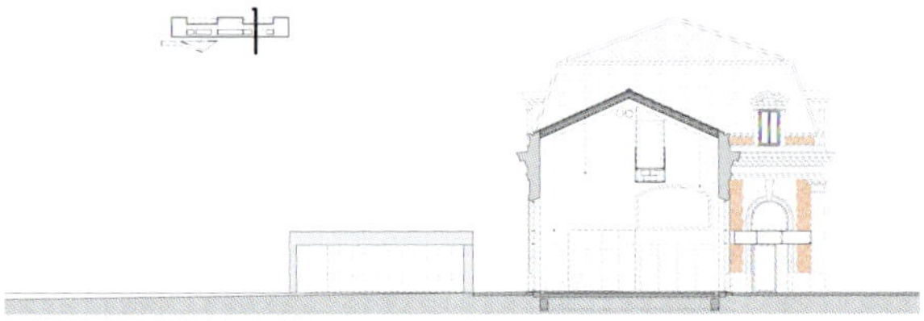

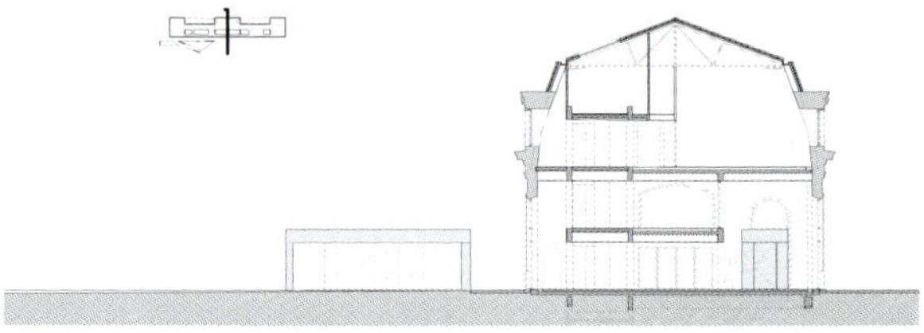

different areas without the need to duplicate communication elements or washrooms. Two canopies penetrate the building, providing access from the station square, and allowing the original space to be recovered. Interior load-bearing walls were taken out on the first floor to achieve a fluid space with visual continuity between the different areas.

The mezzanine slab, which was built in the mid-twentieth century and fragmented the original height of the first floor space, was also taken out. It is only partially retained at the access point from the train station to create a compression of space in comparison to the rest of the building.

New structural porches are generated according to the rhythm of the existing walls in order to support the new slabs and aisle roofs. The upper spaces of the towers are connected by walkways, which are partially supported by the towers' load-bearing walls and partially hung from the structural porticoes of the aisle roofs.

The original structure of the towers, formerly hidden, has been rediscovered. The entire roof was replaced and returned to its original pitch and finished with new black ceramic tiles. All the interior finishes were removed, exposing the brickwork and stonework. This operation, necessary for the rehabilitation of the walls, allows the existing parts of the building to be clearly differentiated from the new ones.

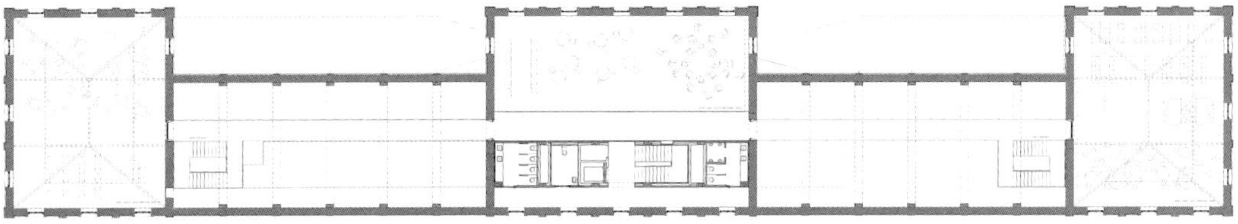

Second-floor plan

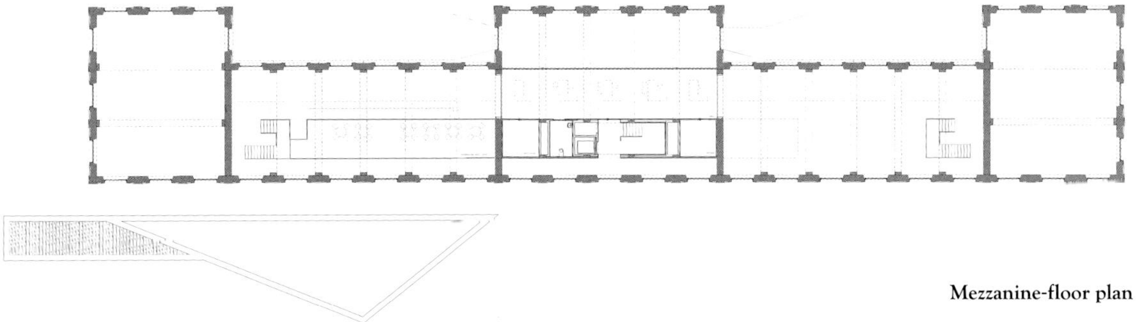

Mezzanine-floor plan

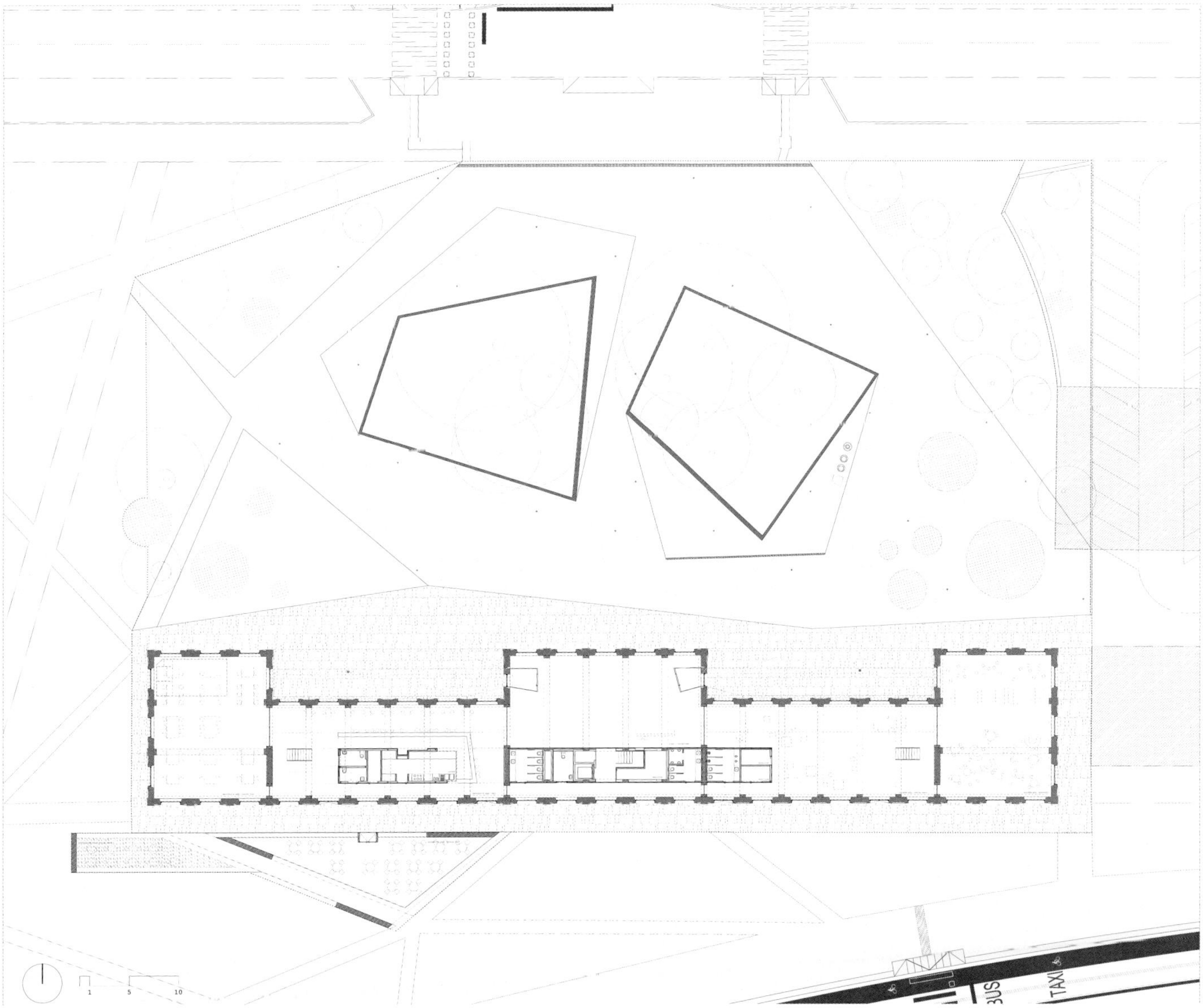

First-floor plan

COTTON LAB

Two distinct and clearly identifiable buildings provide a new retail environment within the large volume of a former industrial factory. Delicately tethered to the enveloping structure, the independent internal buildings have the same profile but differ in construction.

Cotton Lab is located in a former industrial factory in a technology park in Changzhou, Jiangsu. The client had been operating an online clothing store on Tmall and in 2017 they created a store focusing on the aesthetics of clothing and food. They selected a place away from the downtown area to build a new retail environment for the Cotton Lab brand.

In this new commercial model that combines online and offline trading, the virtual store and the physical store have emerged as a display window and a place for experience and consumption. This new internal and external relationship is increasingly prevalent in the design industry in China.

The architecture team faced three challenges: how to coordinate and bridge the gap between the large interior space of a factory and the smaller spaces required for retail and food consumption; how to create an attractive space at low cost; and how to economically make the new space comfortable as the original factory building is simply designed and energy intensive. The architecture team took a "house-in-house" design strategy, building a new independent structure within the main factory building to balance the two major functions.

Two high, transparent chambers run parallel to one another in a north-south direction and have the same profile with a steep and symmetrical double-pitched roof. However, they are different in construction. The chamber for clothing is constructed with a white steel structure suitable for the display of clothing. The other chamber has a steel and timber structure to provide a comfortable environment for food consumption and events.

Architecture:
Atelier Archmixing / Shen Zhuang, Hao Ren, Yu Tang, Jie Zhu
Location:
Changzhou, China
Area:
67,813 square feet (6300 square meters)
Completion:
2018
Photography:
Wu Qingshan, Su Shengliang

棉倉

Schlumberger

The main factory building is naturally ventilated to reduce heat gain, while the two new structures have mechanical ventilation to provide an independent and fully enclosed air-conditioned environment. This application solves the functional problems and serves as a visual tool to anchor the new structures within the larger factory space.

The entrance of the factory connects with the entries of the structures. The space in-between provides an area for sports and various other programs aimed at children and adults. These interstitial spaces evoke public streets or squares where people can wander during their leisure time.

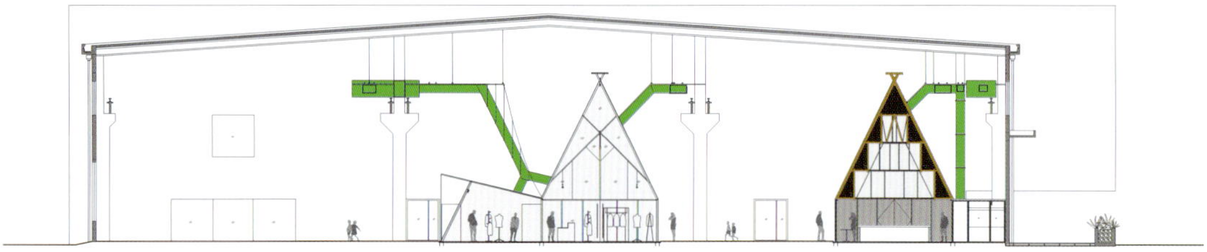

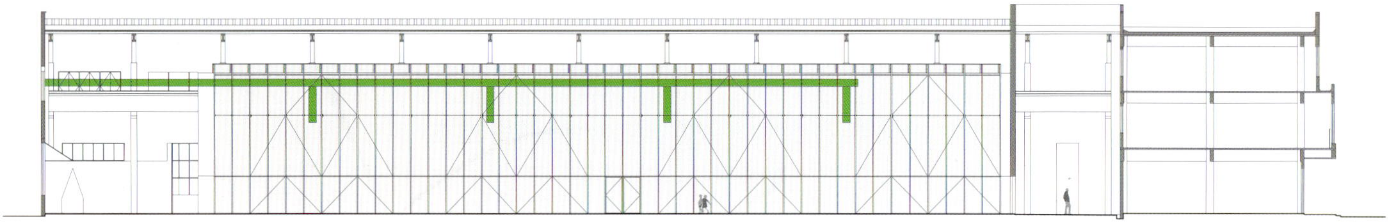

Sections

Floor plan

1. Lobby
2. Outdoor café
3. “Chufan” Restaurant
4. Lecture space
5. “Platform” space
6. Cash
7. Fitting room
8. Clothing retail
9. Baking workshop
10. Device

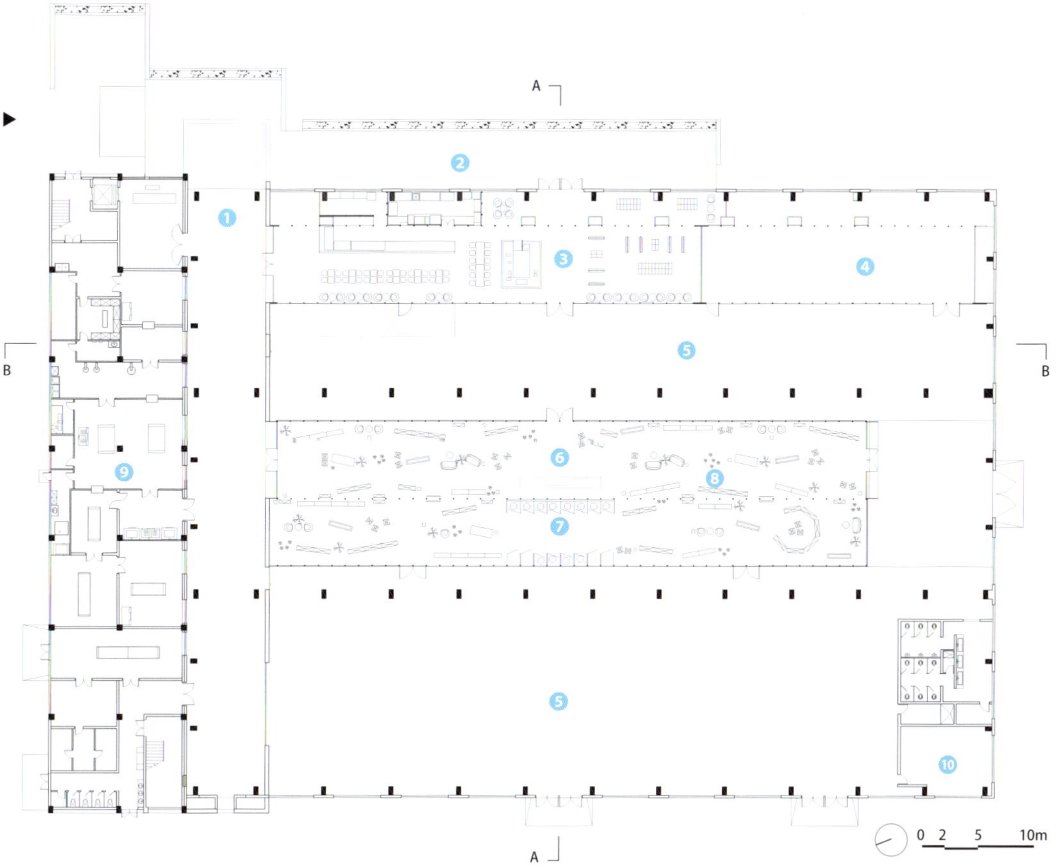

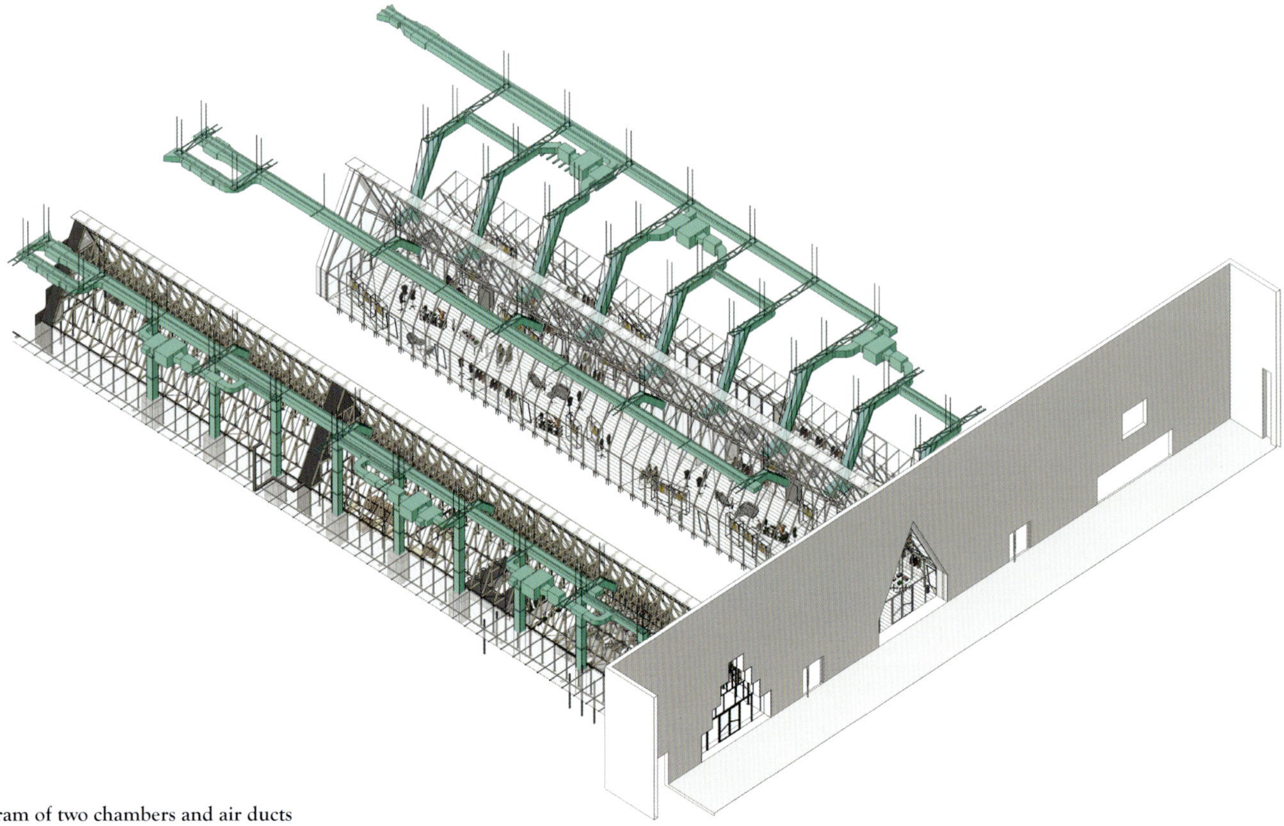

Diagram of two chambers and air ducts

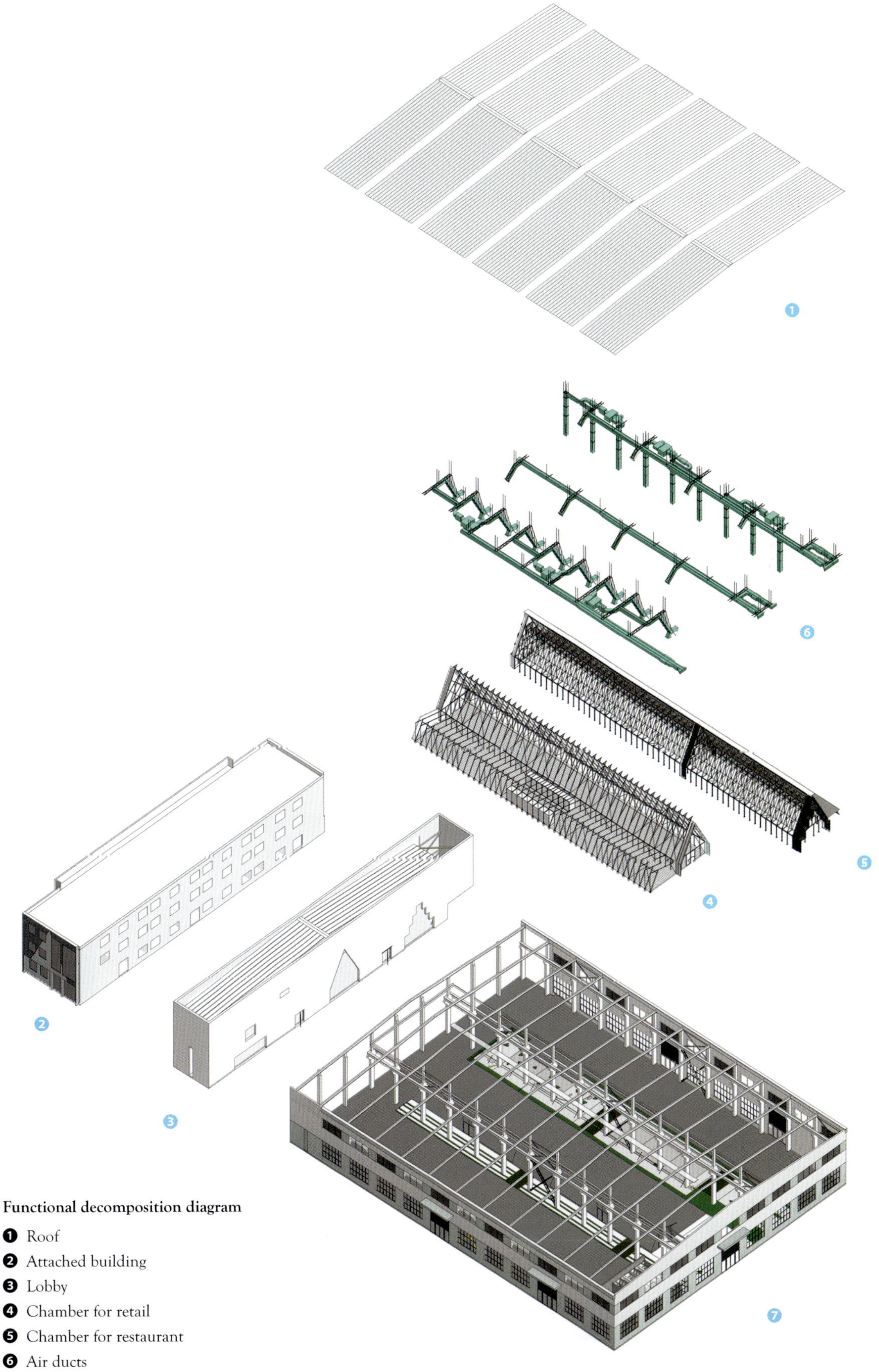

Functional decomposition diagram

1. Roof
2. Attached building
3. Lobby
4. Chamber for retail
5. Chamber for restaurant
6. Air ducts
7. Indoor children's area

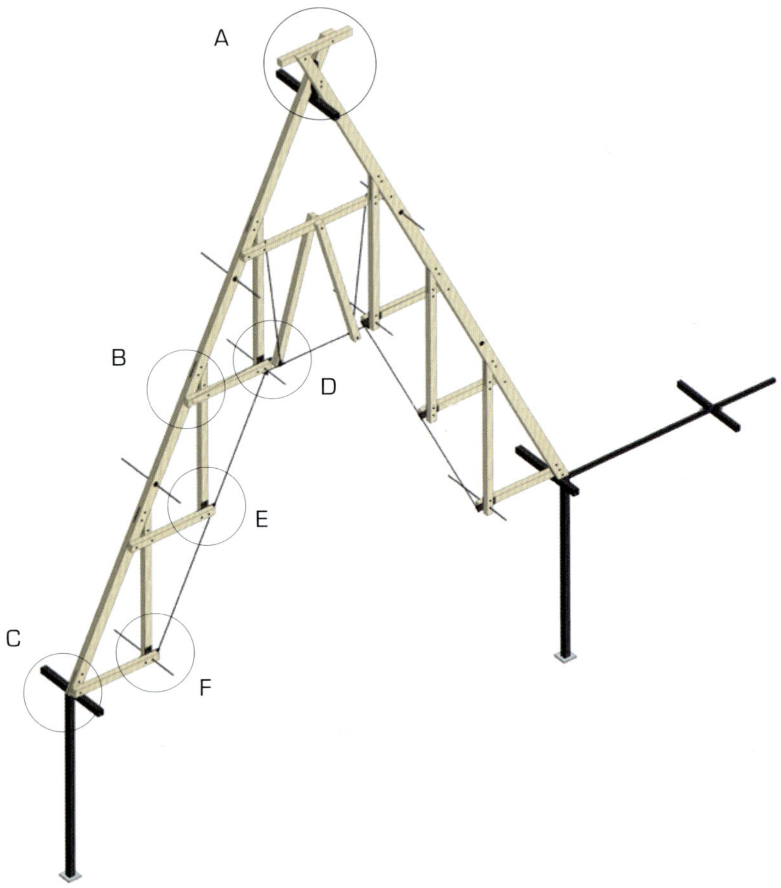

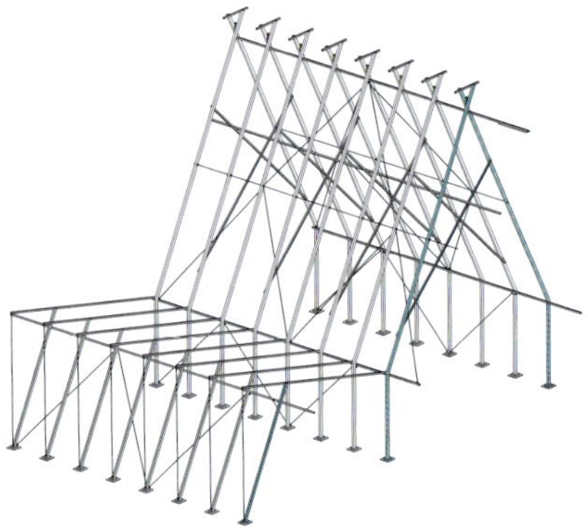

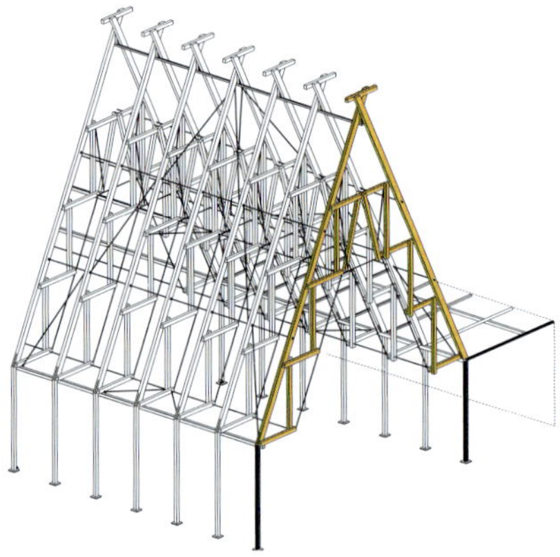

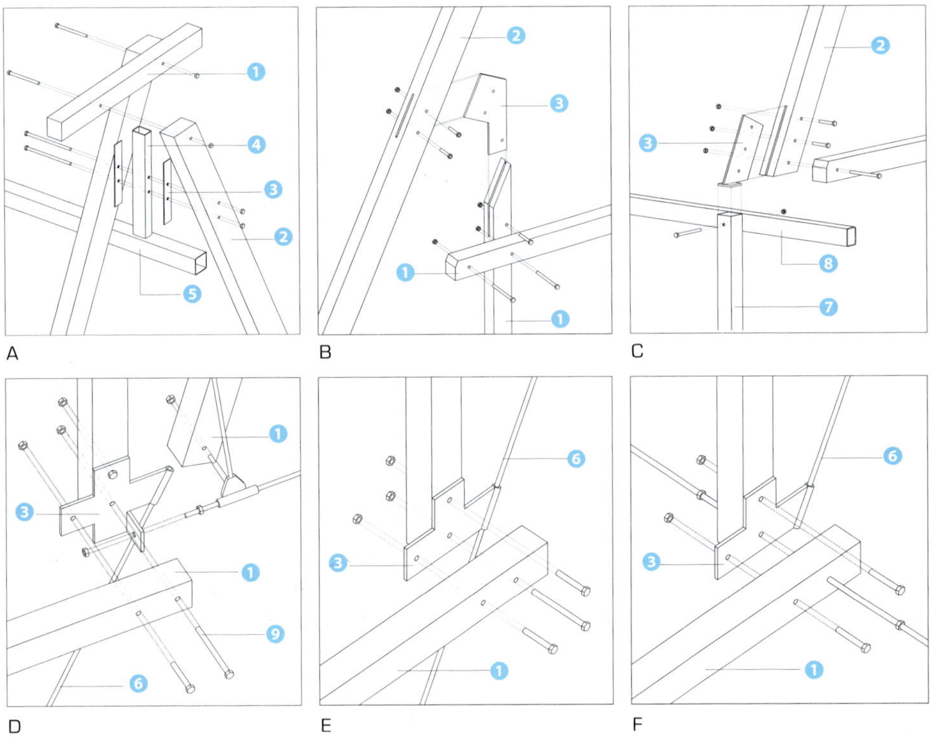

Diagram of restaurant chamber structure

❶ Timber beam 3.5 in × 2.9 in (90 mm × 76 mm)
❷ Oblique timber beam 5.5 in × 2.9 in (140 mm × 76 mm)
❸ Steel joint connector
❹ Steel beam 1.9 in × 2.9 in×0.16 in (50 mm × 76 mm × 4 mm)
❺ Steel beam 1.9 in × 1.9 in × 0.16 in (50 mm × 50 mm × 4 mm)
❻ Steel cable ϕ0.6 in (16 mm)
❼ Steel column 3.1 in × 3.1 in × 0.16 in (80 mm × 80 mm × 4 mm)
❽ Steel beam 3.1 in × 3.1 in × 0.16 in (80 mm × 80 mm × 4 mm)
❾ Bolt

THE WATERDOG

A series of stacked boxes provide offices within this historical building, and sit at one end of the space to allow the former chapel to remain legible. The new construction is independent from the fabric of the original structure, except where it reveals itself as a contemporary metal and glass protrusion through the roof.

The Waterdog is a state-of-the-art workplace in an environment where past, present, and future are inextricably linked. By stacking the offices and meeting rooms, a constant sense of dynamism is created in the workspace.

The Waterdog is the architecture office of Klaarchitectuur. One of the most important requirements at the start of the design process was to reopen the sixteenth-century building to the public. This was achieved by creating a stacked-box construction at one end of the historic chapel, leaving a large and open multifunctional space that can be used for a broad range of activities and events for the community. As such, the building can serve as a source of inspiration for visitors.

The design preserves the building in its full glory despite it being heavily affected by the ravages of time. The design process involved finding creative solutions for the typical challenges posed by renovating a historical building.

It was vital that the building's historical character remained intact due to its heritage-listed status. This was achieved by inserting a new construction within the exterior walls, between the wooden trusses, and integrated into the roof structure of the building. The stacked boxes house the workspaces, meeting rooms, and amenities. They have glass-faced ends for receiving natural light and the the white and black palette stands in sharp contrast to the original building, accentuating the patinated walls, timber roof structure, and gray-tiled floor. The kitchen is located in what was the choir of the chapel—a nineteenth-century addition to the building—and elements are designed as a nod to this former purpose.

Architecture:
Klaarchitectuur
Location:
Sint-Truiden, Belgium
Area:
3229 square feet (300 square meters)
Completion:
2016
Photography:
Valerie Clarysse, Toon Grobet

Sections

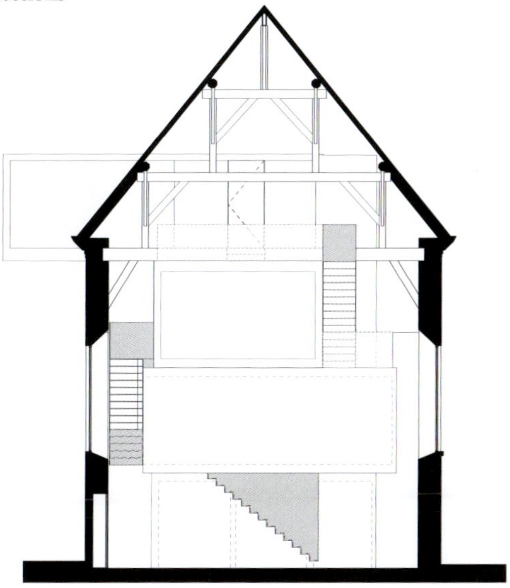

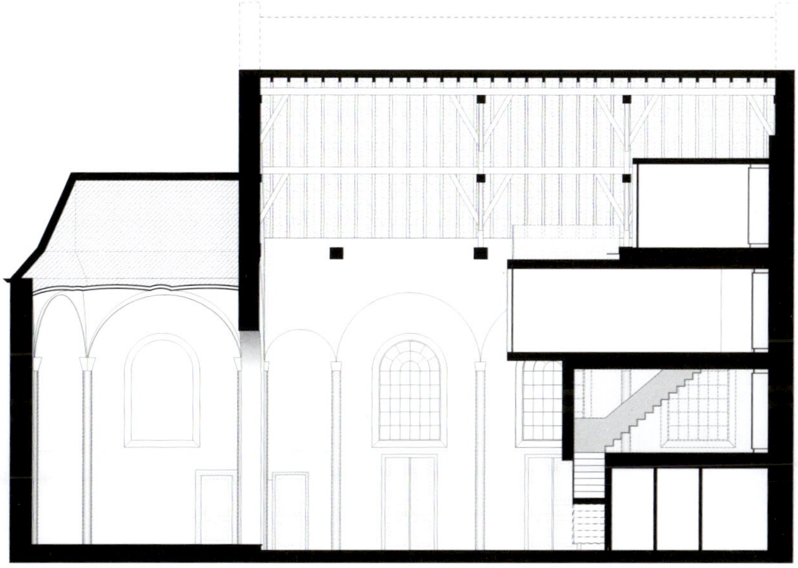

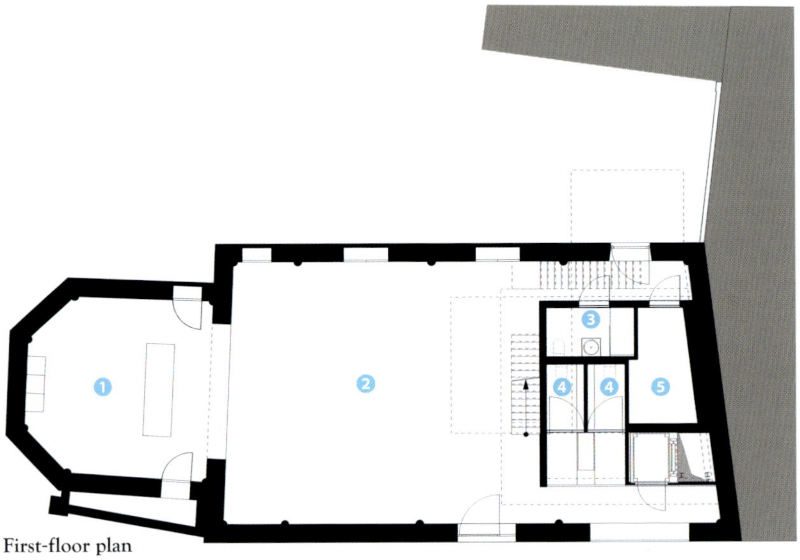

First-floor plan

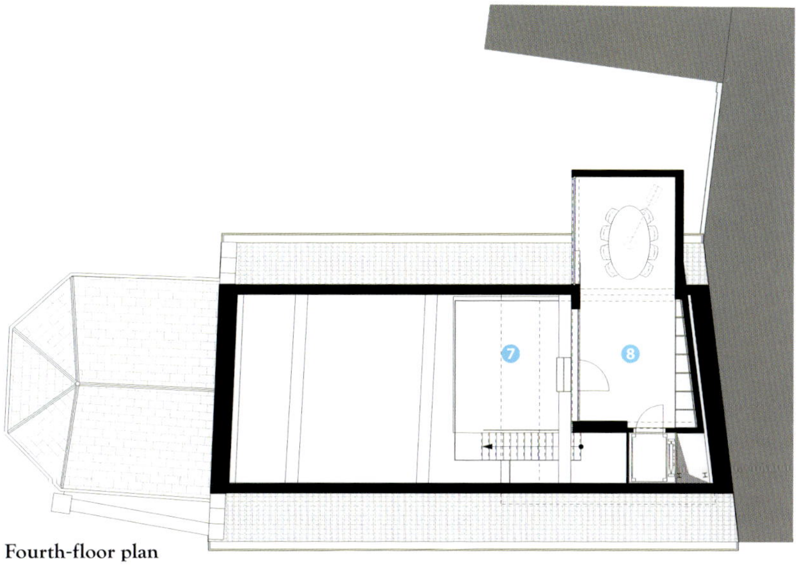

Fourth-floor plan

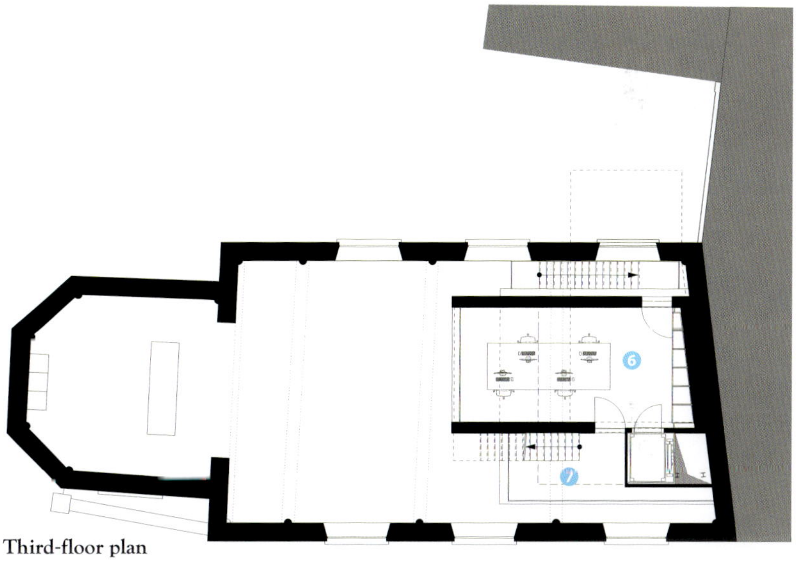

Third-floor plan

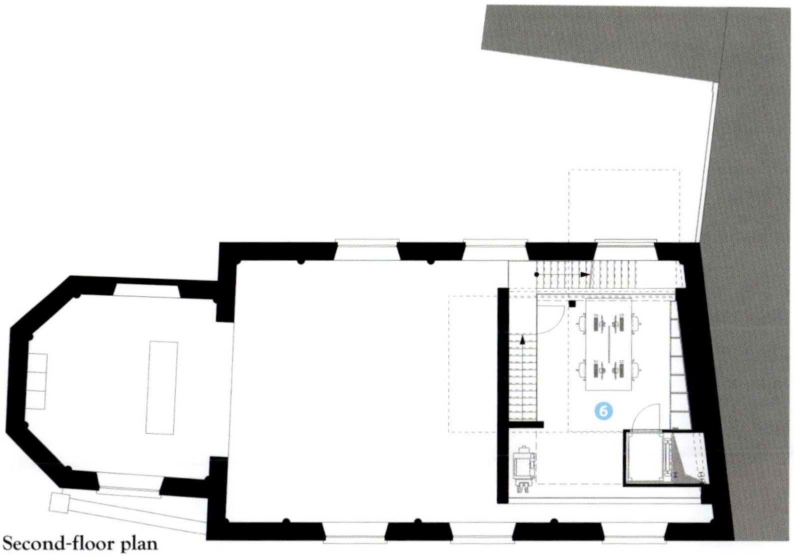

Second-floor plan

❶ Kitchen
❷ Open space
❸ Bathroom
❹ Toilet
❺ Storage
❻ Office
❼ Terrace
❽ Conference room

STRATEGY
2

RENOVATION AND INSERTION

In this strategy, a new insertion lines the interior of an existing structure to accommodate a new function or a new approach to the same function. The intervention can either involve the removal of partitions or floors to open up the space or it can involve the subdivision of a large space into smaller internal volumes. Portions of the existing building might still be legible and the new insertion can be an intentional contrast or it can be a refurbishment using a similar architectural language as the original. The new interior merges with the old one, thereby modifying its character. The original external façade is retained, although it may be renovated or restored.

A key characteristic of this kind of intervention is that the external building envelope is valued, and its authenticity may lie in its form or materiality. This could be because it is part of a larger urban fabric or streetscape that may have heritage value, as is the case with the protected 17th-century houses in Bruges and Three Cusps Chalet. Its value may also lie in the fact that it is a good example of a particular typology of architecture, such as White Pagoda Temple Hutong Courtyard, that can also form part of a particular type of urban fabric or lifestyle. The building envelope may also be valued in and of itself due to its own materiality and construction. In Gouda Cheese Warehouse, which has been transformed into loft apartments, the building envelope is not only valued for its history and aesthetic, but also because of its load-bearing capacity. A building may also have material value because it was designed by a famous practitioner, as is the case with Antoni Gaudí's restored Casa Vicens. Buildings with valued exteriors are often designated as national or historic landmarks, such as Casa Vicens and 660 Congress Street, but they can also have fairly nondescript exteriors. White Pagoda Temple Hutong Courtyard and Three Cusps Chalet, for example, sit comfortably and discreetly within their urban context.

Whether an existing exterior is in a good or bad condition, or whether it has a specific value, will determine how much work is required in terms of renovation. But often "invisible" exterior areas, or portions of a building that are not very visible from the public realm, may be extensively altered. This was particularly evident in the atrium of Gouda Cheese Warehouse, which was fitted with a new glazed roof gently perched between two existing roofs. The internal façades of the atrium were lined with new timber, while the external façades and overall massing of the building were valued and retained. In White Pagoda Temple Hutong Courtyard, previous informal insertions in the central space were removed and new structures added. The renovations of Casa Vicens and the 17th-century houses also had insertions that activated their rooftops, either through the use of cut-outs for balconies or by the inclusion of roof terraces. These external works could be continuations of the internal insertions, for example the new staircase in Casa Vicens, which triumphantly rises to the roof terrace. The form of the staircase is echoed in the landscaping with folded planes and angular planted areas. The external landscaping contrasts with the existing exterior and even though it envelops parts of the building, it creates a space where the original building is displayed as a clearly identifiable object in its own right.

While the exterior may be valued and still be fit for purpose (despite the occasional need for restoration, renovation, or activation), the interior is usually in need of renovation. This could be due to a change of use, such as Casa Vicens, which was transformed from a private residence to a museum. It could be due to extensive damage to the interior, as was the case with 660 Congress Street. Or it could be because of the need for modernization. These different reasons typically have very specific challenges. For a change of use, the need to create new circulation routes often becomes the primary design driver for the insertion. Casa Vicens was meticulously restored on the outside and inside, while a new folded staircase was inserted as a public gesture to link the different levels of the former private residence. Gouda Cheese Warehouse was renovated with a new covered atrium, with elevators and walkways creating a unique experience for residents while providing access to their apartments. Where the reason is due to extensive damage, the remaining fabric may not provide many clues regarding its original form. 660 Congress Street's interior was dilapidated due to abandonment, fire damage, and prolonged water exposure. The insertion of an entirely new interior naturally involves some expense, but it also allows for a certain measure of design freedom since there are less internal constraints. Where the insertion is primarily due to the need for modernization, the challenges could be due to difficulties related to the integration with existing building elements and services, or the need for compliance with changing regulations where some existing items may no longer conform to current building regulations or health and safety norms. There are sometimes spatial opportunities in the existing building and additional interior space can be excavated or activated, for example in White Pagoda Temple Hutong Courtyard where the ground level was lowered, and the ceilings removed to create double-story units with lofts.

As the new and old fabrics merge, their relationship to one another becomes an important consideration. In Casa Vicens, 660 Congress Street, and Three Cusps Chalet, the new insertions are deliberately designed to contrast with the existing fabric in terms of form, materiality, color, and texture. In Cathedral of Szeged and White Pagoda Temple Hutong Courtyard, the new insertions have materials that are clearly distinguishable from the original ones, but the aim was not to create a deliberate juxtaposition. In Casa Vicens, much of the original detailing, which was predominantly constructed out of papier-mâché, contrasts with the new staircase, which is itself somehow reminiscent of undecorated papier-mâché or origami. The contrasting insertion merges with the existing interior to create a new hybrid aesthetic. The two layers are clearly identifiable while

660 Congress Street by PRESENT Architecture ©Robert Deitchler

forming a single entity with thresholds that are sometimes clear and sometimes blurred. Even though the old and new have very different characters, and while the new is not shy or understated, it is nevertheless respectful of the old because of its contrasting calmness, which gives the old the chance to shine without interference or ambiguity. Similarly, in the 17th-century houses, the new is threaded through the building with fragments of the old used as structuring elements that are juxtaposed with the new.

In contrast with Casa Vicens and the 17th-century houses in Bruges, where the existing interior is visible, 660 Congress Street's interior was destroyed by fire and its form had to be inferred by reading the remaining exterior fabric. This reading of an existing building becomes important not just to determine its value, but in some cases to determine its future. The interior volumes in 660 Congress Street were generated by the shape of the mansard roof, while the existing façade was also projected inwards spatially, and the existing openings influenced the planning. The insertion is visually similar to Casa Vicens with its folded and contrasting white planes, but it is an almost completely new intervention in an existing shell (which was also painstakingly restored), and the contrast is primarily visible from the outside where the interior can be seen, like a diorama, through the old. Like 660 Congress Street, Three Cusps Chalet's exterior was also renovated, and a new interior inserted. The layout was influenced by the external level differences, which were essentially projected inwards. Like many other adaptations, the staircase is a key feature that, together with a strategically placed skylight, allows daylight to filter deep into the building. It also allows for the interpenetration of spaces where different rooms are visually and spatially connected with each other.

Because of the merged nature of these designs, the new insertions will not be easy to remove in the future and they inscribe an additional layer onto the existing building. In terms of layering, there are also a number of approaches. For the first approach, the oldest and most original layer is typically valued, but intermediate layers or subsequent insertions, such as those added in Casa Vicens or White Pagoda Temple Hutong

Courtyard after its original completion, may be removed to create a dialogue between the first and latest authors only, instead of allowing a multiplicity of voices. This removal of layers may also reveal unexpected things, for example the luster of the lapis lazuli vaulting that was renewed after cleaning in Casa Vicens, or the Qing dynasty stones that were found in shallow excavation of White Pagoda Temple Hutong Courtyard. These removed layers and exposed objects can be used in the new insertions, serving as an acknowledgement of their inherent material value. The stones discovered in White Pagoda Temple Hutong Courtyard were installed as features, and gray tiles found during the demolition of previous insertions in the courtyard space were also reused. In other cases, such as the 17th-century houses in Bruges, all the previous layers are valued in situ, and the latest intervention is regarded as one of many. But older layers can also be retained as strategic features as in Gouda Cheese Warehouse, where cheese boards and cheese shelves have been repurposed. Some projects, like Cathedral of Szeged, take the layered approach a step further and have layers within layers. Here it is sometimes difficult to distinguish the hand of the new architects from previous ones. This is especially challenging due to the continuing practice of borrowing from and reinterpreting the old. The Cathedral of Szeged was originally designed and built using a variety of traditional and modern styles and construction systems, while the latest interventions similarly make use of a variety of approaches. In some instances, the clearly contemporary additions contrast with the old, and in some cases the old was adapted to make it seem more contemporary. The new sleek white plaster in the crypt is a case in point. The multilayered approach often results in a more challenging reading of a building and it can create a blurring of old and new, while a more purist approach can result in improved legibility, but also includes a measure of erasure of the past.

In renovation and insertion, the old is sometimes used to frame the new, or the new creates a stage set for the old. In 660 Congress Street and Three Cusps Chalet, the old façade frames the new interior. In Gouda Cheese Warehouse, existing building forms frame the new atrium on section, while in White Pagoda Temple Hutong Courtyard, the new interventions are framed by the older courtyard's form on plan. In Cathedral of Szeged, the 17th-century houses, and Casa Vicens, new insertions provide a stage for the old, or a platform from which to view the old. Some renovations and insertions suggest new ways of inhabiting familiar spaces. Gouda Cheese Warehouse introduced a new dwelling type into the area and was well received, while White Pagoda Temple Hutong Courtyard reconceptualized courtyard life for a modern generation. In all cases, however, the new and old become inextricably linked to form a new hybrid condition.

CASA VICENS

Architecture:

Martínez Lapeña - Torres Arquitectos, Daw Office

Location:

Barcelona, Spain

Area:

13,336 square feet (1239 square meters)

Completion:

2017

Photography:

Pol Viladoms · Casa Vicens

Buildings by famous designers, especially ones with such an exuberant character as Casa Vicens by Antonio Gaudí, can often be challenging to adapt. A new origami-like staircase replaces the phantom of Gaudí's original staircase, and the new work is clearly differentiated but engages with the old on equal footing.

Casa Vicens, built in 1885, is the first house designed by architect Antoni Gaudí. Joan Baptista Serra de Martínez extended the house in 1925, transforming the single-family summer residence into three dwellings with one per floor. Between 1935 and 1964, the house underwent several further changes, which significantly modified the northeast façade and made it difficult to understand what the original building looked like. Casa Vicens was declared a UNESCO World Heritage site in 2005, and opened to the public as a museum in 2017 following the restoration.

The restoration seeks to recover and showcase Gaudí's original work, including the façade and interior, as well as most of Martínez's additional work. The later extensions were demolished in the restoration, all of the inner parts removed, and a new staircase and elevator introduced.

The new staircase meets the current building codes and replaces the phantom of Gaudí's original staircase. It occupies the central heart of the building and relates Gaudí's original design to the volume added in 1925. The landings lead to the original Casa Vicens rooms and the new staircase swells polygonally into the twentieth-century floors. The stair emerges on the roof as a new and complementary geometrical addition to the Moorish style of the house.

This is the project in which Gaudí designed his first passable roof. This is where visitors can observe the influence of Moorish architecture in the corner domes and towers. The restoration process waterproofed the roof and repaired all roof elements.

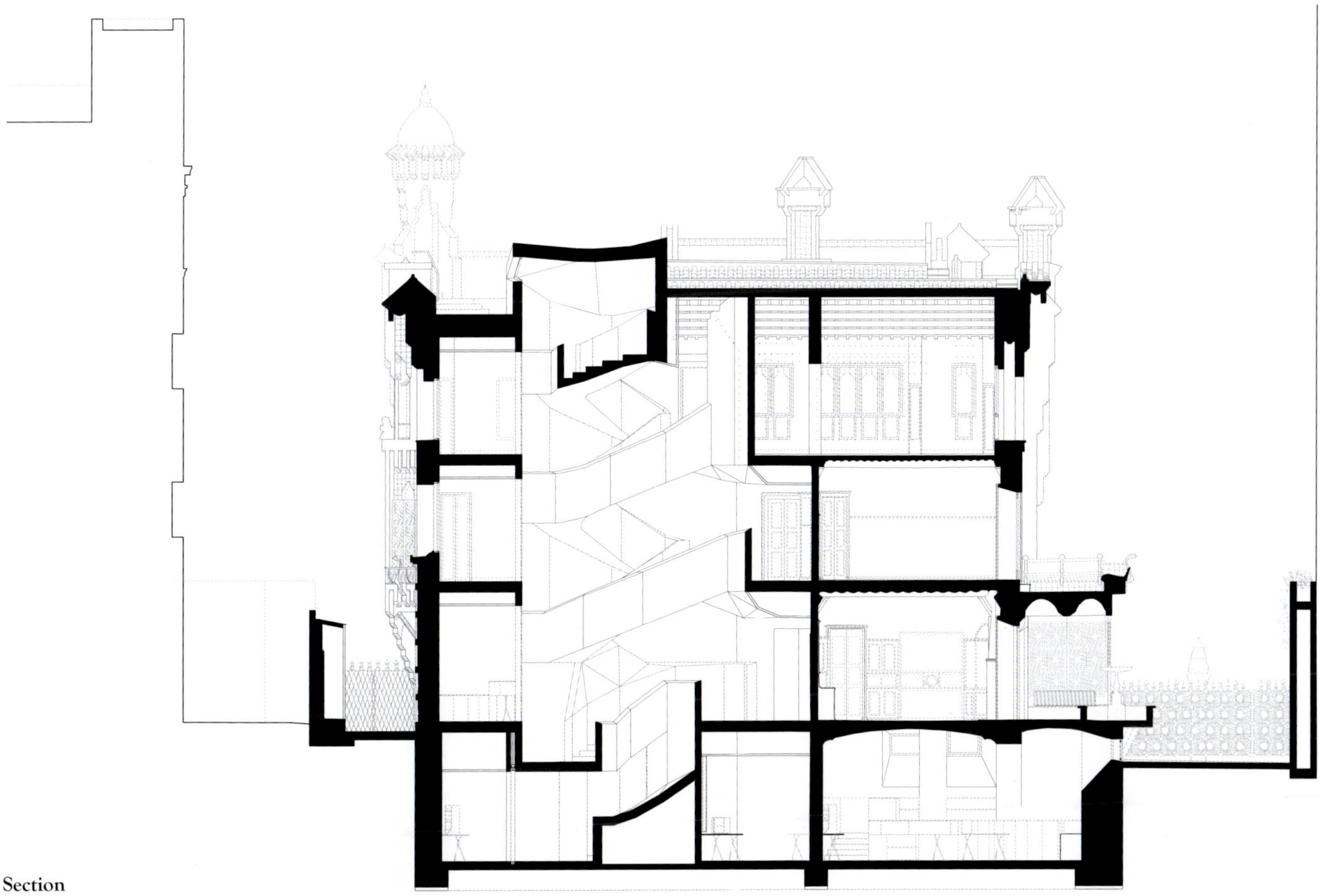

Section

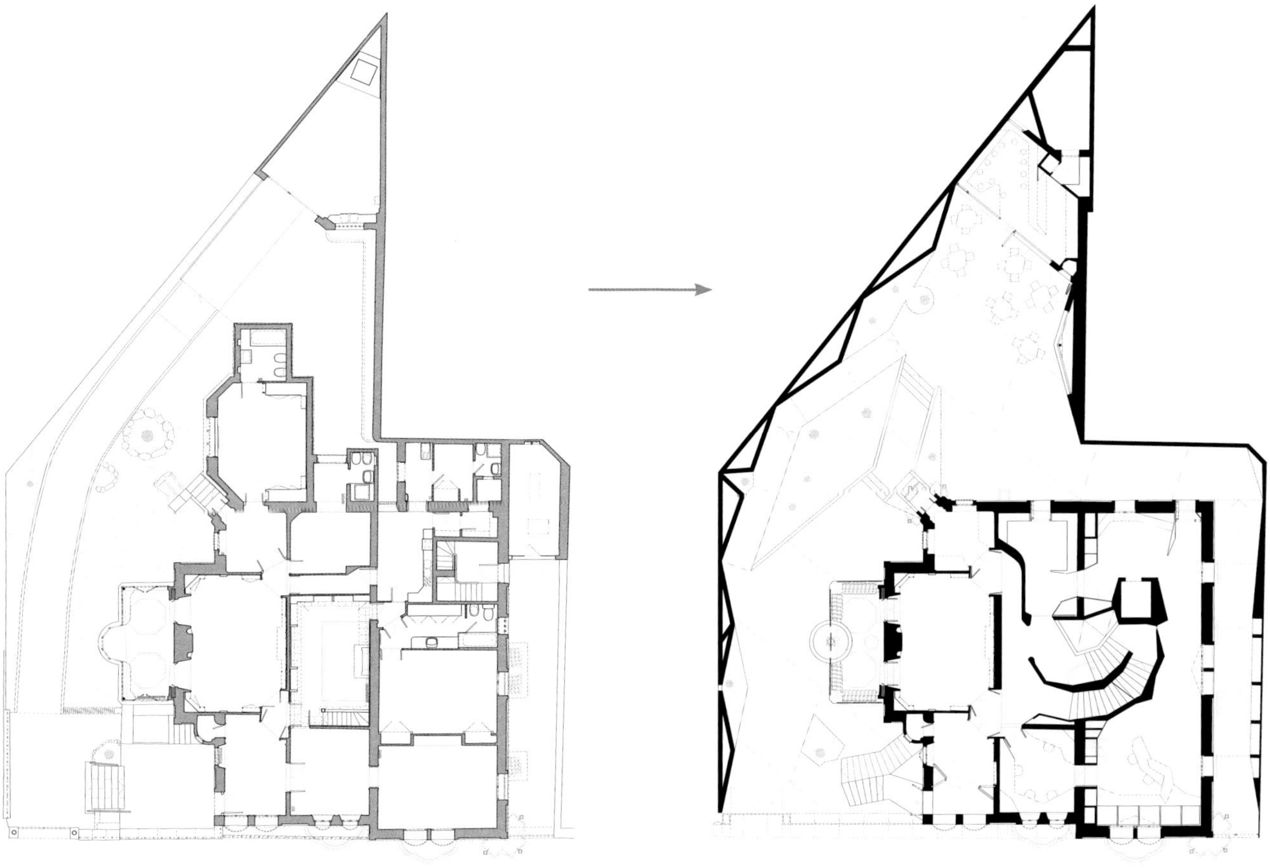

First-floor plan

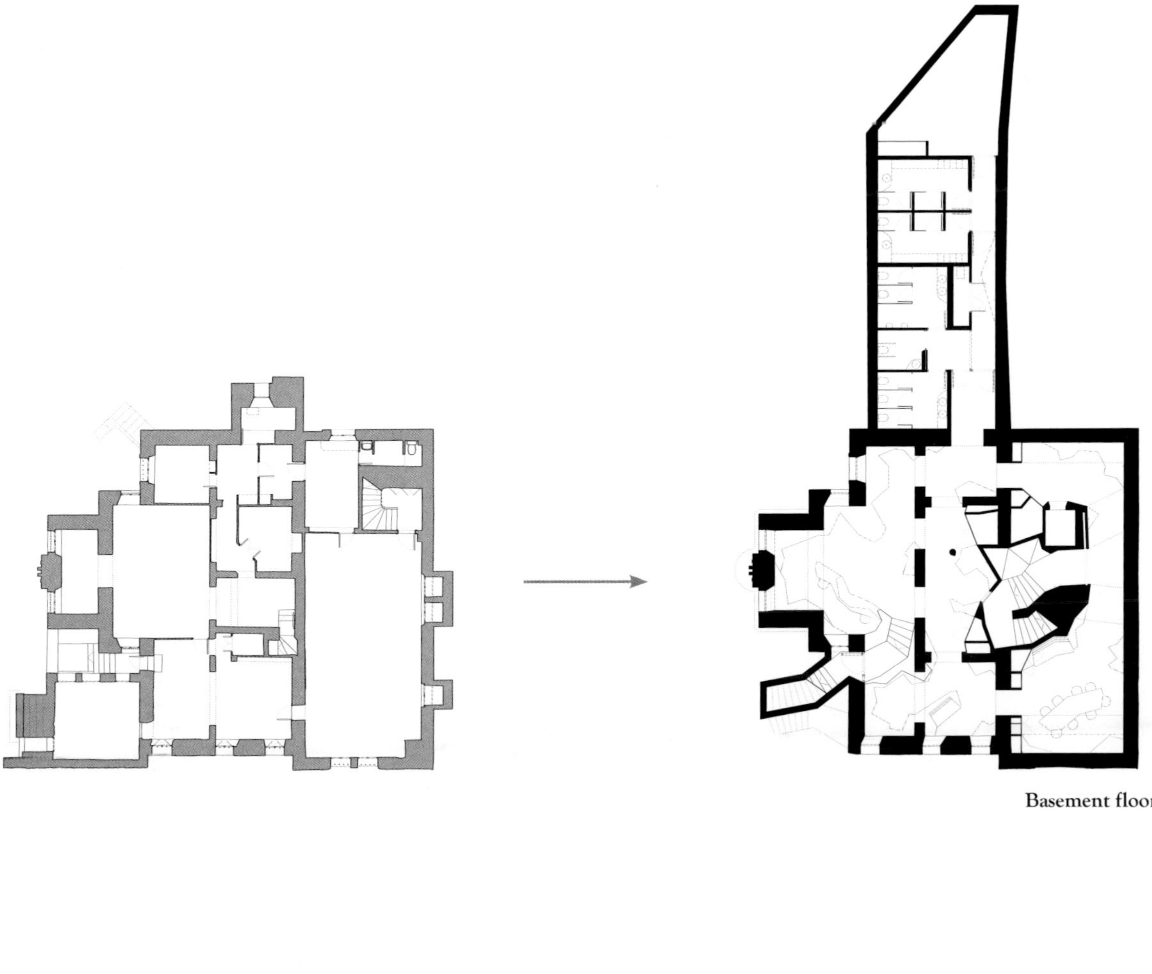

Basement floor plan

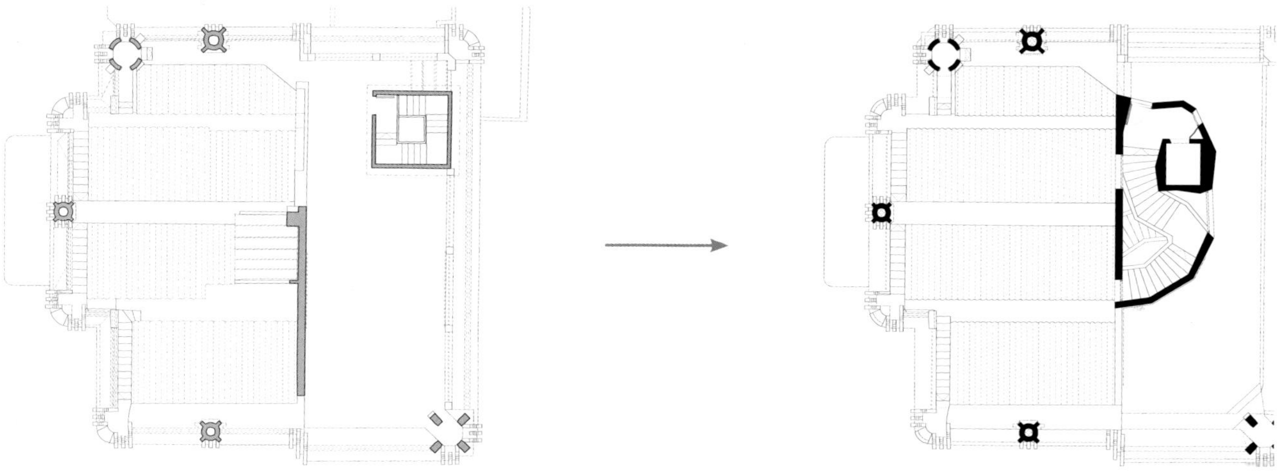

Rooftop plan

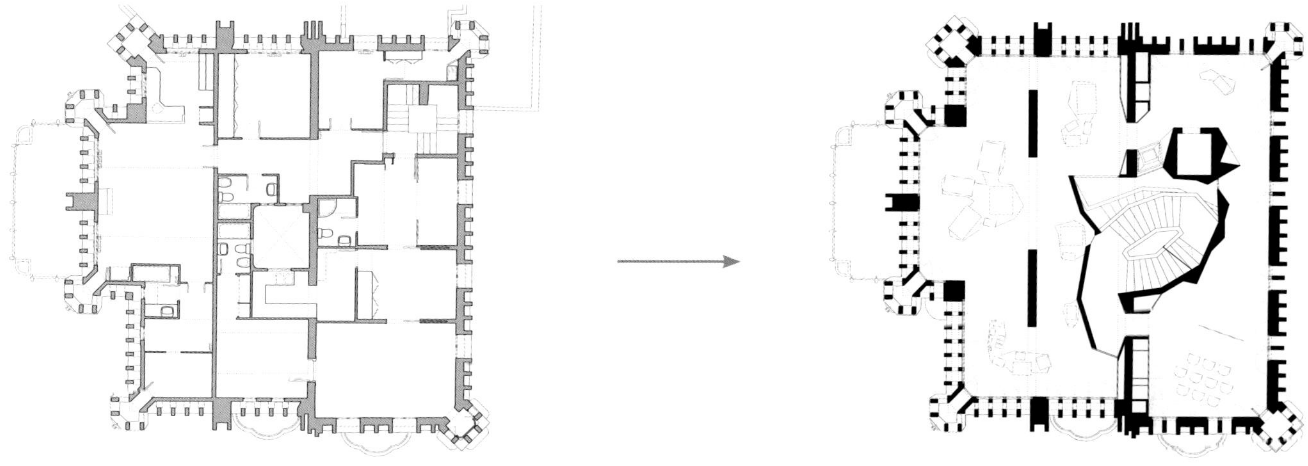

Third-floor plan

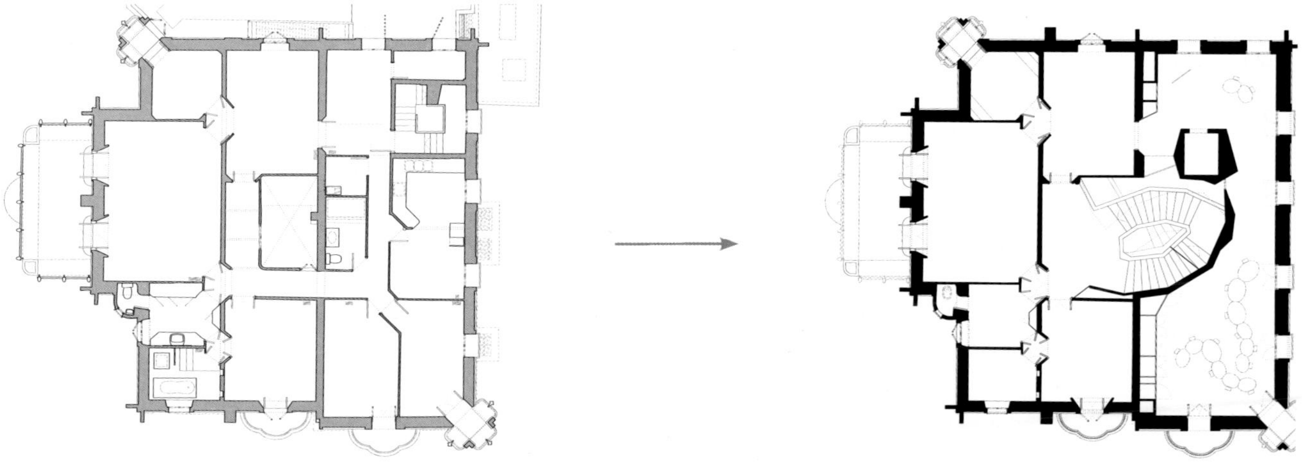

Second-floor plan

660 CONGRESS STREET

This fire-damaged building is rehabilitated to provide two apartments, a commercial space, and retail area. The insertion is spatially informed by the building's exterior and mansard roof, and the façade is carefully restored and now serves as a frame through which the contrasting new interior can be viewed.

The George S. Hunt Block at 660 Congress Street in Portland, Maine, originally built in 1886, had been abandoned for many years when a fire, followed by prolonged water exposure, destroyed the interior. In 2011, a new owner surveyed the compromised structure and deteriorating brick façade and decided a comprehensive rehabilitation was urgently needed to save the building. The architecture team approached the design with a vision to revitalize the landmark façade and modernize the building's interior, allowing the spaces to flow fluidly together.

The architecture team wanted to design a building that was aware of the past, but not bound to it. The refurbished 7500-square-feet (697-square-meter) building includes a pair of two-bedroom apartments on the second and third floors, a light-filled commercial space on the first floor, and a spacious retail area in the basement.

The initial design challenge was to develop an approach to the interior without any existing documentation of its historical past. The architect looked to the historical façade of the building, and traced the silhouette of the mansard roof with gently curving walls. The expansive volume of the roof is revealed at the ceiling with dramatic coffers that bring light into the interior through skylights and hidden lighting fixtures.

Fragments of history were left untouched in the arched doorways, fireplaces, and brickwork. The new entrance to the apartments is via a black-steel staircase with solid white-oak treads, fabricated by a local Maine welder. The thin industrial lines of the steel balusters cast shadows from the overhead

Architecture:
PRESENT Architecture
Location:
Portland, United States
Area:
7500 square feet (697 square meters)
Completion:
2016
Photography:
Robert Deitchler

658
7-5188
SALON

Avon
ONE WAY
ANTIQUES

Front elevation

Section

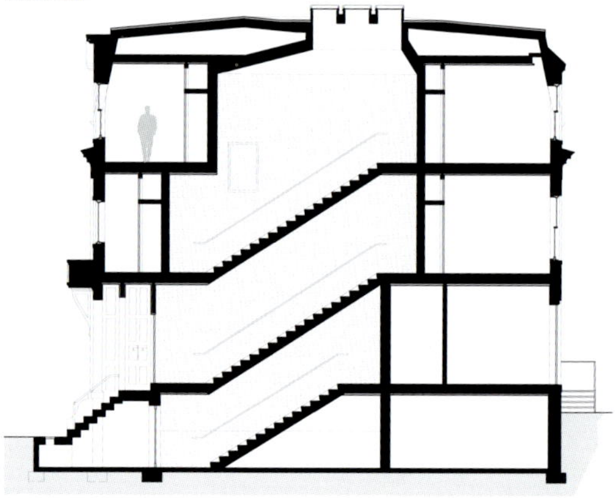

skylights onto the exposed historic brick. Many of the improvements are hidden from view, such as new HVAC and utilities, code-compliant structural work, and upgraded environmental and life-safety systems.

The façade was the most important historical aspect of the project. It was meticulously rehabilitated and included repair of the slate mansard roof, cleaning and spot repointing of deteriorated brick, replacement of the double-hung windows with energy-efficient aluminum-clad timber windows, and the rehabilitation of the surviving leaded-glass transoms and multi-pane double-hung windows.

New copper roofs were installed, and unsightly downspouts, which had been haphazardly attached to the façade over the years, were returned to their original concealed brick pockets. The pressed-tin frieze and dentil ornamentation were carefully restored on-site, while the rotted timber storefront window frames were replaced in kind. This was accomplished on a logistically complicated site with limited private property available for staging.

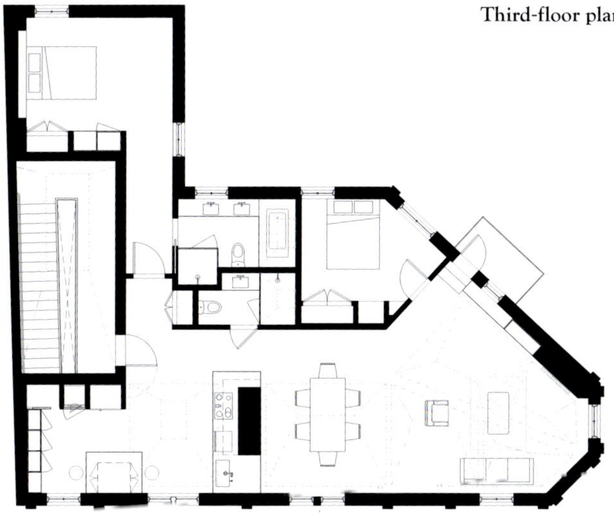

Third-floor plan

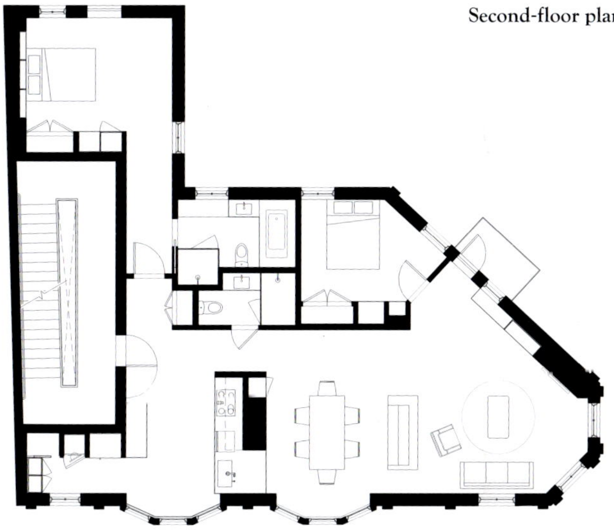

Second-floor plan

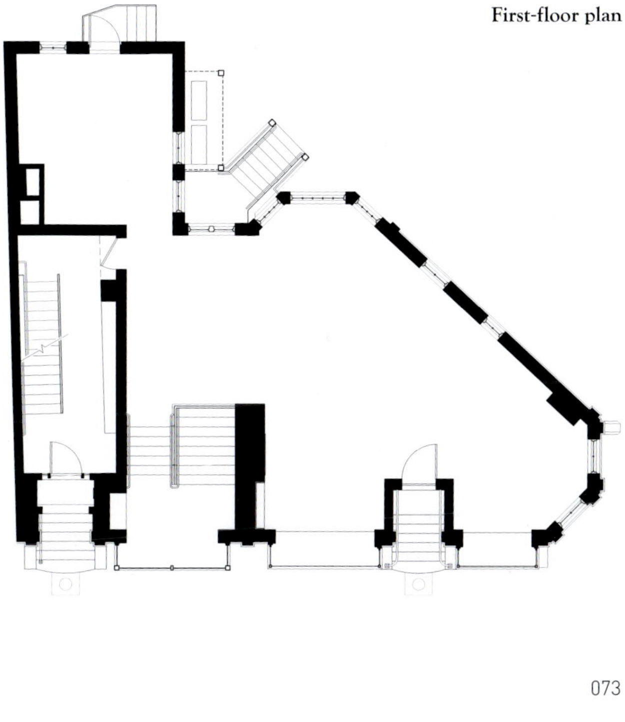

First-floor plan

PROTECTED SEVENTEENTH-CENTURY HOUSES

The layered history of these buildings is respected and a new contemporary interior woven through the existing elements. The façades remain unaltered as the buildings front an historic public square. A cubic form protrudes at the back of the building and an interior void brings light inside.

Atelier Tom Vanhee transformed two disused protected seventeenth-century houses on a brewery site in Bruges into a family home, while retaining existing retail and storage space.

The different window types and added rear façade are evidence of successive conversions over time, and the design begins from these changes and adds another layer. The historical and authentic parts have been kept or reconstructed and structurally improved where necessary. These elements, including doors, fireplaces, beams, and stairs, go hand in hand with the new elements and remain legible.

A patio and a sloping roof between the existing gable roofs transform the attic into a fully usable space and activate the residual area between the roofs. The darkest space—the dining area—opens up onto the roof ridge. There is a view of the brewery activities in the inner square through an industrial-looking balcony.

A void connects the different floors and brings light from the patio and the trapezoidal window in the attic into the heart of the home. A new staircase makes the formerly unused attics accessible, thereby enlarging the house. The stair, void, and patio activate a leftover space.

Restored doors conceal a bathroom and a shaft for a future elevator. An old passageway has been reopened, and the existing spatial format at the front accommodates the more private functions of the house.

Architecture:
Atelier Tom Vanhee
Location:
Bruges, Belgium
Area:
3282 square feet (305 square meters)
Completion:
2016
Photography:
Filip Dujardin

Fascino HATS & CAPS

Waste heat from the adjoining brewery warms the house and rainwater is harvested. The site is close to public transport in the touristic area of Bruges, so the interventions were designed to be invisible from the lively public square at the front of the building.

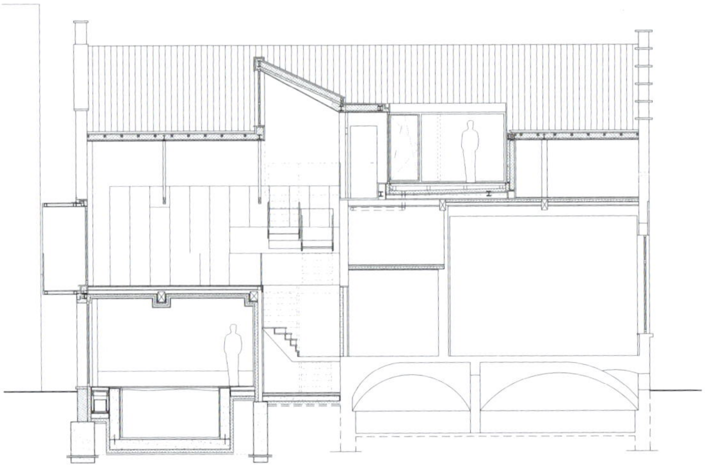

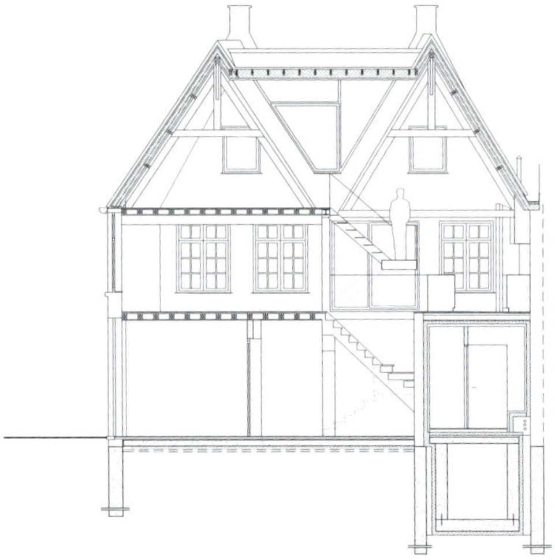

Sections

Elevations

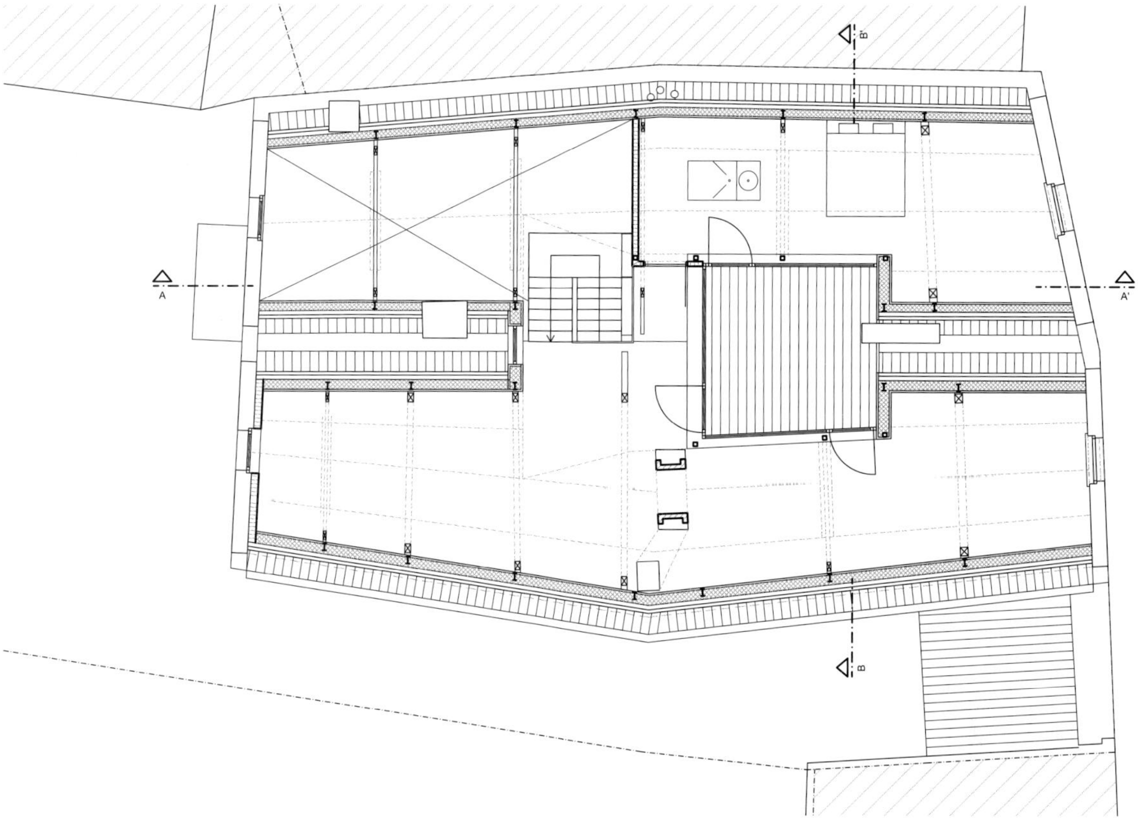

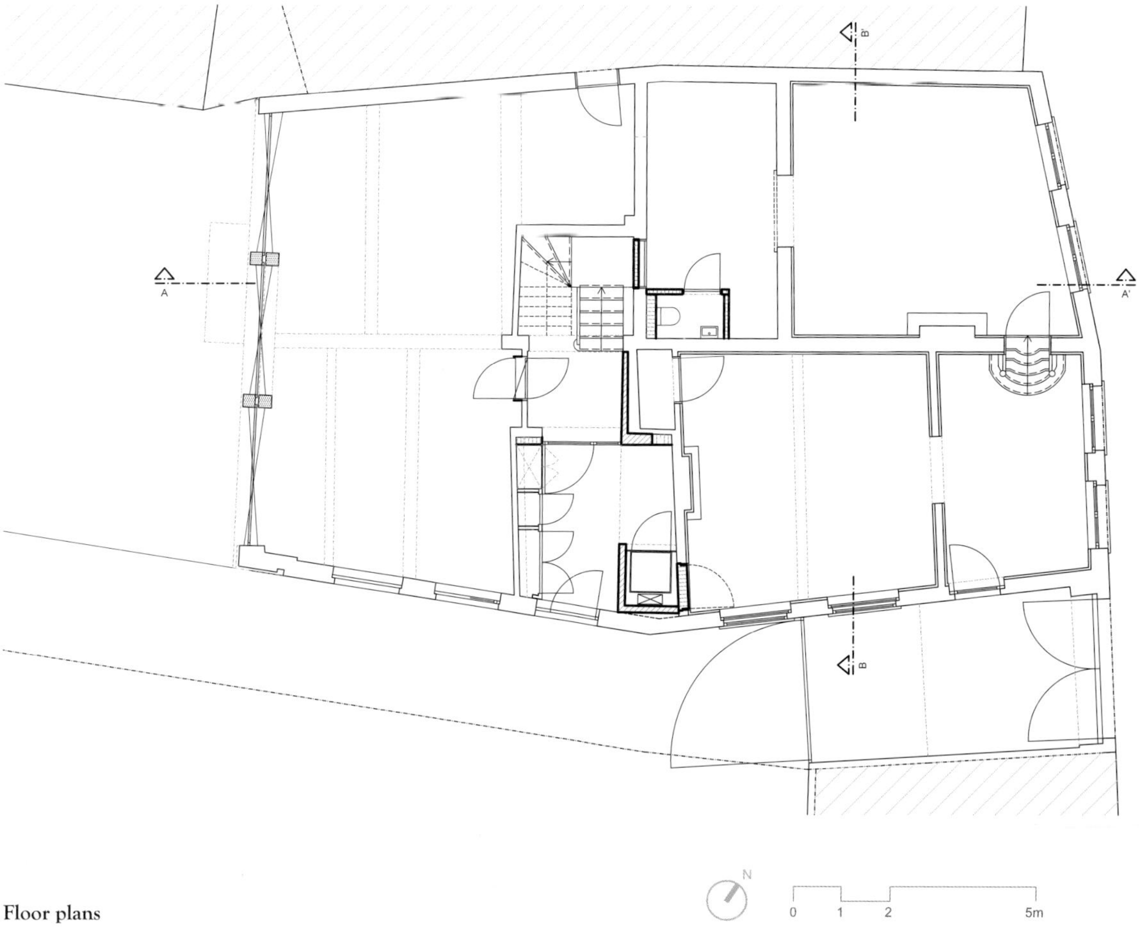

Floor plans

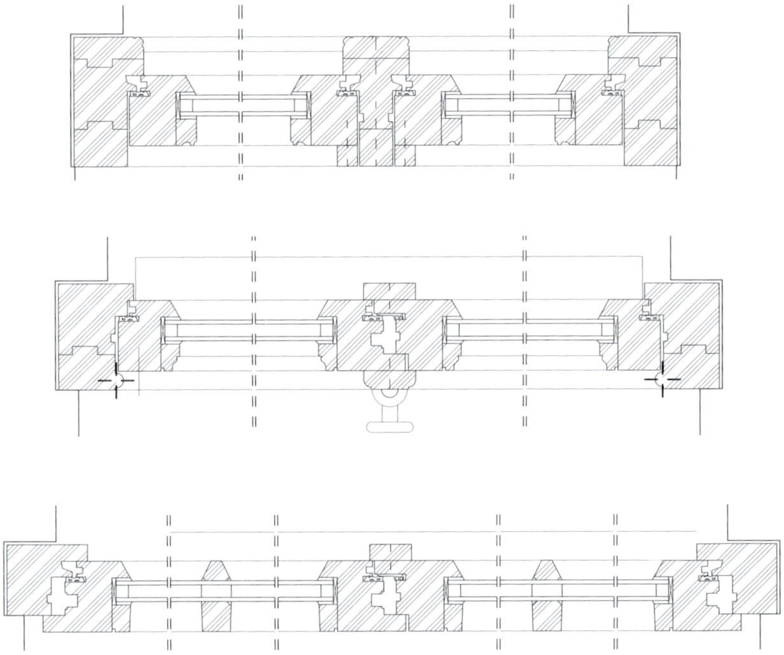

Detailed drawings of joinery

CATHEDRAL OF SZEGED

Built in the early twentieth century, this cathedral tracks the evolution of building technologies and styles from historicist to modernist. Restoration, reconstruction, and transformation create a subtle and often undiscernible merging of contemporary and historic layers to emphasize the beauty of the cathedral and improve its accessibility as a cultural space.

The core of the project was to develop the tourism aspect of the iconic Cathedral of Szeged and to give visitors and churchgoers an insight into the past and present of the 1000-year-old Diocese of Szeged-Csanád. The comprehensive development program emphasizes the beauty of the cathedral and makes it accessible to all. It also strengthens community-building features and transforms the church and its cultural spaces into a venue for visitors, churchgoers, and inhabitants of Szeged.

The renovation was not only an aesthetic intervention, but also a reconsideration—a transformation—of the key elements of the complex, such as the undercroft, liturgical space, western tower, and twelfth-century Demetrius (Dömötör) Tower. This refurbishment sees the church of the past became a focal point for the present, utilizing previously abandoned spaces and opening up closed-off areas.

The intervention clarifies the relationship between the original building and the superimposed layers. On the one hand, the building has been restored to its original state. On the other hand, the changes reinterpret the building according to contemporary standards and knowledge. The architecture team found it particularly difficult to address because of areas with multiple layers of historical development and the more recent being were of undeniable artistic merit. For example, the baptistery of the Demetrius Tower had been reconstructed on the basis of Béla Rerrich's vision, which was complemented with modern elements.

Architecture:
3h architecture + Váncza Művek Studio
Location:
Szeged, Hungary
Area:
80,212 square feet (7452 square meters)
Completion:
2015
Photography:
Tamás Bujnovszky, 3h architecture

The undercroft provides a reserve space or buffer zone. This section also provides protection against underground water and flooding. The area bounded by the piers and the cross vaults results in a captivating space. The intention was not to transform this space, but rather to reveal it and gently interpret it—not to interfere, but to carefully understand its logic. The spaces defined by the brick vaults bear the marks of history, yet in their position and utility they relate to contemporary architecture. This gives a specific charm, which the architecture team tried to keep and strengthen.

Since the cathedral was built at the end of the historicist era of architecture and at the dawn of modernism, it neatly tracks the evolution of building technologies and styles. This is particularly evident with respect to the towers. The undercroft was built with sturdy, solid-brick cross vaults resting on square and rectangular pillars, and the basilica level also employs this building technique. The closing vaults of the chapels under the towers are however made of reinforced concrete. The particularly solid ribbed concrete slabs of the towers are stacked up and rotated through 90 degrees.

The architecture team's aim was incorporate two important characteristics of historical architecture—symmetry and decoration—so as to reinterpret them from today's perspective and apply them to new additions. Both symmetry and decoration appear in the newly designed parts, adding local flavor and doing away with sterility. An attempt was made to clarify the extent to which decorative motifs used in the 1930s are still legible, pursuable, and how much deviation they allow.

Sections

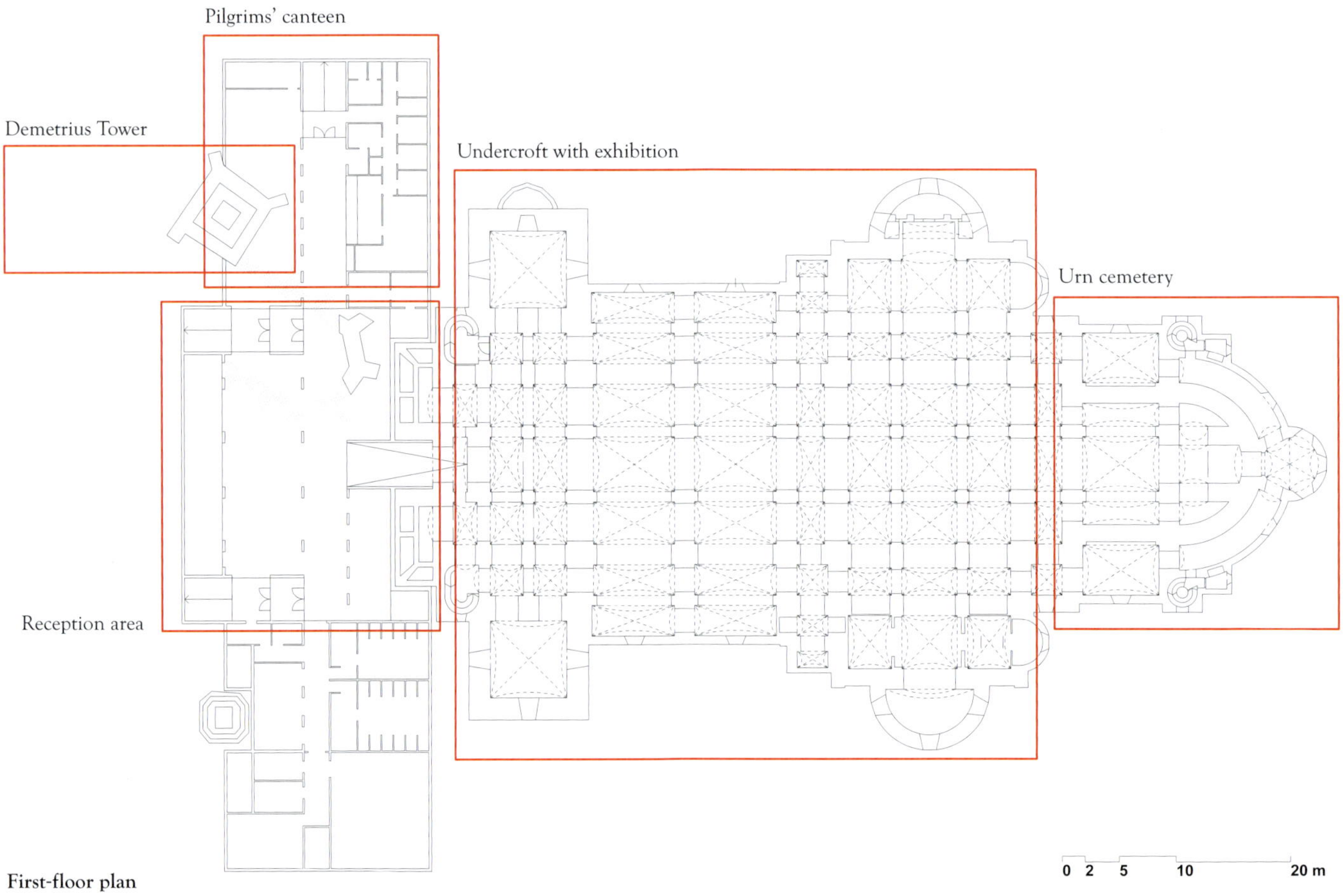

First-floor plan

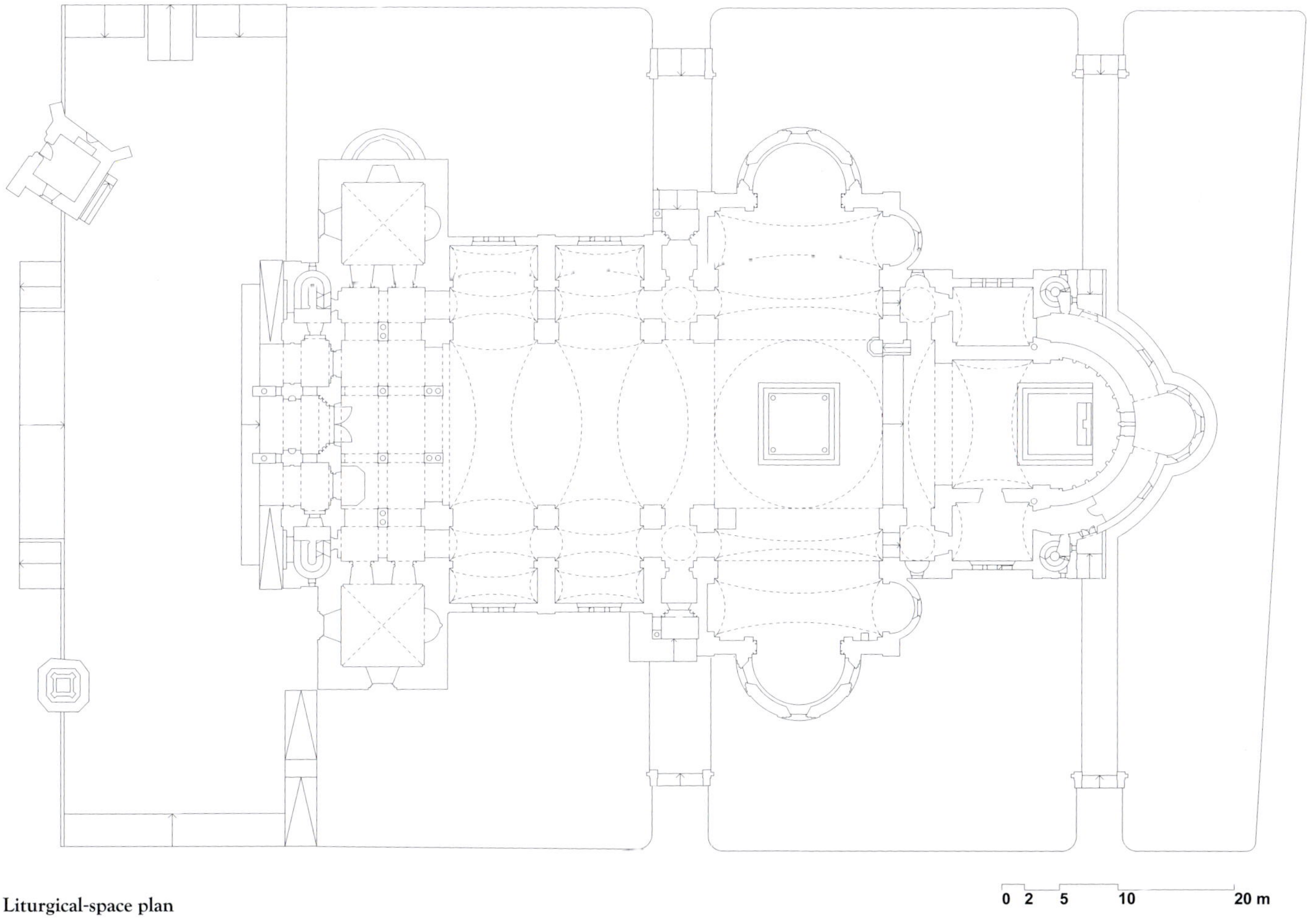

Liturgical-space plan

THREE CUSPS CHALET

A new light-filled interior within this former annex serves as a private residence and work studio. The design responds to the change in level between the street and rear courtyard, while maximizing the internal space and allowing light to filter down through the staircase.

Three Cusps Chalet is a very peculiar building, documenting Braga's history and diaspora, and combining typical nineteenth-century Portuguese architecture and urban design with an unexpected alpine influence. This influence was brought by an historic wave of rich Portuguese returning from Brazil in the eighteenth century, significantly influenced by Brazil's second industrial revolution.

The building was conceived as an annex serving the small palace next door and sitting at the heart of both the Roman and medieval walls of Braga. It is a particularly sunny building, enjoying all-day natural light.

The program required the cohabitation of a work studio and a private residence. A 4.9-foot (1.5-meter) height difference between the street and the block's interior plaza allowed the architecture team to place the working area on the first level where it faces westward and relates to the street.

The façade was returned to its original glory, and the interior recuperated the original spacious and functional distribution, timber floors, ceiling structures, and original staircase. Portuguese Estremoz marble has been introduced in the wet areas and on the first floor, and white is used for walls, ceilings, carpentry, and marble.

The layout relates to the interior plaza and the morning light. The plaza has several orange trees, which provide shade during the summer and display a beautiful show during winter, covered with bright fruits. Spaces are hierarchized by floor with work space on the first floor, social areas on the

Architecture:
Tiago do Vale Architects
Location:
Braga, Portugal
Area:
1840 square feet (171 square meters)
Completion:
2014
Photography:
João Morgado

Elevation

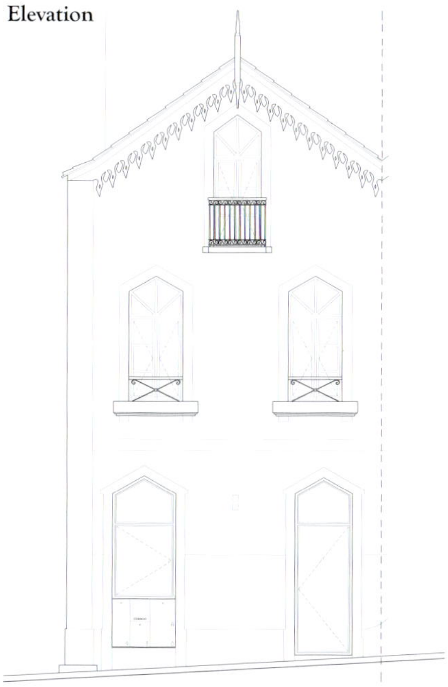

second floor, and bedrooms on the top floor. The stairs become narrower with each flight, informing the changing nature of the spaces it connects.

The staircase geometry filters the visual relations between the work space and residence while still allowing for natural light to seep down from the upper levels. The staircase defines the perimeters of the kitchen and living room, with light entering through the kitchen window in the morning, and from the staircase's skylight and from the living room in the afternoon.

The ceiling of the bedrooms is exposed and painted white. As a counterpoint, the wardrobe on the top floor of the building reads as a small wooden box with floor, walls, roof structure, and joinery doors in natural timber.

Elevation

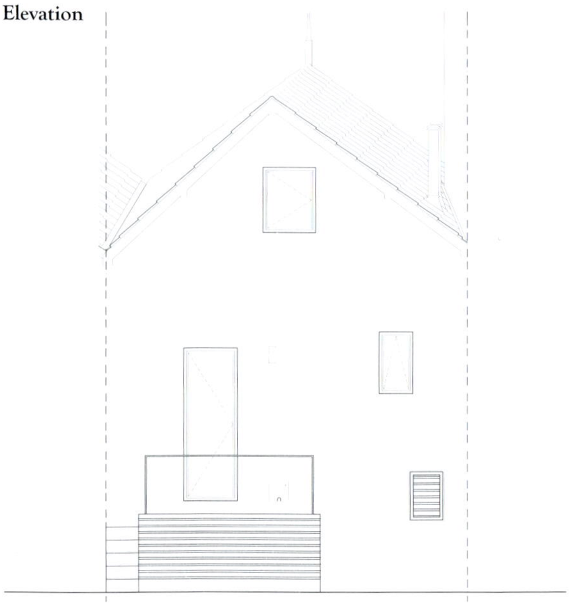

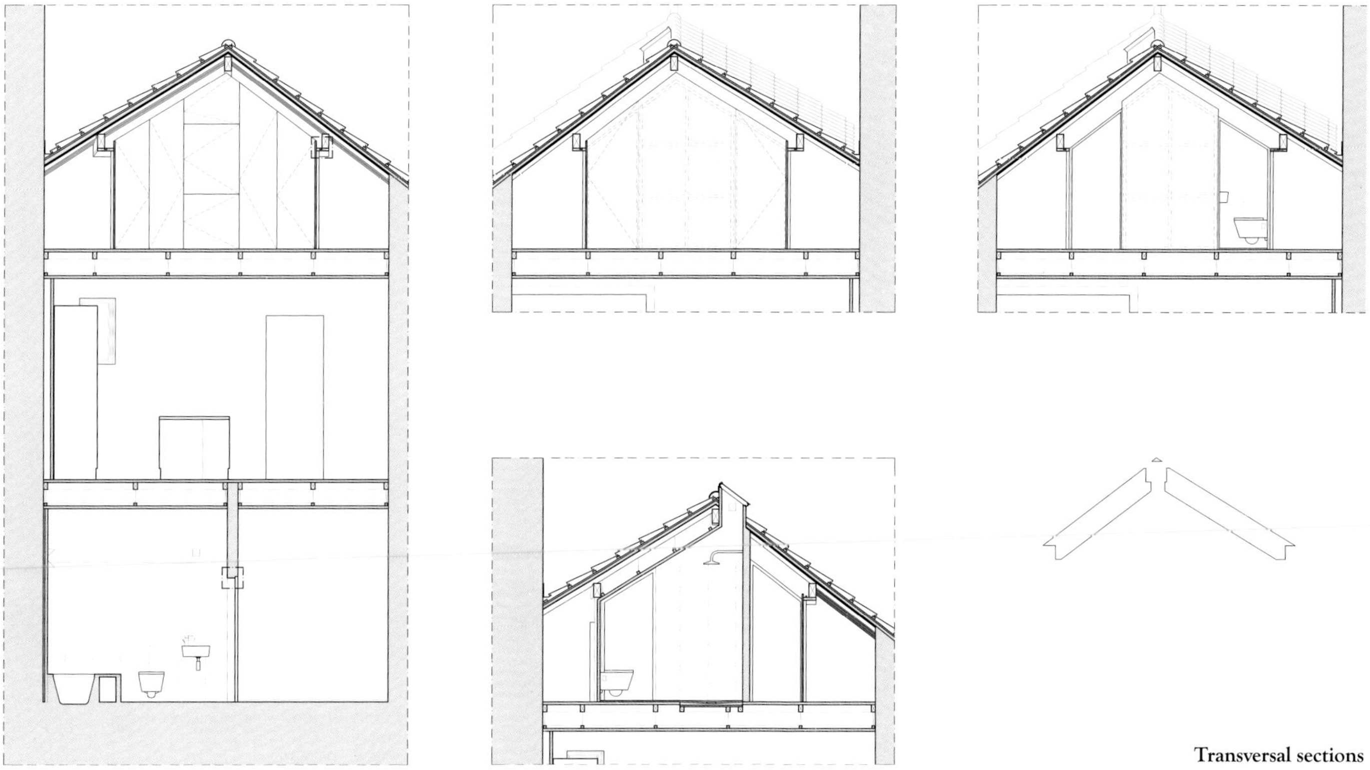

Transversal sections

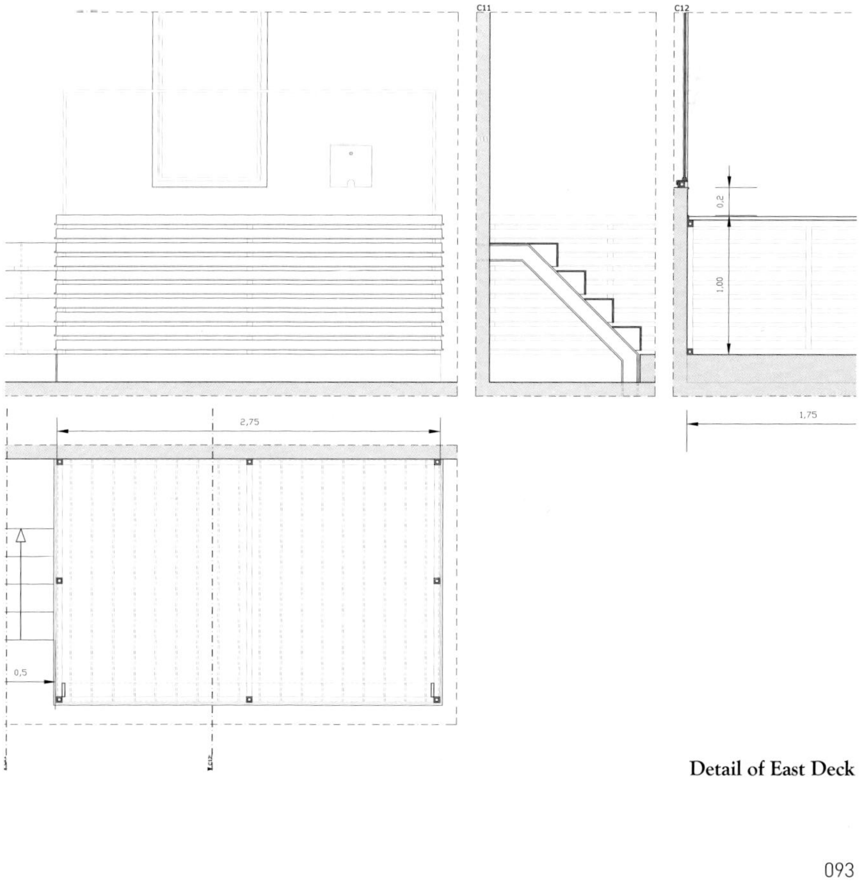

Detail of East Deck

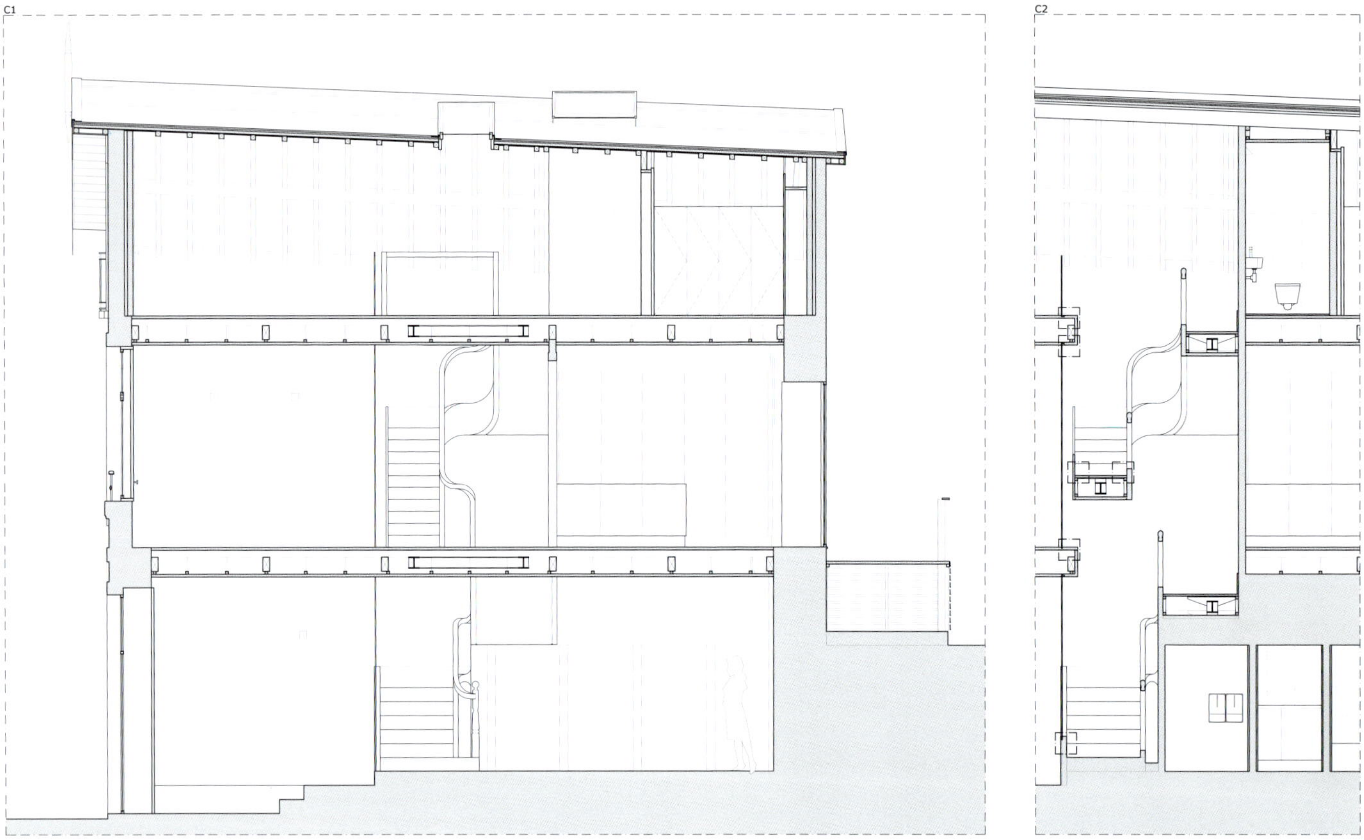

Longitudinal sections

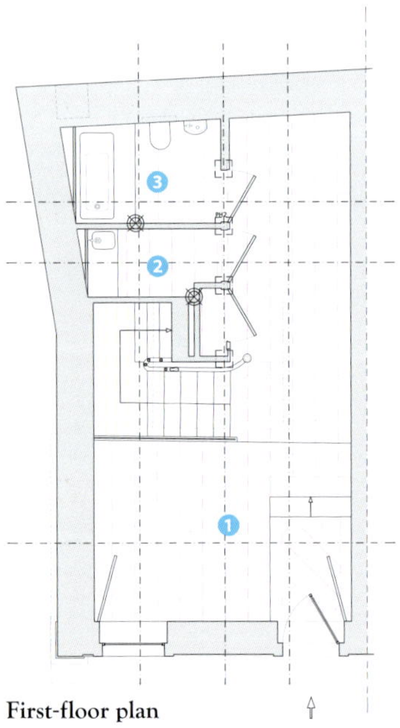

First-floor plan

1. Hall
2. Laundry
3. Bathroom

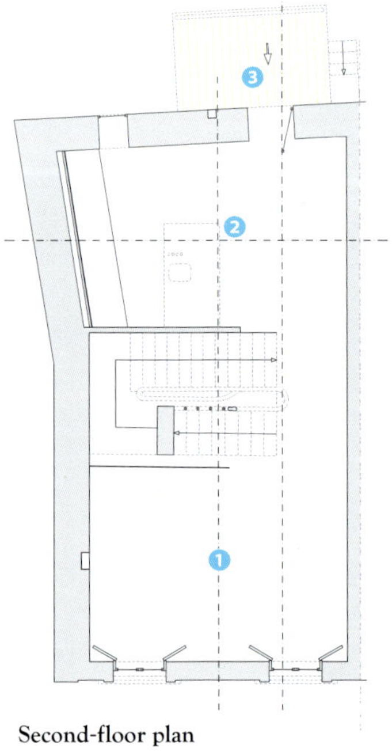

Second-floor plan

1. Living room
2. Kitchen
3. Deck

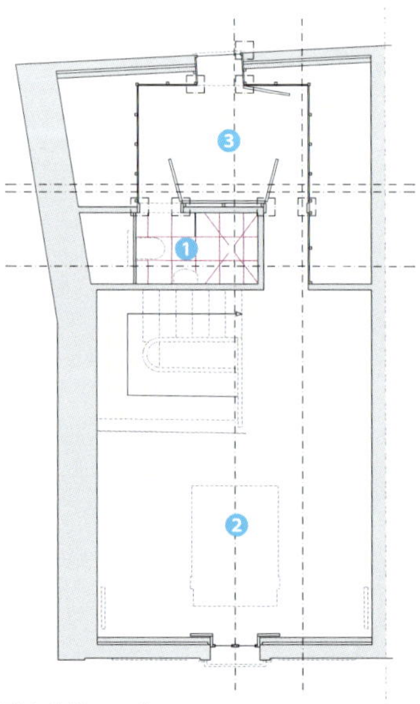

Third-floor plan

1. Bathroom
2. Bedroom
3. Dressing room

GOUDA CHEESE WAREHOUSE

The transformation of this former cheese warehouse is only visible inside. Removing the core of the building creates a spacious atrium, and elements of the former warehouse are reused in the new construction to pay homage to building's history.

Mei architects and planners transformed the cheese warehouse De Producent in Gouda, the capital of the famous Dutch cheese, into residential lofts. A spacious atrium in the heart of the building is enclosed by 52 loft apartments, and elements from the former cheese warehouse, such as the original cheese boards, have been innovatively reused.

De Producent is a national monument. Therefore, the main changes of the transformation are only visible inside the building. The removal of flooring and façades on both sides of the original ventilation alley, and the addition of a glass roof, create a spacious atrium that brings natural light into the building. Parts of the ventilation alley façade have been retained as a hoistway for two glass elevators that provide access to apartments on the four floors.

The architecture team retained as many elements as possible from the former cheese warehouse, giving them a second life in the new construction. The shelves where cheese ripened are reused as cladding on the façades of the apartments facing the atrium. Signs of use remain visible and they have been treated with monomers to meet the fire-resistance requirements. Some of the cheese shelves have been carved with sentences that add an extra layer of extra meaning. These sentences make reference to the history of cheese making and come from a Dutch board game found in the archive of De Producent. Some of the original trays that were hung onto the shelves to manage the maturation process have been reused for the apartment numbers.

Architecture:
Mei architects and planners
Location:
Gouda, Netherlands
Area:
53,819 square feet (5000 square meters)
Completion:
2017
Photography:
Ossip van Duivenbode, Jeroen Musch

The warehouse had two separate construction systems to bear the weight of a million kilograms of cheese: one for the building and one for the cheese. The original construction—steel columns, wooden ceilings, concrete ceilings, and wooden attic beams—is maintained unfinished and is visible in the loft apartments. The existing timber floors are used as permanent formwork for the new concrete floors so that the original ceilings remain visible and give a historic touch to the apartments.

A diverse range of apartment floor plans was possible due to the strategic placement of loggias in the façade, which maintain the rhythm of characteristic small windows. All loft apartments are different, varying from 646 square feet (60 square meters) to 1937 square feet (180 square meters), and tailored to individual wishes. Upon purchase, every buyer received a personal consultation with the architect.

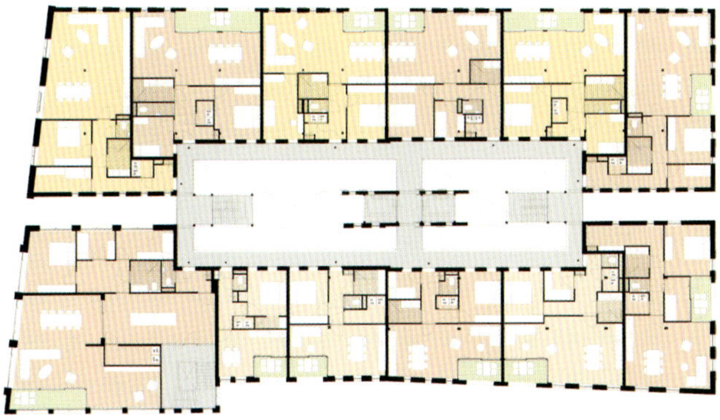

Fourth-floor plan

Fifth-floor plan

Second-floor plan

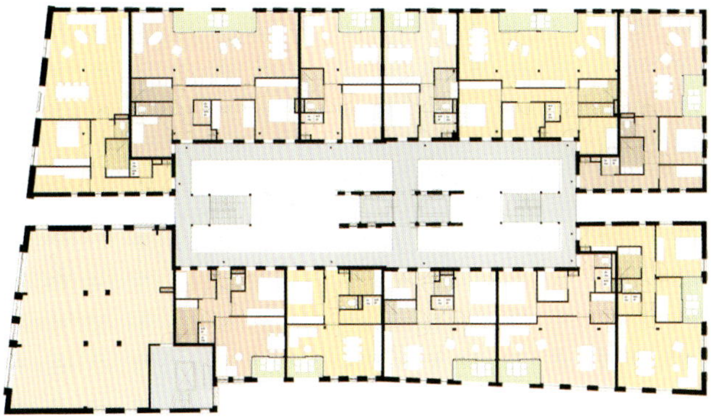

Third-floor plan

First-floor plan

WHITE PAGODA TEMPLE HUTONG COURTYARD

The renewal of this courtyard allows it to become a central focus for the residents of six surrounding guest rooms. While emphasis is placed on transforming the courtyard into a living space for a contemporary lifestyle, the building's materiality reflects a mix of old and new.

An increasing number of young people now choose to leave their old houses in the Beijing *hutongs* to settle in new areas of the city. The site of the project is in a historical and cultural district in Fucheng Men that contains 33 traditional blocks and 807 courtyards. An essential objective of the urban renewal of this area is to encourage the younger generation to return to the old city. The renewal includes the renovation of White Pagoda Temple Hutong Courtyard, which respects the existing spatial organization while transforming it into a living space suitable for the contemporary lifestyle.

The courtyard, which originally housed eight families, sits at a Y-shaped intersection where two façades are fully exposed to the street and can be viewed by pedestrians. Illegal additions were commonly made to maximize the usable space for the large number of residents. Consequently, the additional building components in the center of the courtyard needed to be removed in order to reveal its original spatial composition.

Six guest rooms form a square-shaped courtyard. The courtyard and roof space provide additional living areas, and a new exhibition space on the rooftop was formed after reinforcing the original structure of the building. The rooftop can be accessed via a new staircase on the southern side of the courtyard. The staircase shaft was built using recycled bricks from the demolished parts of the building, with glass bricks embedded in the walls. Other reused items include seven large rectangular stones from the Qing dynasty, which were discovered 3.3 feet (1 meter) below the ground surface during excavations.

Architecture:
B.L.U.E. Architecture Studio
Location:
Beijing, China
Area:
2648 square feet (246 square meters)
Completion:
2018
Photography:
Zhi Xia

The renovation of the courtyard is not limited to static aesthetics. It also aims to preserve the lived experience. Living in a courtyard surrounded by trees and having the opportunity to participate in an open and connected community within the city is what forms the unique cultural experience of the *hutongs*.

Axonometric diagram

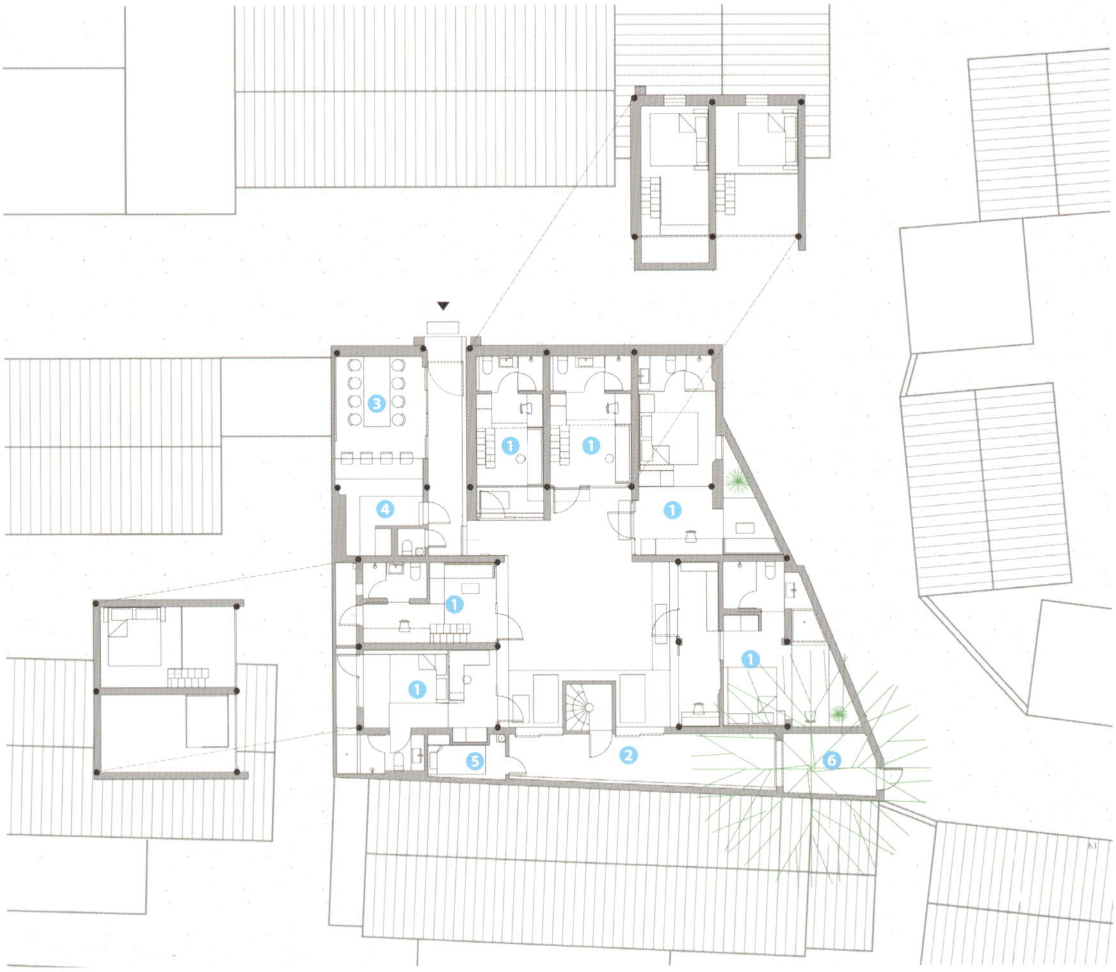

Floor plan

1. Guest room
2. Gallery
3. Café and reception
4. Kitchen
5. Staff room
6. Garden

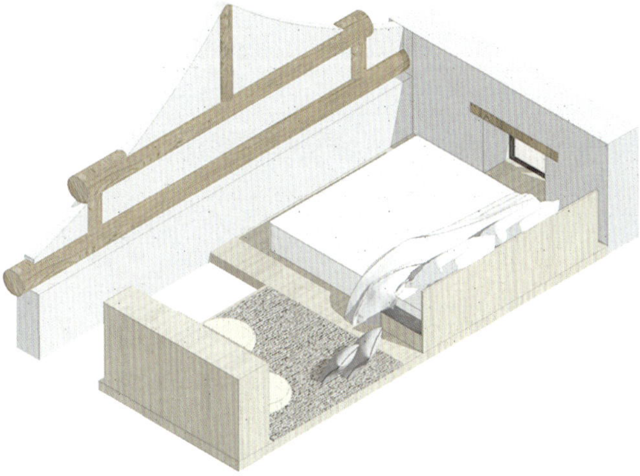

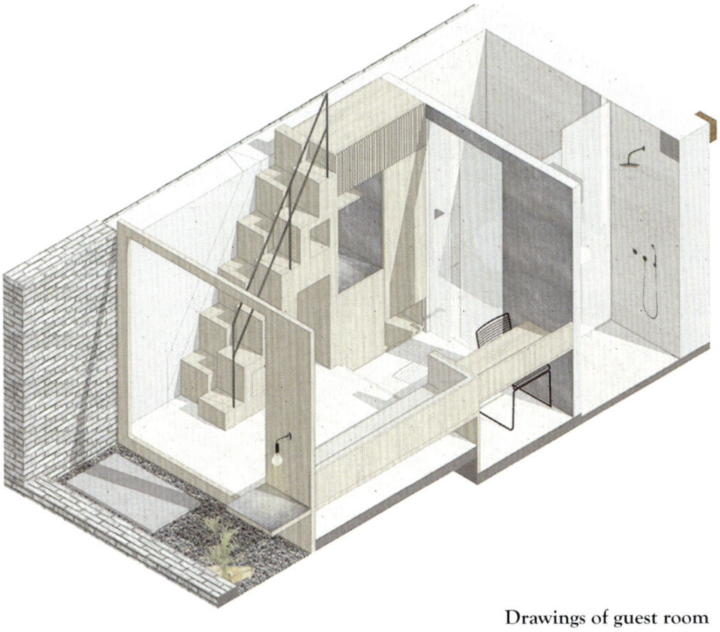

Drawings of guest room

STRATEGY
3

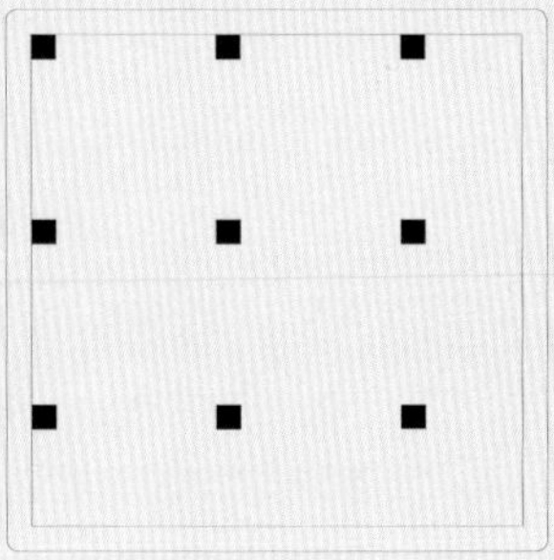

STRUCTURAL MODIFICATION

The very fabric of the existing building is altered where structural modification takes place. The existing structural system is modified by the new intervention, which either acts as a prosthesis to replace a missing structural element, or as a structural support or a cast to reinforce the existing structure. The intervention may affect both the interior and exterior façades, and the new structure contributes to the modification of the building's existing spatial qualities.

There are various reasons for using structural modification as a key driver for an intervention. In all instances the structure of the old building is not able to support the new program without a structural intervention. In the projects presented, this structural necessity also becomes the catalyst for the dialogue between old and new, which becomes legible in the language of the end result.

The new structure can serve to recover and therefore reinforce the original volumes of the old building, or to challenge and transform them. When the envelope has been retained, the structural intervention may assist a frail structure that may otherwise crumble, or it may permit a new spatial configuration in the interior that is derived from the requirements of the new program.

The creative employment of a new structure can be used to unlock a building's spatial potential, permitting the demands of the new program to be met, as was done in Zeitz Museum of Contemporary African Art (MOCAA) and M.Y. Lab Wood Workshop. It can also be used, sometimes unavoidably so, to save a building from ruin. A ruin is often unable to support or enclose functional space without the addition of new structural members or the reconstruction of the existing structure.

There may have been different causes for a building's current state of disrepair. It may be due to long-term abandonment and gradual decay, such as Ixi'im Restaurant, or it may be due to a traumatic event, as in the bombing of Santa María de Vilanova de la Barca during the Spanish Civil War.

The first step of structural modification may involve a partial demolition of the building either to make it safe, or in the case of Zeitz MOCAA, to unlock its latent spatial potential, first through a process of subtraction and then through a process of addition. The existing fabric also usually requires some maintenance and stabilization. The old buttress arches and walls at Ixi'im Restaurant had to be repaired, using traditional techniques and local materials, before the new structural insertions could be made. The new structural insertions can often be highly complex to visualize, calculate, design, and construct. Zeitz MOCAA and Santa María de Vilanova de la Barca are both examples where the capacity of the original structure had to be carefully analyzed before a challenging process of design and construction could commence.

In the case of a ruin, one approach is to add a separate and clearly identifiable structure that takes over the structural responsibilities of the original fragments. At Ixi'im Restaurant, a new steel framework is threaded between the remains of a former engine room, and in places it seems to act like a crutch or a prop that keeps the existing pieces upright. The framework creates new spaces set back from the old. It is an architecture that celebrates the distance between new and old and it creates a tension between the two. The new intervention contrasts with the color, texture, and materiality of the ruin, and is respectfully pulled away from the existing fabric to articulate this difference. The structural modification therefore also serves to challenge the enclosing volume of the original building to produce a new set of relationships between inside and outside.

Contrary to this oppositional approach is one of adjacency, where the gaps between remnants are filled in, similar to reconstructive surgery, and continuity is created between new and old. The new structure's primary purpose is to retain and support, and it must therefore be located close to the original. In Zeitz MOCAA and Santa María de Vilanova de la Barca, the new and old portions merge to take joint responsibility for the structure and enclosure.

The sense of ephemerality or transience versus permanence can be interpreted differently depending on which approach is used. At Ixi'im Restaurant, the new steel structure and its contents could be seen to be permanent in one way, being climatically controlled and maintained, while the ruined fragments can be regarded as ephemeral, since they are left outside the building envelope and actively continue to weather and decay. In another sense, since the steel structure is clearly separated from the older fabric, it would theoretically be possible to remove it without much impact on the older fragments, so it too can be seen to be potentially transient. In other cases, such as Santa María de Vilanova de la Barca, the old fragments are included as part of the enclosure and have a greater sense of permanence than the new elements.

The decision whether to reveal and express or conceal the structure becomes an important consideration. A new structural insertion is often concealed to minimize visual interference in cases where the remains of a building are fragmented, and they are included in the new composition as separate pieces.

The new structure can be autonomous and independent of the old, such as at Ixi'im Restaurant, or it can form a composite structure where the old and new structures both contribute to the building's load-bearing duties. Where the existing silos at Zeitz MOCAA were too thin to accommodate the hollowing out of the new atrium, new concrete sleeves were cast inside them in order to form a new layered structure capable of withstanding the complex structural stresses. In M.Y. Lab Wood Workshop, a partially concealed structure that makes use of new columns and beams in conjunction with the existing walls was used to create a large open space with minimal structural interference. At Santa María de Vilanova de la Barca and House Z22 and Warehouse F88, the old and new structural skins form a merged building envelope.

The structure can be used to delineate movement or accentuate an architectural promenade and a number of projects demonstrate the use of the structure not purely as a load-bearing element, but also as a structuring element that has a spatial and sensory function. In Ixi'im Restaurant and House Z22 and Warehouse F88, the structure is used to define and express movement routes through the buildings. In Zeitz MOCAA and M.Y. Lab Wood Workshop, the structural modification enables the creation of movement routes and spatial linkages that would not have been possible in the buildings' original configurations. This is an especially important consideration in gallery spaces, and it is closely linked to the need for natural light.

A structural frame generally allows for larger openings, while a load-bearing wall usually only allows for the smaller "punched" openings unless an innovative technique or material is used to generate a continuous permeable façade. In the adjacent hotel building of Zeitz MOCAA, the structural concrete frame allowed for the installation of its bubble-like windows and the reinforced silos provided the opportunity to remove the silo caps and replace them with glass floors. The steel framework in Ixi'im Restaurant allowed for the installation of large glazed panels and for natural light to enter through the gaps between old and new. The structure of M.Y. Lab Wood Workshop enabled a large raking ceiling with high-level windows, which allow natural light deep into the internal space. On the other hand, the special opaque ceramic outer shell of Santa María de Vilanova de la Barca and its perforated internal brick skin creates a luminous interior without the inclusion of conventional window openings.

Structure can be used to make a building legible in terms of spatial division, threshold, and movement, but it can also be used to make a building's temporal nature and materiality easier to read. At House Z22 and Warehouse F88, the natural stone walls were deliberately exposed to reveal the materiality and craftsmanship, while the new interventions—in concrete, plaster, and wood—were left in their raw natural state, and contrast with the old by revealing their own material make-up and manufacture. The old and new elements are in dialogue with each other in terms of their structure, materiality, and modes of craftsmanship, which are indicative of their respective times, and the architects purposefully did not privilege a particular era over the other. It is a truthful and respectful conversation where neither the old nor the new is subservient to, or dominant over, the past. Similarly, in Zeitz MOCAA, the old and new concrete silos were exposed on their cut lines and left in their natural state. The new polished skin is clearly differentiated through its color, aggregate, and texture, and it enables a clear reading of the different constructive periods.

In the projects presented, the celebration of structure is often echoed in non-load-bearing architectural elements in an emblematic display of, or reference to, other structural principles. These can be appreciative references to former structural innovations, such as the traditional timber arch bridge suspended over the reception area of M.Y. Lab Wood Workshop,

Zeitz Museum of Contemporary African Art by Heatherwick Studio and VDMMA©Mark Williams

or the henequen strings installed on the ceiling of Ixi'im Restaurant. They can also be used to demonstrate principles that relate to the transmission of forces like the Gaudí-esque chandelier in Santa María de Vilanova de la Barca, which was fitted with draped catenary arches that provide a light counterpoint to the massive stone walls.

In cases of structural modification, both the old and the new structure is valued, whether it is in terms of load-bearing capacity, spatial potential, its expression of craftsmanship, or for its aesthetic appeal, which can be related to its visible strength or its ephemerality. The relationship between the old and new is generally non-hierarchical and the structural modification is used to generate dialogue between the existing fabric and the new interventions. The introduction of a new structure has been motivated by the need to preserve the old building without compromising the spatial demands of the new program. It is in finding this balance that the designers have determined the concept that inspires the spatial qualities of the collaboration between old and new.

IXI'IM RESTAURANT

An old engine house is transformed into a modern restaurant with a steel structure that gently supports the existing walls and creates a new interstitial space between heritage and intervention. The spatial sequence allows visitors to move from the ruin to contemporary addition, which is physically and visually integrated with the main square.

Ixi'im Restaurant comprises the reuse of the engine house of an old henequen farm. Its productive splendor in the second half of the nineteenth century and subsequent decline in the second half of the twentieth century provided an opportunity to generate a new use for this element of Mexico's built cultural heritage. The site has several independent structures, including the engine room, which shape the public space or main square. After years of abandonment, the engine room's ruins were covered with a layer of weed and grass and faced the risk of collapse.

After creating a register of the structural damage, the architecture team undertook restoration repairs where possible, including the buttress arches and walls, always using the original building technique and stones found scattered around the building. Once the building was in safe condition, the design related the architectural program and visitor experience to the full context of the site in which a north-south axis connects the hacienda with other nearby settlements.

The design establishes a pause in this circulation through a subtle threshold in the access space to the ruin. Referring to the original activity of the farm and its industrial elements, the intervention strategy is materialized in a large metallic enclosure that weaves the new architectural program through the existing building. This articulating frame, whose internal offset liberates the existing walls from structural responsibility, generates a new interstitial space between heritage and intervention. At the same time, it allows the filtering of indirect natural light, thermally confining the interior, and supporting a large display of crafted liquors.

Architecture:
Central de Proyectos SCP, Jorge Bolio Arquitectura, Mauricio Gallegos Arquitectos, Lavalle + Peniche Arquitectura
Location:
Chocholá, Mexico
Area:
4478 square feet (416 square meters)
Completion:
2016
Photography:
Eduardo Calvo Santisbón

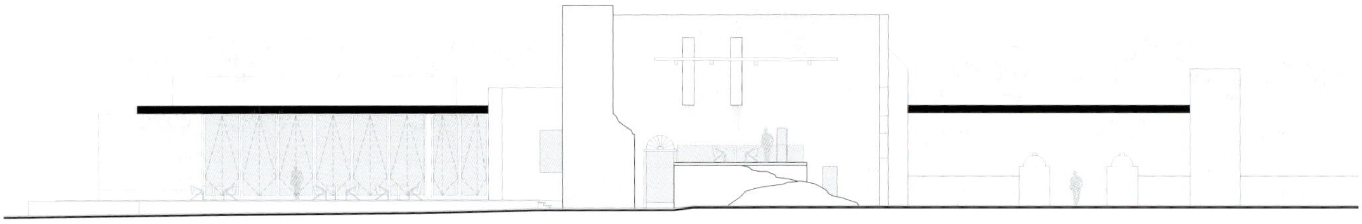

Northern elevation

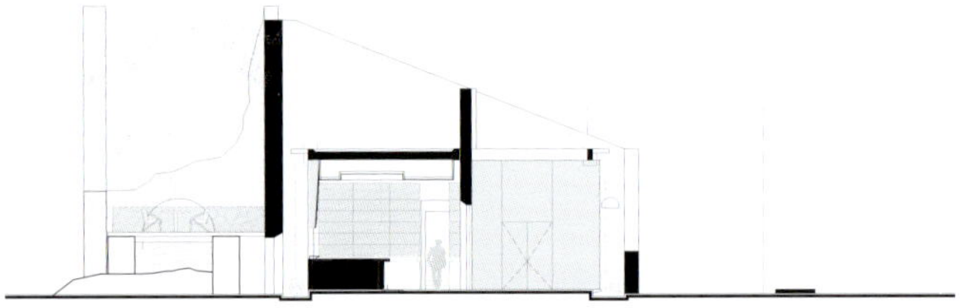

Section A-A'

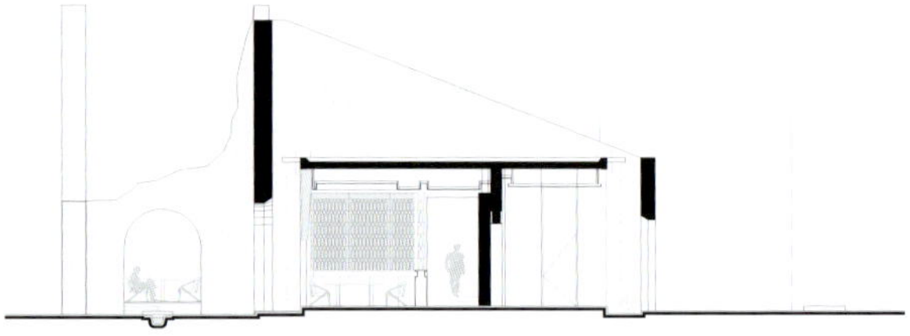

Section B-B'

Ideograma

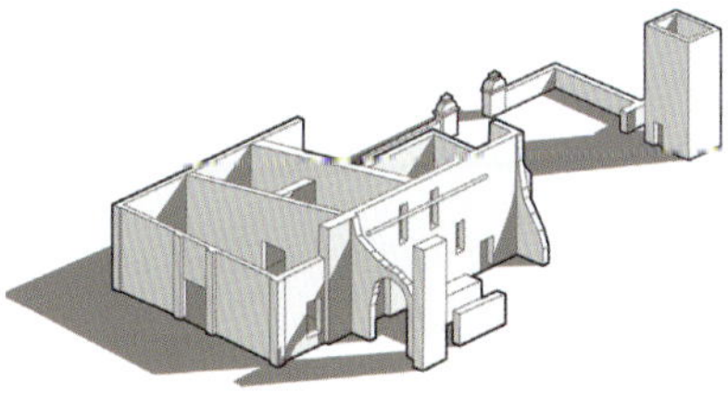

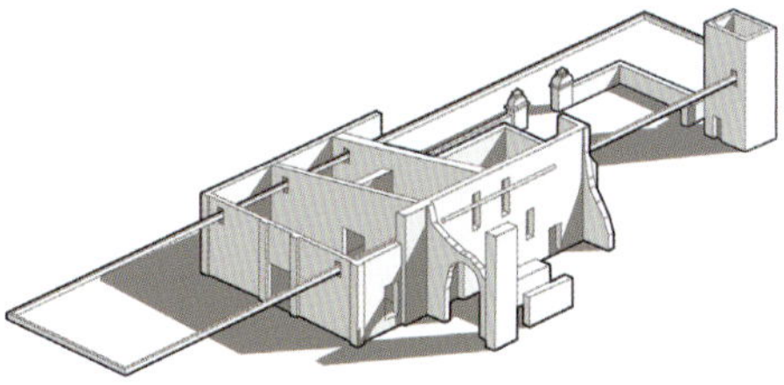

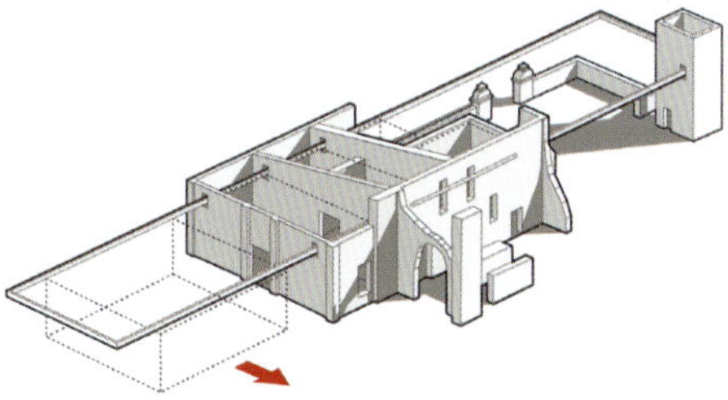

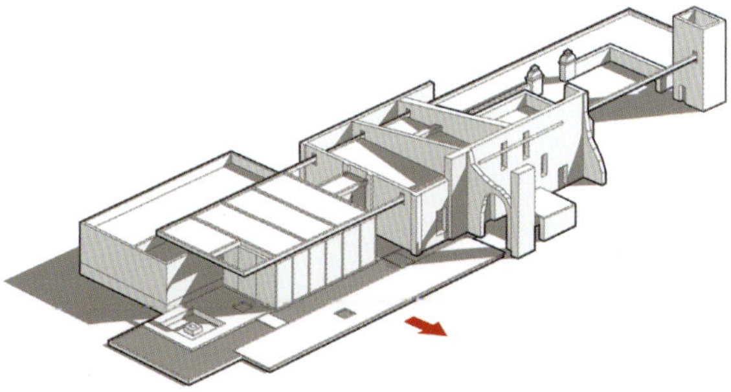

In the interior, the suspended henequen strings, produced by the last active rope factory in Yucatan, provide an acoustic function and reference the plant for which the building was originally constructed. The spatial sequence allows visitors to transit between epochs, finishing in the contemporary addition, which is physically and visually integrated with the main square and its components.

IXI'IM

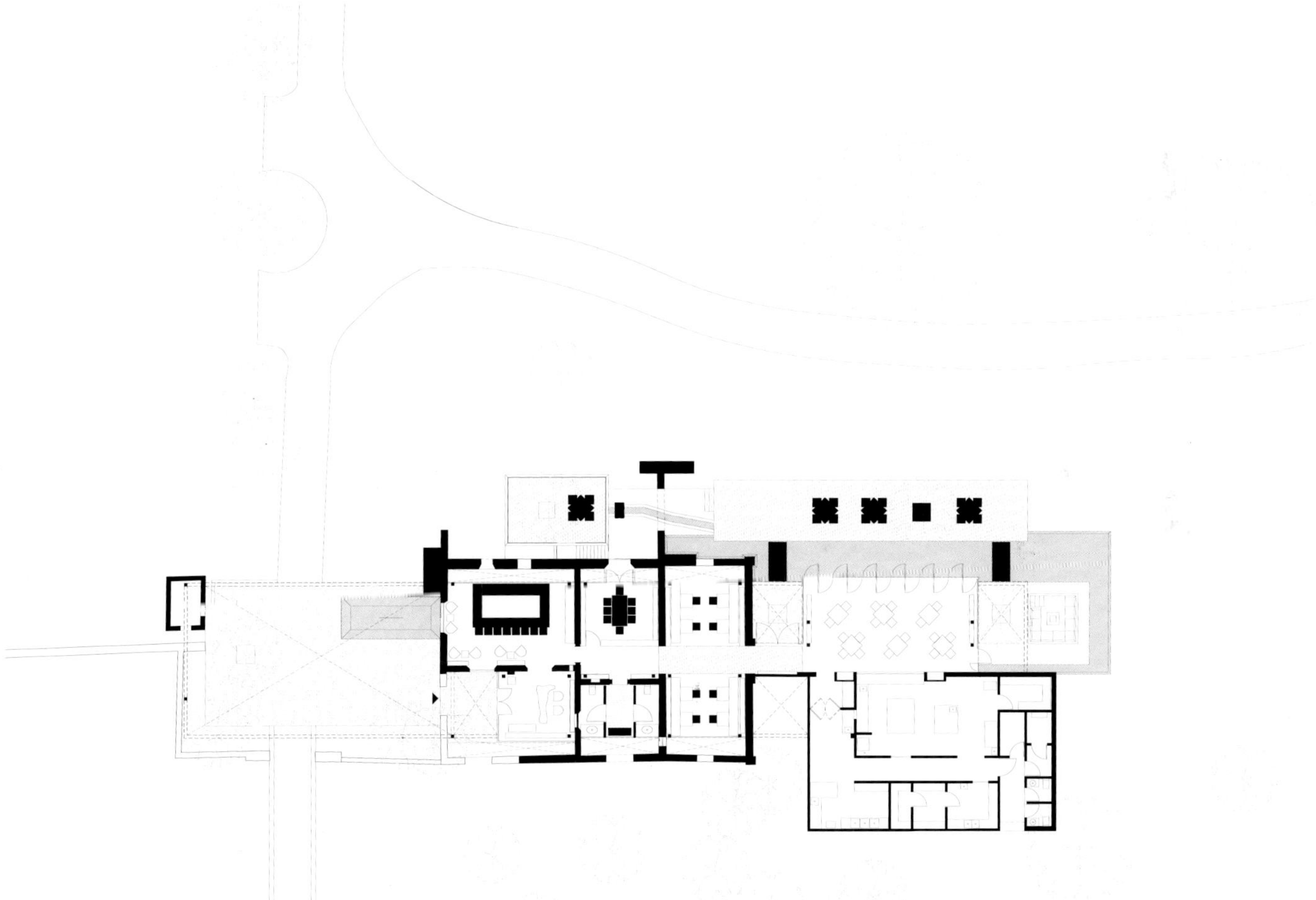

Floor plan

HOUSE Z22 AND WAREHOUSE F88

Large stone walls in this contemporary home are exposed to reveal their craftsmanship, while new concrete and timber insertions showcase the characteristics of the natural materials. The old and new complement each other through the harmony of raw finishes and textures.

House Z22 and Warehouse F88 is the reconstruction of a multi-family house with workshop rooms, which was originally built 170 years ago. Located in Seefeld in Zürich, the house is in a heritage area where new regulations protect the outlines of the existing volumes, and the project had to be developed in conjunction with the conservation of monuments.

The project is a contextual dialogue with history. The massive stone walls provided the starting point for applying new contemporary forms of living, which includes five small apartments in the house and four residential ateliers in the former workshops. The architecture team removed the plaster layer of the stone walls to expose the natural stone, which remained hidden.

The original bourgeois house is still the same from the outside, but plays a minor part in the interior redesign. The architecture team developed a free-flowing space within the confined area of the stone walls. A new "promenade architectural" typology unfolds and has a dialogue with the periphery—the natural stone wall. Lightweight built-in structures are plastered to create a rocky appearance. The built-in furniture is made of raw concrete, timber, and plaster. The windows were mounted directly onto the natural stone slabs with solid wooden frames.

In the workshops, the architecture team responded to the large stone arches with a topography of concrete—a contemporary response to a strong historical element. A stone landscape is understated in appearance to emphasize forms and light.

Architecture:
Gus Wüstemann Architects
Location:
Zürich, Switzerland
Area:
9795 square feet (910 square meters)
Completion:
2017
Photography:
Bruno Helbling

Section

The architecture team created a conversation about the craft of making with 3.2-foot-deep (1-meter-deep) solid stone walls, concrete furniture, and wooden windows with a 7.9-inch-deep (20-centimeter-deep) solid frame. This relates to the historical context of the building and how it was made. Large stone blocks were originally stacked together, but today's structures are formed with reinforced concrete. All elements were returned to their raw original state or built without additional finishes.

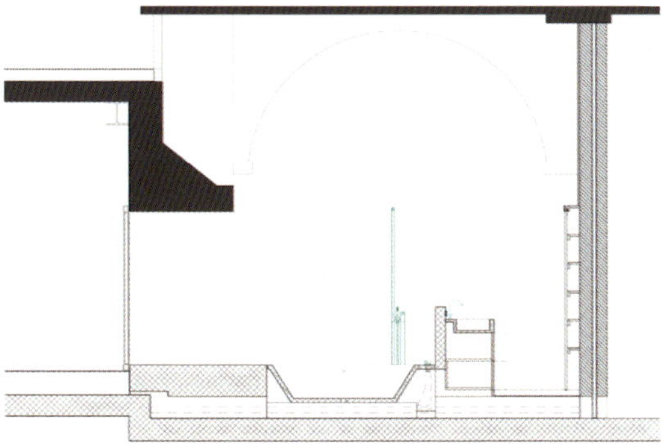

Detail of bathroom

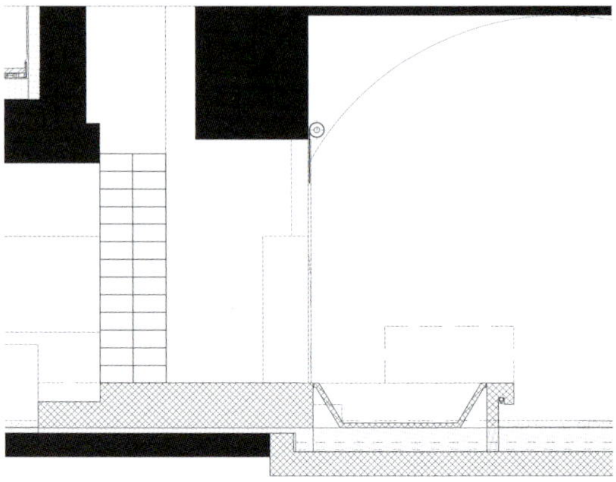

Detail of bathroom

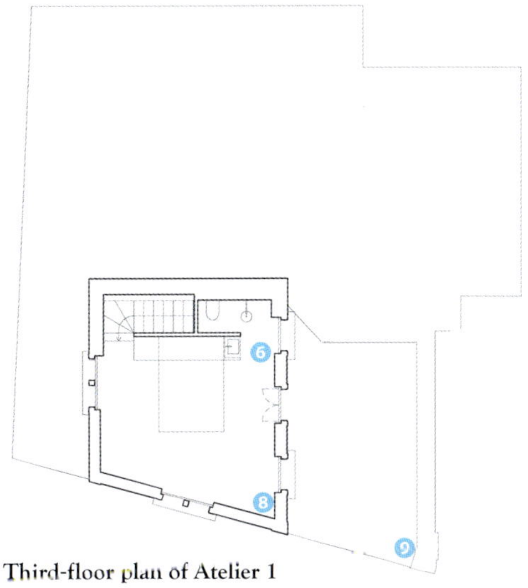

Third-floor plan of Atelier 1

Atelier 2

1. Living room
2. Kitchen
3. Bathroom
4. Garden
5. Bedroom
6. Toilet
7. Terrace

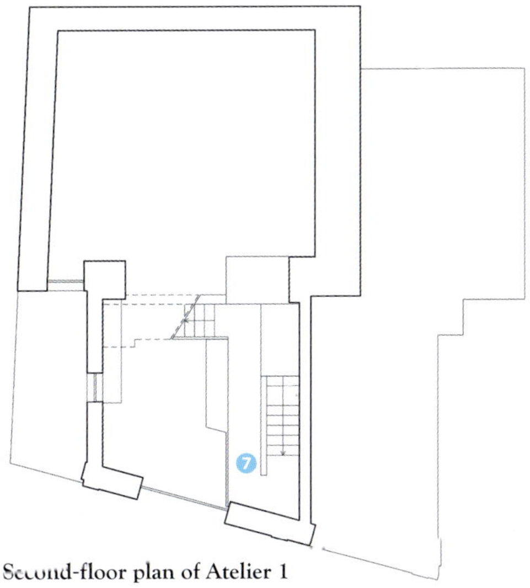

Second-floor plan of Atelier 1

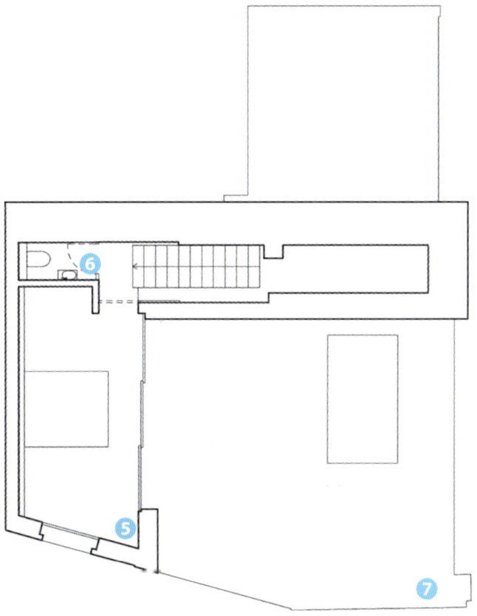

Second-floor plan of Atelier 2

Atelier 1

1. Living room
2. Wardrobe
3. Bedroom
4. Toilet
5. Kitchen
6. Bathroom
7. Gallery
8. Bedroom
9. Terrace

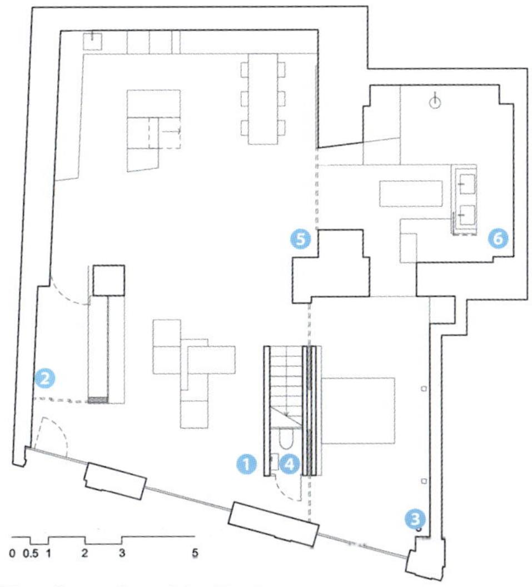

First-floor plan of Atelier 1

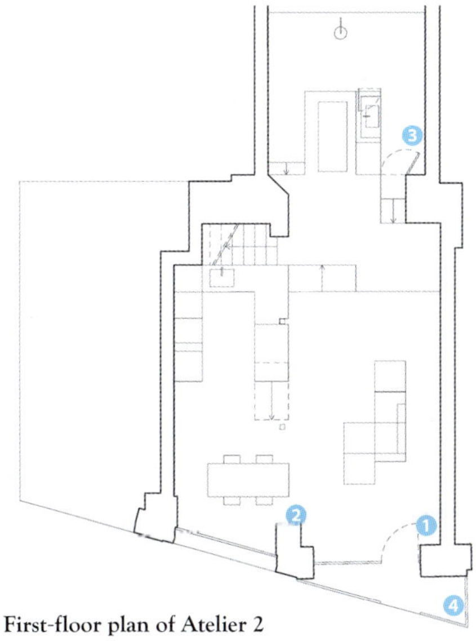

First-floor plan of Atelier 2

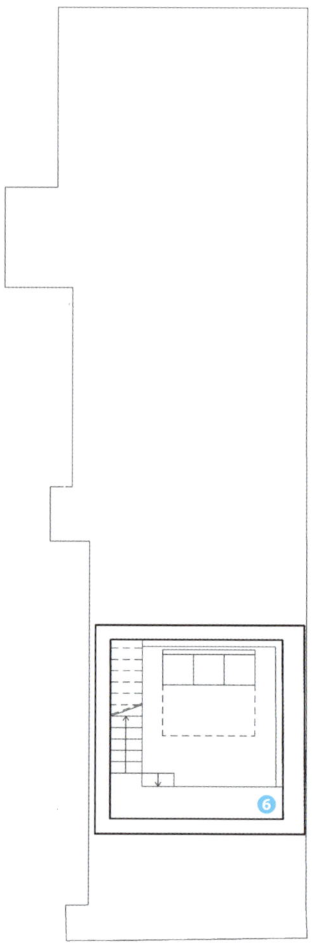

Basement floor plan of Atelier 3

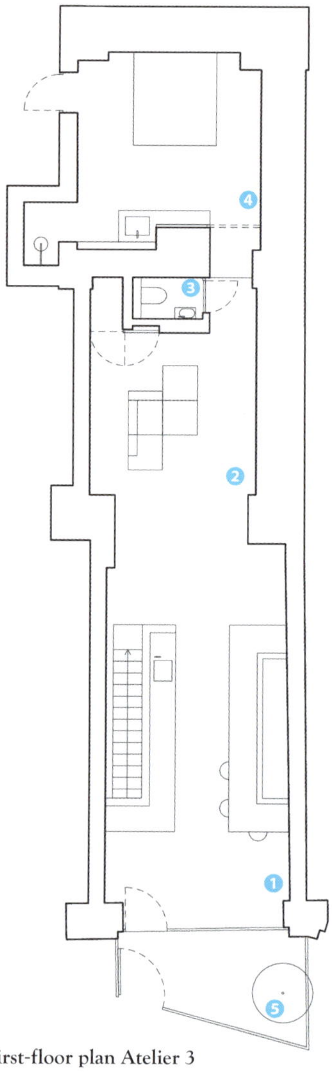

First-floor plan Atelier 3

Atelier 3

1. Kitchen
2. Living room
3. Bathroom
4. Bedroom
5. Garden
6. TV room

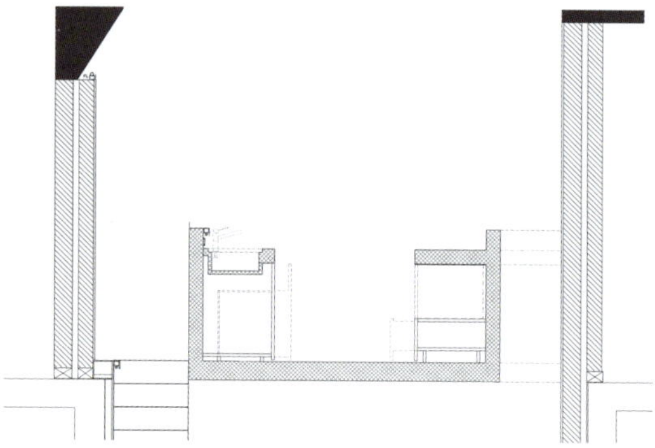

Drawing of kitchen

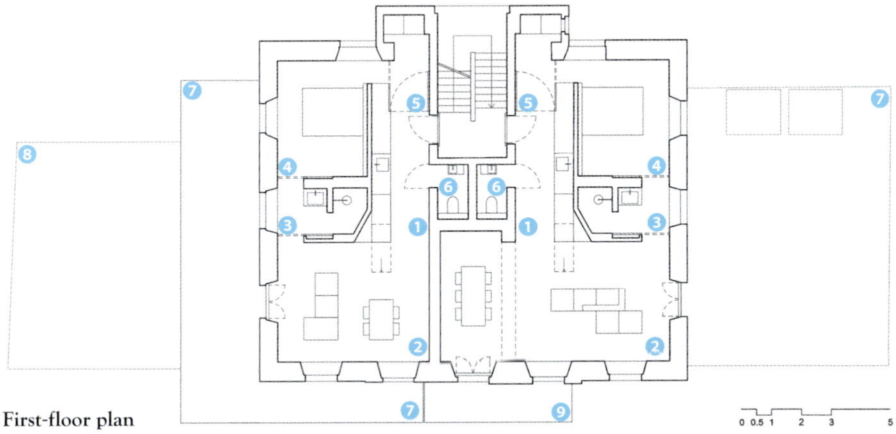

First-floor plan

Apartments 5 and 6

1. Kitchen
2. Living room
3. Bathroom
4. Bedroom
5. Wardrob
6. Toilet
7. Terrace
8. Garden
9. Balcony

ZEITZ MUSEUM OF CONTEMPORARY ART AFRICA

The structural modification of the silos gives what this iconic building a new lease on life. The exterior is distinct for tubular concrete forms and bubble-like windows, while the interior has a cavernous internal atrium created through a process of internal excavation.

The prominent grain silo on Cape Town's Victoria & Alfred Waterfront had stored and graded corn from across South Africa since the 1920s. Following its decommission in the 1990s, Victoria & Alfred Waterfront approached Heatherwick Studio to develop ideas for adapting the silo and the site. Although the waterfront was already a vibrant area, it lacked a major cultural institution. At the same time, Zeitz Foundation was seeking a new permanent home for its collection of contemporary art from Africa and its diaspora. The two programs coincided and the grain silo was transformed into a new contemporary art museum.

Although the concrete building looks like a single structure, it is composed of two parts: a grading tower and 42 tall, cellular silos. The main challenge was to convert these tightly packed concrete tubes into spaces suitable for displaying art while retaining the building's industrial heritage. The architecture team developed a concept to carve out a central atrium from the center of the building, like a vaulted cathedral. The atrium provides access to the gallery floors that are organized around it.

The carved tubes were technically challenging. The rounded shape was modelled on a single grain of corn, scaled to fill the 89-foot-high (27-meter-high) volume, and then translated into thousands of coordinates, each defining a point within the silo's tubes. Physically mapped out with nails, the brittle concrete tubes, which are only 6.7-inches (170-millimeters) thick, were then lined with partial inner sleeves of reinforced concrete. These concrete sleeves created a stable composite structure 16.5-inches

Architecture:
Heatherwick Studio (lead design architects), VDMMA (executive architects), Rick Brown Associates Architects (hotel fit out), Jacobs Parker Architecture & Interior Design (museum fit out)
Location:
Cape Town, South Africa
Area:
102,000 square feet (9476 square feet)
Completion:
2017
Photography:
Mark Williams

North elevation

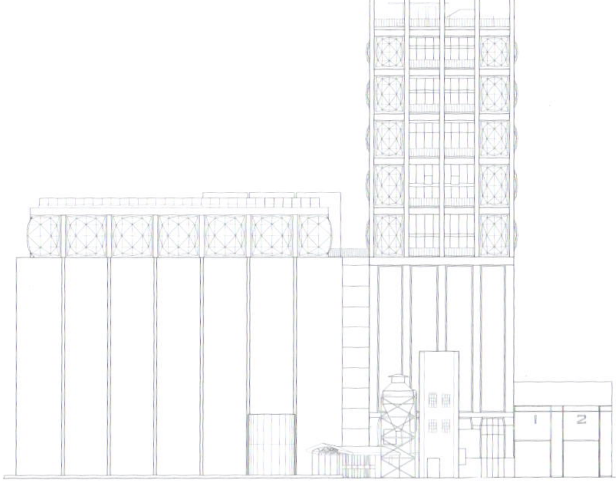

(420-millimeters) thick and provided a cutting guide for removing portions of the old silos. The existing tubes were pared back to reveal the curved geometries of the 162,447-cubic-feet (4600-cubic-meter) atrium. The cut edges were polished to give a mirrored finish that contrasts with the building's rough aggregate concrete.

Each of the carved tubes is capped with a 20-foot (6-meter) diameter panel of laminated glass that brings daylight into the atrium. The glass carries a frit specially commissioned from the late African artist El Loko, based on his *Cosmic Alphabet* works. As well as mitigating heat gain, the frits create a safe, walkable surface for the sculpture garden. The remaining internal tubes were removed to make space for 80 gallery spaces providing 64,583 square feet (6000 square meters) of exhibition space. Underground tunnels have been adapted for site specific works.

The proportions of the tower portion of the silo complex made it unsuitable for exhibition space. The architecture team conceived this structure as an illuminated beacon. Inspired by the bulging glazed texture of a Venetian lamp, they developed a method using facets of glass to subtley create a convex shape. Built with structural glass, the composition strengthens the steel-bar frames to make a transparent shell. The glazing forms a kaleidoscope of changing textures and colors, and creates irregular, sparkling patterns and provides far-reaching views. At night, the building acts as a lantern for the harbor and the city beyond.

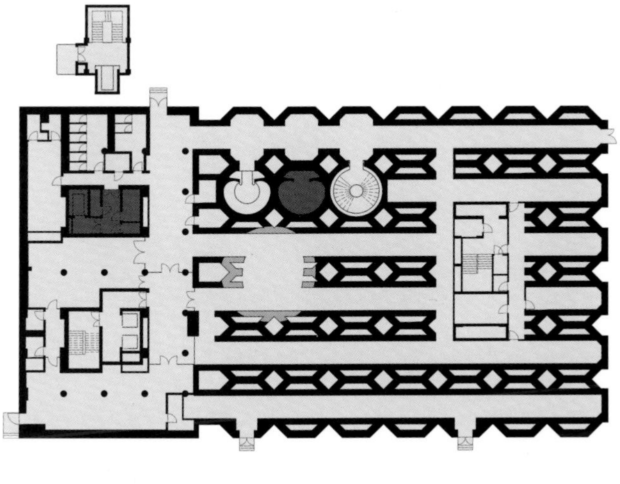

Basement floor plan

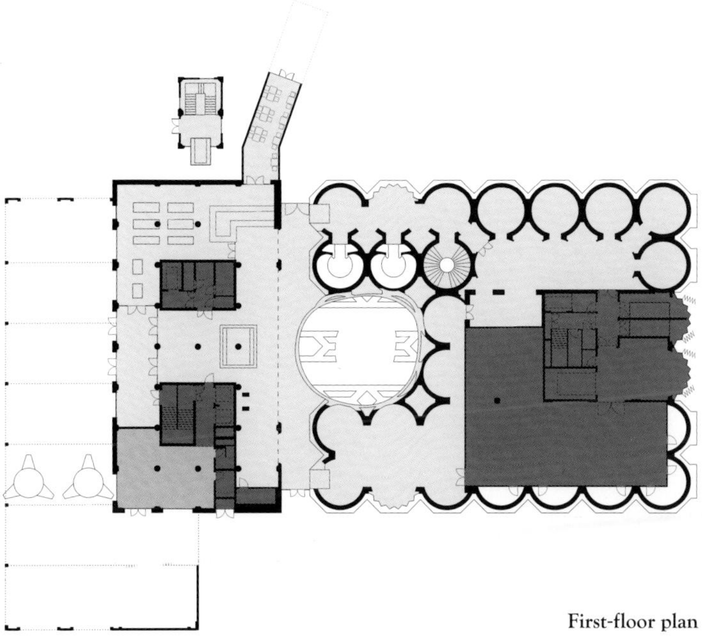

First-floor plan

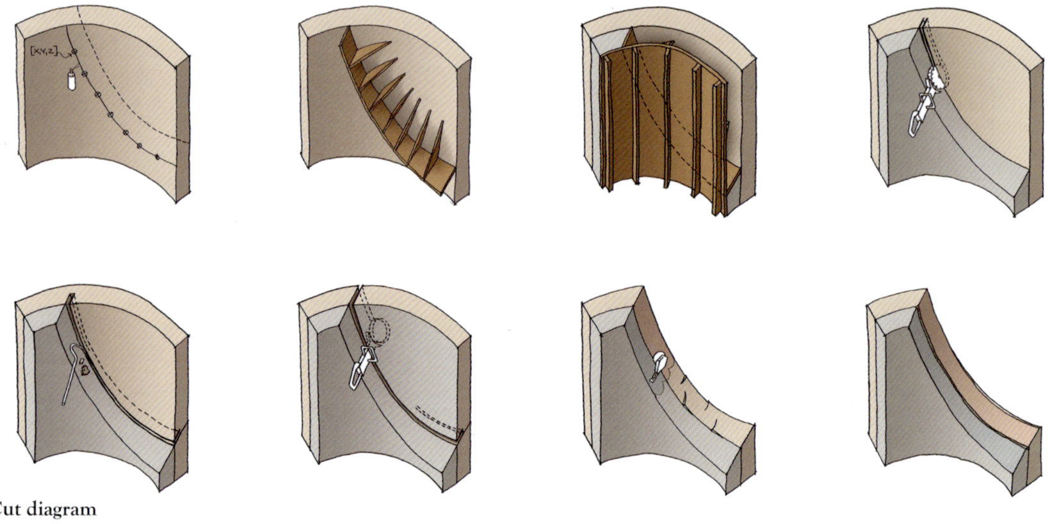

Cut diagram

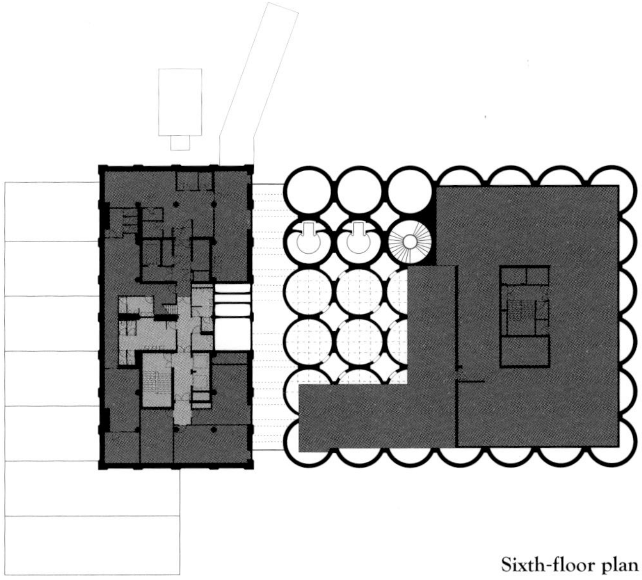

Sixth-floor plan

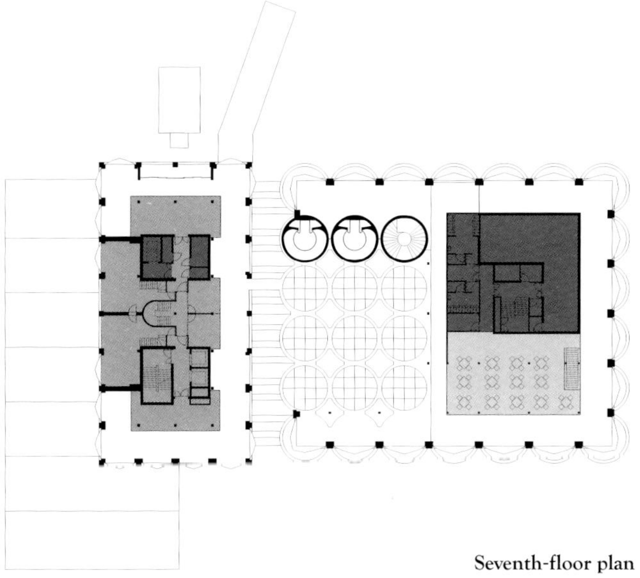

Seventh-floor plan

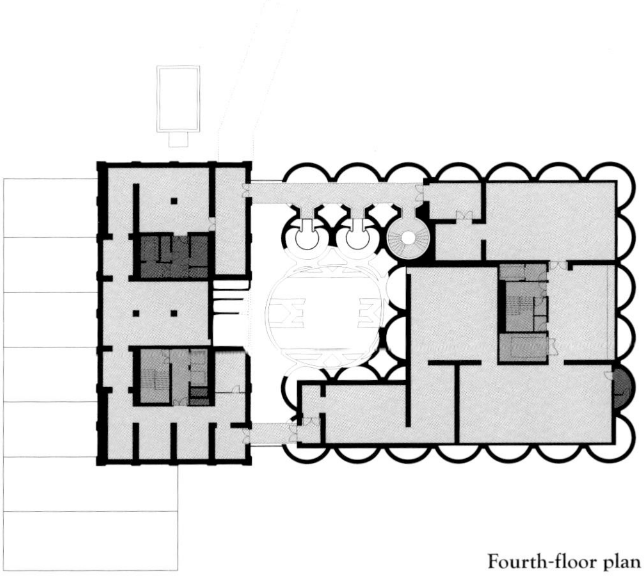

Fourth-floor plan

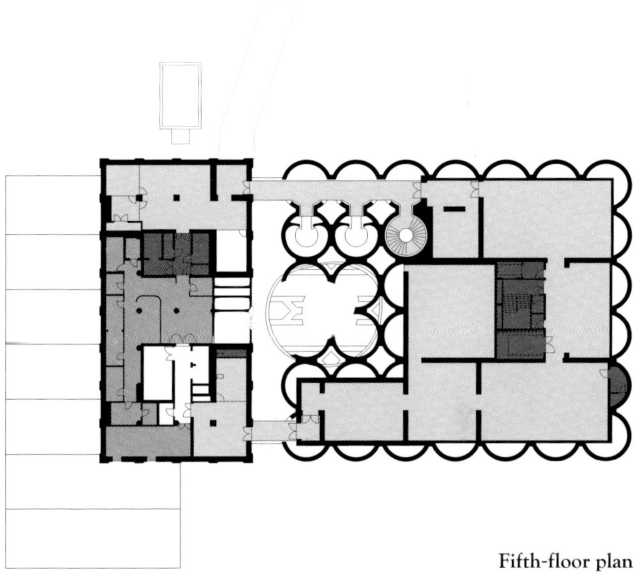

Fifth-floor plan

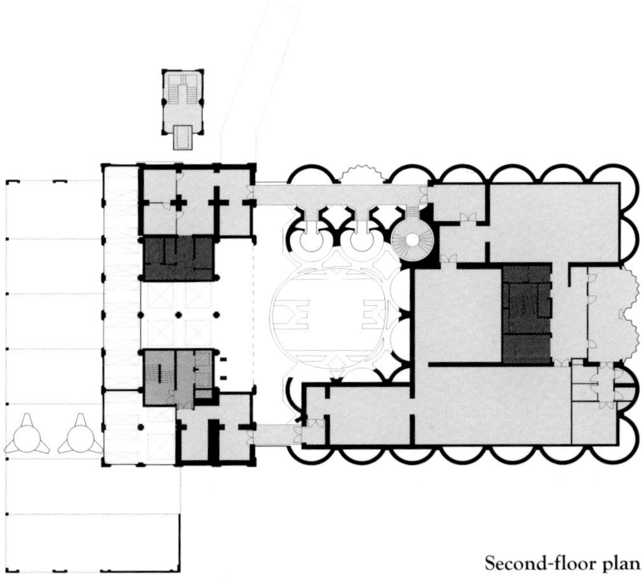

Second-floor plan

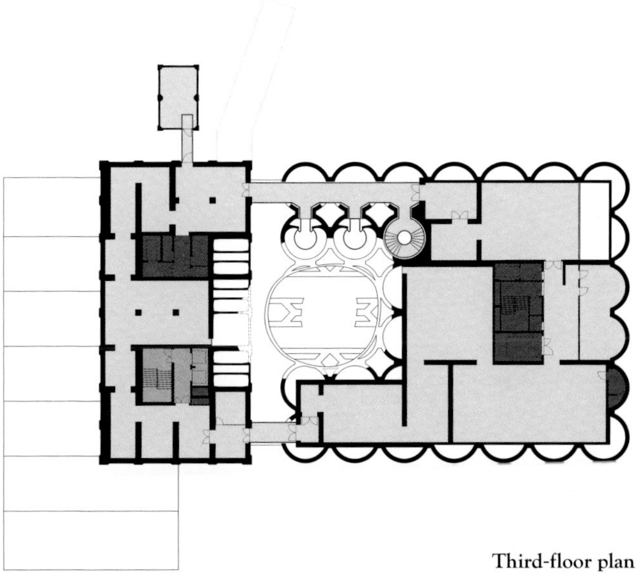

Third-floor plan

M.Y. LAB WOOD WORKSHOP

The addition of a second level within this former warehouse generates a dynamic open space used for woodworking. A hybrid load-bearing system helps achieve a large open workshop floor with only a limited number of visible supports, while high-level windows and a raked ceiling allow natural light to penetrate deep into the space.

M.Y. Lab Wood Workshop is located in the former Dongfeng Sofa Factory in Changning District, Shanghai. The project refurbished the 3229-square-feet (300-square-meters) one-story warehouse into a two-story commercial space for a woodworking learning center.

This design inserts an "archaeological excavation site" recreation into the original 16-foot-high (5-meter-high) space. The main woodworking room is on a sunken floor behind the main entrance, and enclosed by a low terrazzo wall with a pitched black-metal-mesh ceiling above. Sunlight spills into the room from the top of a walkway from where visitors can overlook the woodworking operations.

Utilizing the triangular space formed by the sloping ceiling, a second level increases the internal area. Two black metal "boxes" are introduced. One, enclosing a staircase between the two floors, has a tilted top form that parallels the pitch of the ceiling. The other, a tearoom, interlocks with the main space and the garden to bring formative diversity into the interior, and provide a niche-like space where students take breaks.

The load-bearing structures enhance the floating sensation of the second level. The primary beams of this floor have been lifted with only five columns, two of which are hidden within walls. Multi-ribbed secondary beams extend out of the primary beams and attach to the original walls for reinforcement. This leaves the main space as open as possible.

Architecture:
Continuation Studio
Location:
Shanghai, China
Area:
4951 square feet (460 square meters)
Completion:
2017
Photography:
SHIROMIO Studio

2

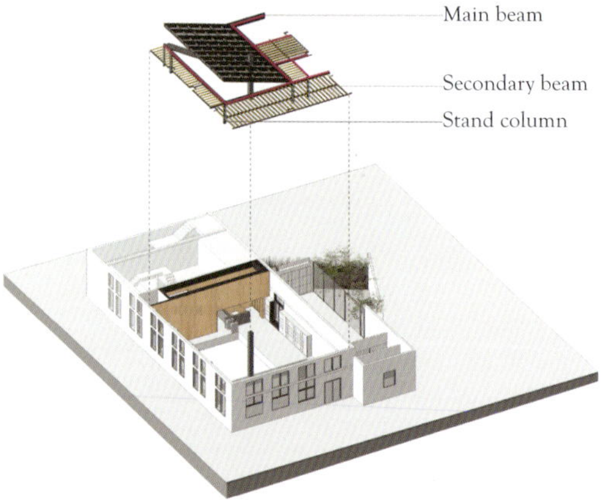

Diagram of added structure

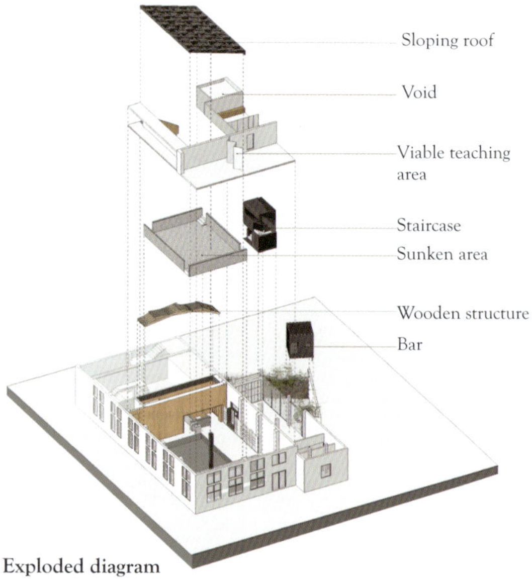

Exploded diagram

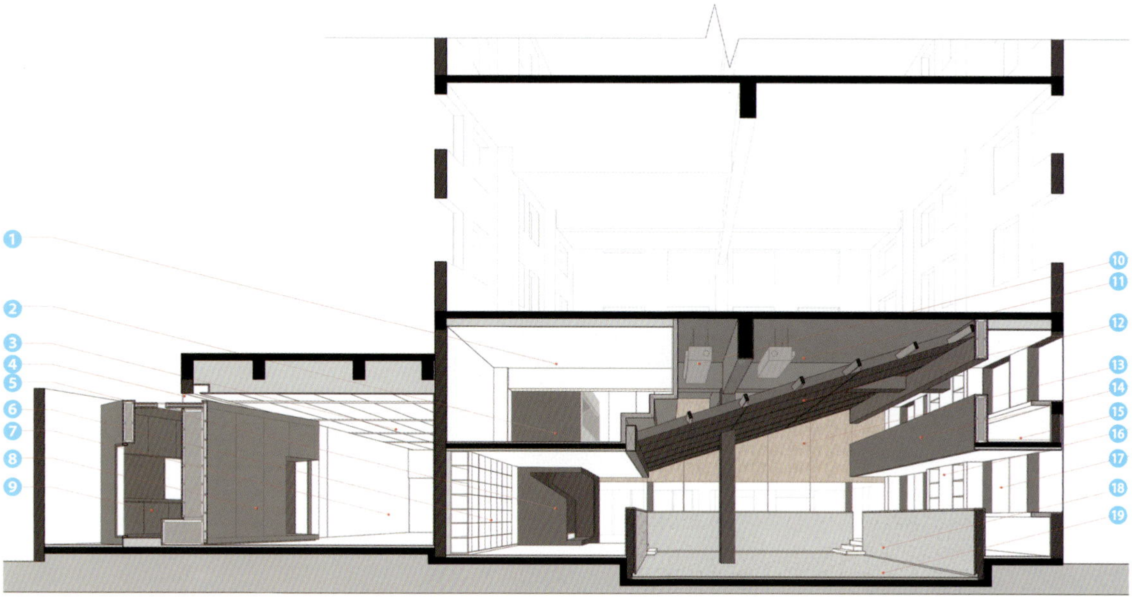

Perspective section

1. White latex paint
2. Terrace classroom
3. Perforated drywall
4. Skylight
5. Staircase
6. Lockers
7. Operation area
8. Galvanized iron sheet
9. Tearoom
10. Air conditioner
11. Deep latex paint
12. Black metal mesh
13. Wooden overcoating
14. Black steel
15. Reading area along window
16. White paint-free plate
17. Stalinite
18. Terrazzo wall
19. Terrazzo ground

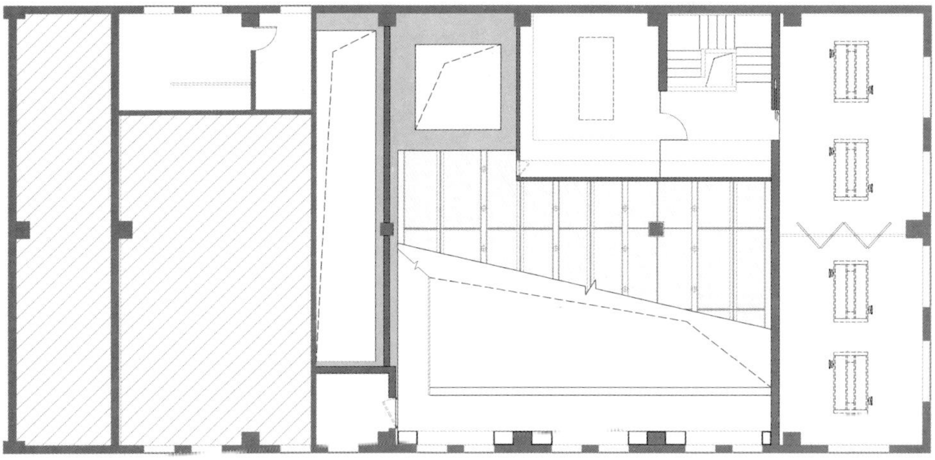

Second-floor plan

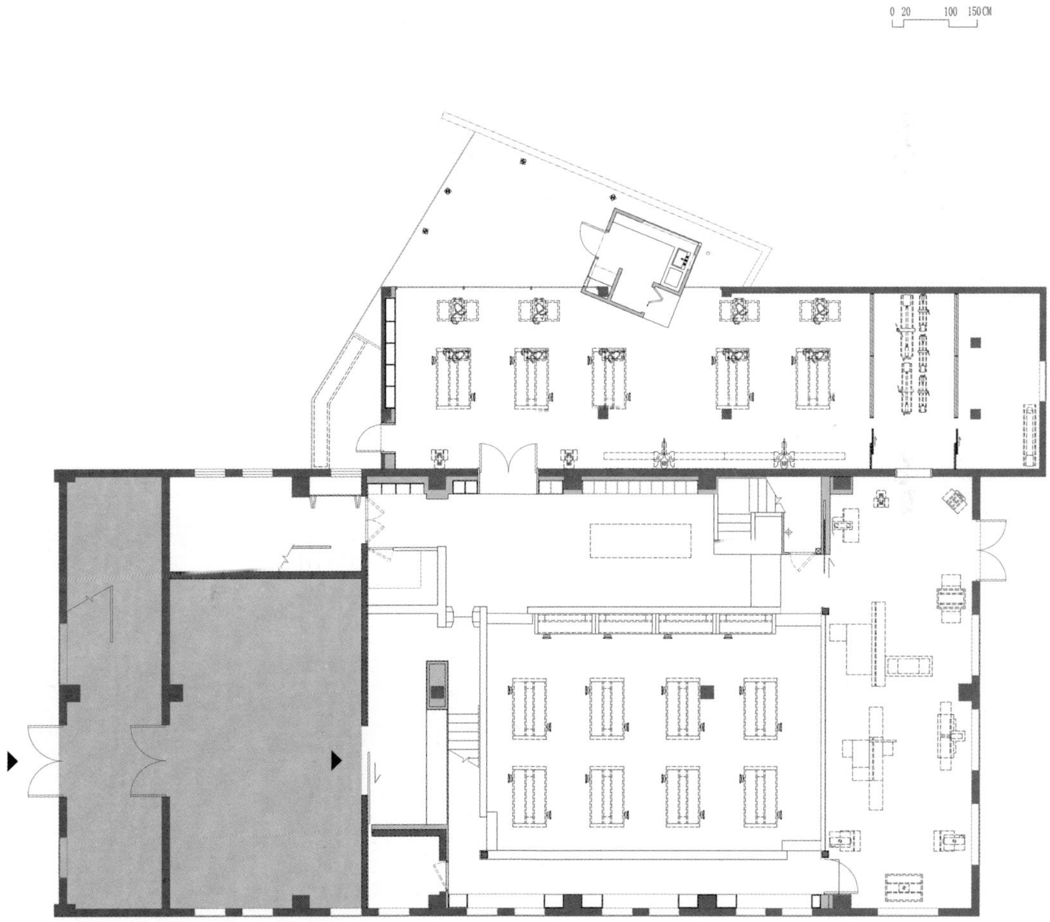

First-floor plan

1. Skylight
2. Overhead cupboard
3. Rain pipe
4. Kitchen counter
5. Seat
6. Cupboard
7. Sloping roof
8. Stairs
9. Exhibition area
10. Storage

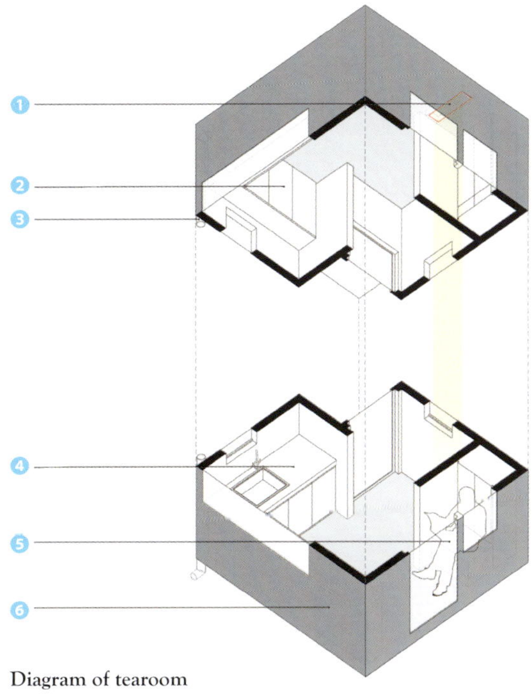

Diagram of tearoom

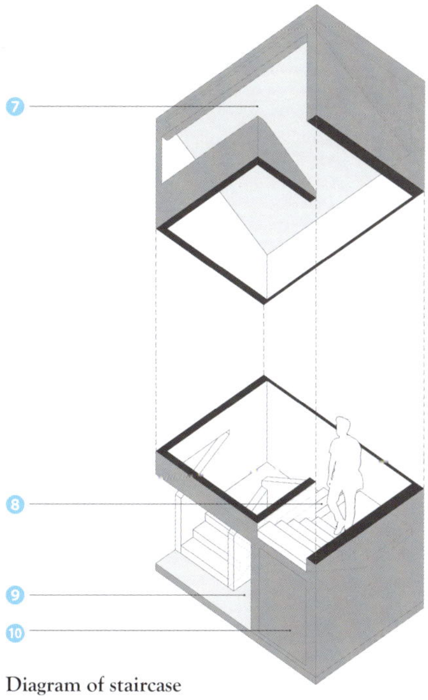

Diagram of staircase

SANTA MARÍA DE VILANOVA DE LA BARCA

Damaged and disused, this old stone church finds new life with the introduction of a brick envelope that mirrors the textures of the stone on the exterior, while providing contrast on the interior.

The old church of Vilanova de la Barca is a thirteenth-century Gothic building that was partially demolished in 1936 as a result of the bombings during the Spanish Civil War. Since then, the church had been in a general state of ruin, preserving the apse, fragments of the naves, and the west façade.

The restoration project aimed to recover the ancient church and restore its original appearance while transforming the structure into a new multipurpose hall. The project aims to establish an architectural dialogue between the old and new elements, the past and present.

The original church has a basilica-style floor plan with two naves, a presbytery, and lateral chapels. The building is 72-feet (22-meters) long and 23-feet (7-meters) wide, with an interior space rising up to 33 feet (10 meters). The surviving construction had two impressive lateral buttresses, probably of Romanesque origin, and a seventeenth-century ribbed vault in a late-Gothic style in the apse. The church was built with local stone ashlar, which was largely damaged by the weather conditions and erosion. More recently, the church has been severely affected by the construction of an attached single-family house in the former graveyard.

The most important part of the intervention focused on the covering of the façade and roof, which have been conceived as a new architectural ceramic shell gently supported above the remains of the ancient walls. The new brick façade is based on a latticework texture and a new gabled roof has Arab tiles.

Architecture:
AleaOlea architecture & landscape
Location:
Lleida, Spain
Area:
3229 square feet (300 square meters)
Completion:
2016
Photography:
Adrià Goula

The exterior façade rises hermetic, opaque, and windowless, as a textured background that reproduces the wrinkled, dense, and irregular texture of the stone ashlars, creating visual continuity and integration with the original fabric. On the other hand, the interior façade has white perforated brickwork that reinforces the contrast and discontinuity between the old and new. The perception of the old church is restored from the outside, and the restful and introspective atmosphere preserved on the inside.

There is a new alternative entrance to the building through the former graveyard located between the church and attached single-family house. It replaces the previous access point of the apse—a door introduced after the demolition of the church—and creates a new entrance patio, dignifying the former graveyard after years of being suffocated by the large adjacent dividing wall. The pergola, trees, vegetation, and water chain provide a new scenography that serves as an entrance threshold to the church's interior.

Elevations

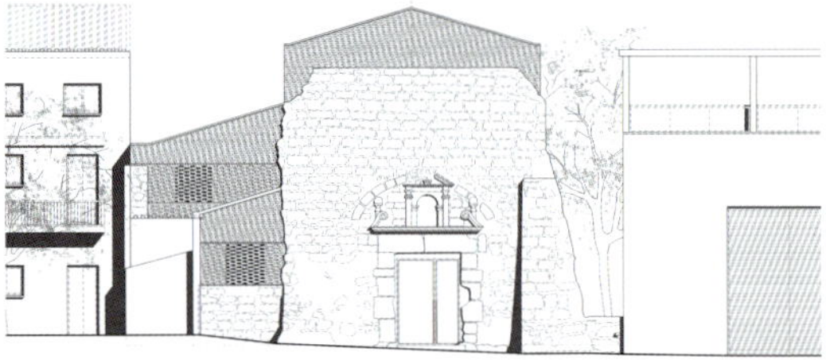

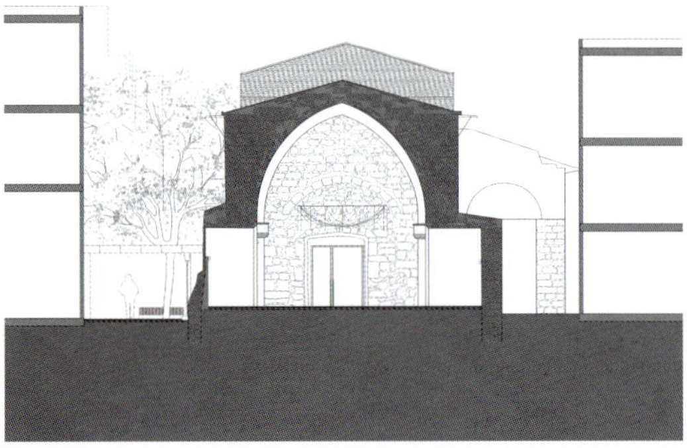

Floor plan

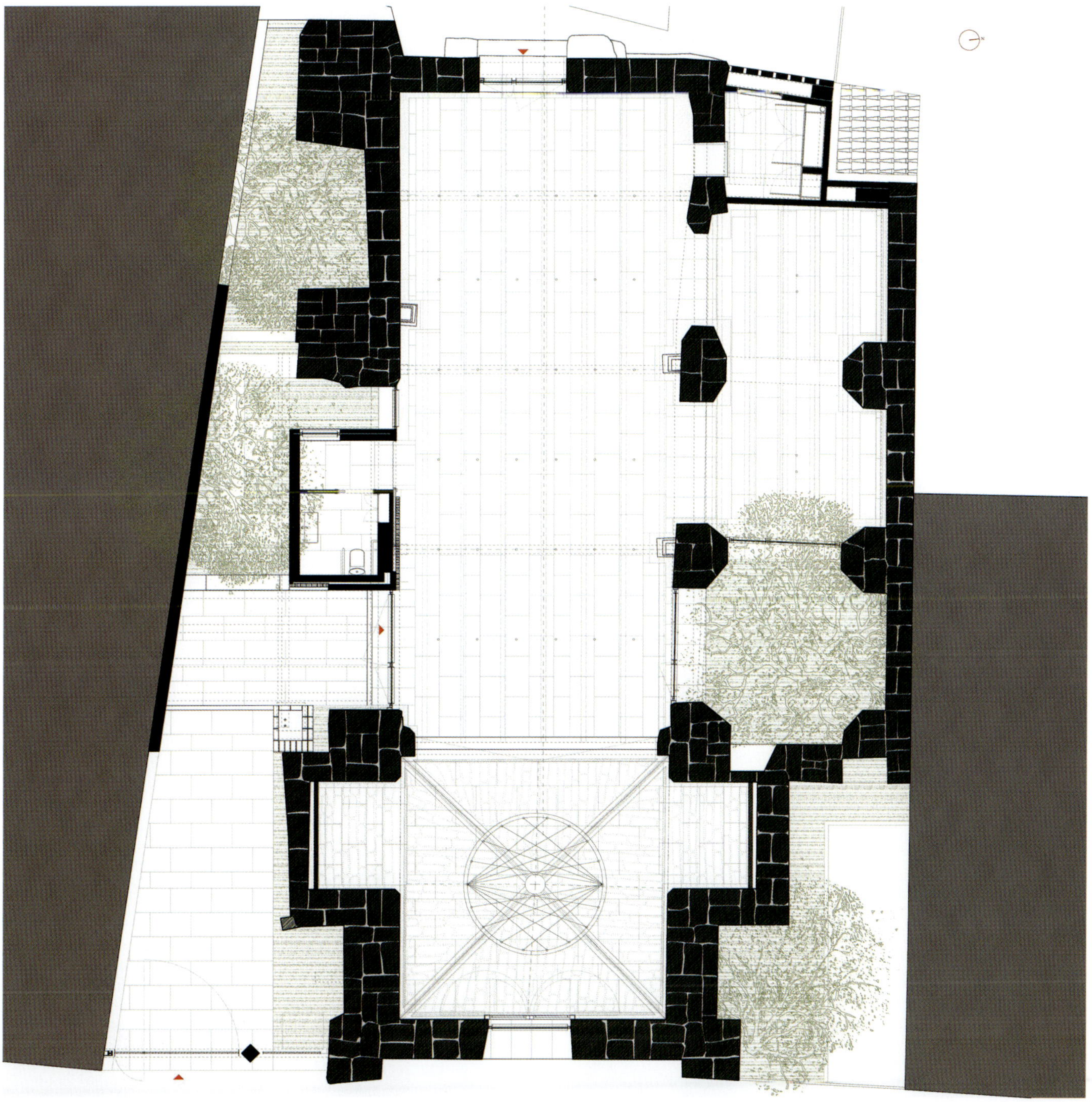

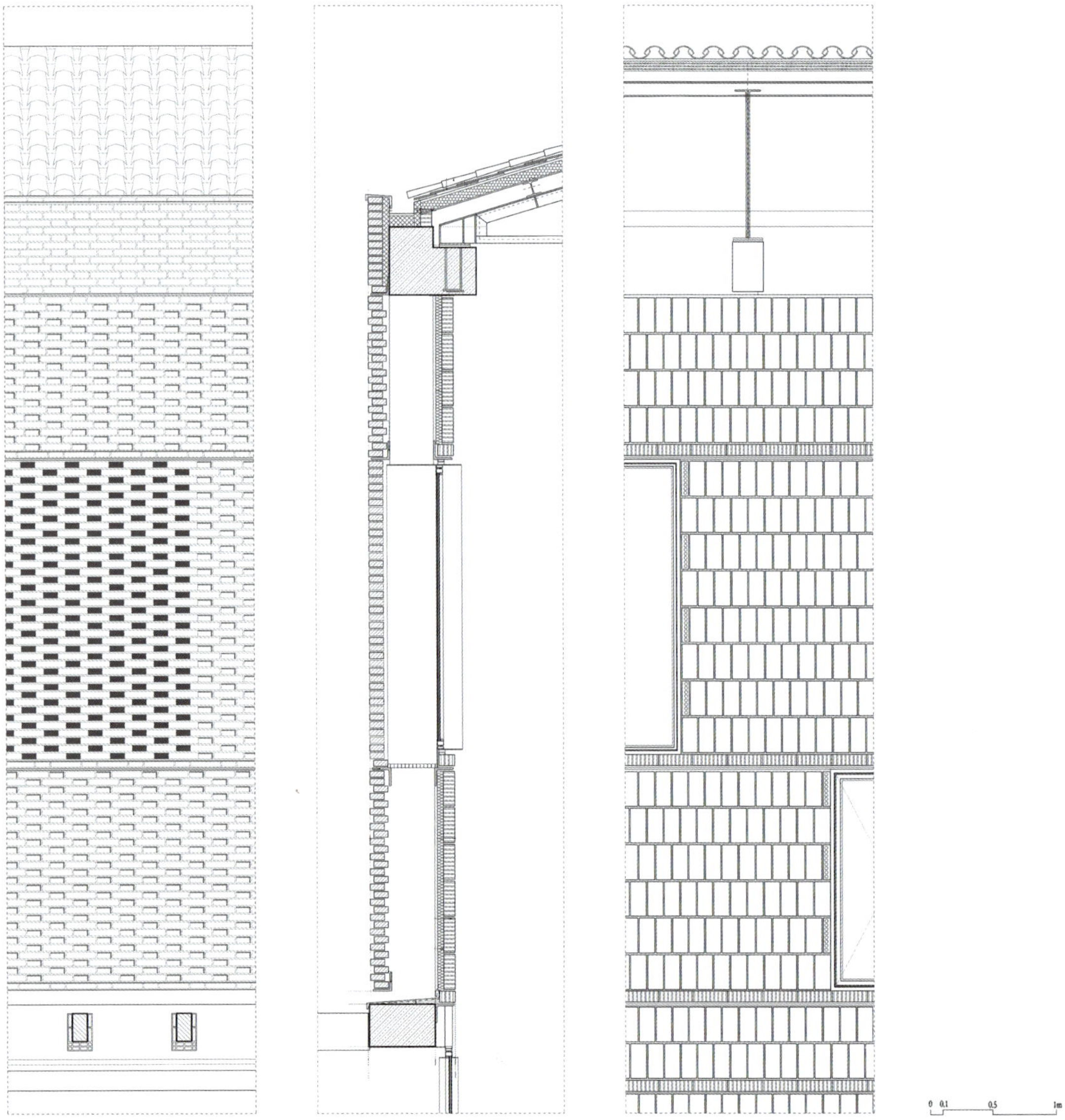

Detailed drawings

STRATEGY
4

EXTERNAL JUXTAPOSITION

In this strategy a new structure, independent of the old, is added to or built adjacent to an existing structure. While the existing building may be modified in various ways, including some or all of the preceding strategies, the primary aim is the external juxtaposition of two distinct building forms—the new and the old—which are in dialogue with each other. This dialogue may be sensitive, but it may also be confrontational.

This strategy, in many ways, is similar to the first strategy, "architecture as furniture," in which the new is treated as separate and distinct from the old. Only here, the intervention is at the scale of the building, and dialogue occurs on the exterior rather than interior. The projects in this section present a number of ways in which the dialogue between old and new may take place. External juxtapositions usually occur when the new program requires a substantially larger volume than that provided by the host structure. This strategy offers the most freedom for the new design to have a language quite separate from the old. Nevertheless, the examples presented here demonstrate how these new interventions can have a dialogue with the existing in various ways, even if they sit apart from the old structure. The techniques used include the referencing of existing rhythms, mirroring of volumes, reflection of elements, and continuity through circulation and intermediary spaces.

Malmö Saluhall and Studio Molière represent external juxtaposition by mirroring the form or image of the old building with a degree of translation or distortion of the reflected image. The dialogue therefore is constructed through similarity and difference. The massing and scale of both examples are imitated, and the difference is found in the architectural language that nonetheless is a modern translation of the old. At Malmö Saluhall, the volume of the shed is mirrored such that the new touches the old and adopts the same form. The new however differs in materials, although it stays within the limited color palette of the original shed. It differs further through the distortions of the volume generated by the site constraints and, as a consequence, produces a dynamic relationship: The exterior presence of the new building sets up a responsive relationship to the surrounding urban fabric. The new school building at Studio Molière is built a short distance from the historical building, and the glass façade of the new reflects the façade of the old. Placing the new building opposite the old one makes it possible for occupants to view each building from the interior of the other. This has the effect of collapsing the two elevations onto each other, bringing the

Malmö Saluhall by Wingårdh Arkitektkontor ©Wingårdhs

similarities and differences between the two façades to the fore through their reflections. The new building complements the old through the harmonious proportions of the window openings, and matching the floor and eave heights for continuity between the two.

Collage is where seemingly disparate images or buildings are brought together to form a new coherent entity with a different meaning. Gucci Hub represents the strategy of external juxtaposition through collage—uniting several distinctly different buildings as objects in one composition. It comprises a complex set of individual buildings. The various components, old and new, sit juxtaposed next to each other, each with distinct massing and architectural language. While contrast is used to identify old from new, various techniques are used to hold the complexes together to read as one.

The spaces between the distinct buildings become important moments with layered characteristics generated by the language of the buildings that enclose them. It is in these open spaces that the dialogue between old and new becomes apparent.

At Gucci Hub, a disused airplane factory made up of large industrial sheds has been modified by subtraction and addition to create functional spaces and internal and external circulation across the site. Portions of sheds are carved out to produce outdoor spaces, and new elements are inserted into existing courtyards to bring cohesion to the complex. The old buildings are treated in a uniform manner to unite them in contrast to the new interventions. The glass and black metal of the new intervention contrasts against the red brick walls and roof tiles of the old. The verticality of the new six-story tower against the horizontal

B30 by KAAN Architecten ©Karin Borghouts

spaces of the large warehouse buildings creates another juxtaposition, and the ribbed façade of the new, which repeats the structural rhythm of the warehouse trusses, unites the complex.

The external juxtaposition in B30 serves to connect the two main wings of the historical building. It is essentially an erasure and overwriting of a previous adaptation to create a new dialogue with the existing building. The original is valued through the erasure of the previous alterations. The current alteration has a reduced overall height to allow the roof of the historical building to regain its prominence. Continuity between old and new is achieved through mimicry. The coffered ceilings provided inspiration for the new angular light wells, and the tones of the new materials were chosen to match those of the original building. The juxtaposition is subtle and the internal thresholds between old and new are blurred. This juxtaposition presents itself as an evolution of the architectural language of the older building, which is reflective of an evolution of governance. This shift is registered in the new intervention that is open, transparent, and inviting, juxtaposed against the hierarchical and enclosed language of the historical building.

The last two examples of external juxtaposition stand in stark contrast to one another. They present two very different ways in which the juxtaposition of a new intervention can take place from within the courtyard of an existing building. The difference hinges around the scale of the interventions. Layering Courtyard works at the scale of a room and looks inward, while Antwerp Port House is a large intervention that offers views out over the port and the city and can be seen from afar.

Layering Courtyard radically transforms the quality of spaces in a courtyard building, typical of the Republican period in China, through a delicate placement of a new separate building within the old courtyard, thus creating a new set of rooms open to the sky. This building that once had one relatively large courtyard now has a series of smaller outside spaces that mediate a transition from public to private, providing gentle qualities of light and views into and through green spaces. In addition, more subtle design approaches to the existing building add to the layering of the whole. The first courtyard is created by pulling back the line of enclosure at the street front to deepen the entry threshold. The thick stone wall of the old building offers the first material layer in the transition from public to private. This is followed by a new glass wall set back from the street, and with the removal of roof tiles, establishes the first courtyard providing a threshold barrier to the noisy street. The next series of courtyards are generated through the juxtaposition of new elements against the existing structure. The new building in the courtyard mimics some of the architectural characteristics of the existing in its roof shape and proportions, but is made of a set of new materials—metal and glass—that establish a contrast against the original textured timber and stone. As in "renovation and insertion," the existing and new interiors are held together by way of the renovation. A smooth white finish merges the two, while the introduction of a minimalist timber lining brings a modern yet warm finish to the interiors, in contrast to the textured timber structure.

While Antwerp Port House also emerges as a juxtaposition from within the courtyard of the building, it has a dialogue with the physical and historical context outside. The derelict fire station was once intended to be a tower, which prompted the designers to elevate the intervention high above the roofscape of the old building, providing users with a panoramic view of the port and surrounding city. The language of the new takes its cues from the water, rather than the old building. This is translated into a crystal-like form made of faceted structural glass that reflects the tones of the water and sky, as well as being an expression of the diamond trade in Antwerp. The external juxtaposition presents itself to the city of Antwerp from the interior courtyard of the old fire station, not only as a reflection of the physical qualities of its surroundings but also as a reflection of its historical and economic narratives. The new structure is supported by the old, floating above it, in contrast to the old building that is firmly anchored to the ground.

In general, when existing buildings are extended through external juxtaposition, the one common characteristic is that the spaces between old and new have an important role to play in the experience of the composition. In each case the new provides a translation of the old, expressing similarities and differences that signal a respect for the past and a belief in the future.

MALMÖ SALUHALL

This market hall finds its appeal in the decision to design through similarity and difference. The overall form of the new intervention mirrors that of the old and then deviates from it by allowing the site constraints to impose alterations to the mirrored image.

The old freight depot west of Malmö Central Station was no more than a roofless shell when siblings Nina Totté and Martin Karyd bought the building to create a market hall for approximately 20 vendors and restaurateurs. The initial intention was to add a similar volume onto the existing oblong brick building, but the plans changed when several layers of underground utilities were discovered on the site, reducing the buildable area of the lot.

The addition imitates the gabled silhouette of the existing building, but only occupies a portion of the site. A gap in the roof between the building and the addition brings daylight to the old brick façade. The new façade cladding of weathering corrugated steel provides an echo of the industrial character that has historically dominated the district. Vertical steel profiles give the façade rhythm and its rust-red color serves as a backdrop for vegetation that grows over the lattices. Vegetation also fills the narrow space between the market hall and adjacent parking structure.

The main hall on Gibraltar Street has a large protruding roof to provide a covered entrance. The market hall provides a robust framework within which different traders can develop and sell their products. Food and ingredients are showcased through a straightforward layout and simple, solid material palette. Service areas (warehouses, storage rooms, staff rooms, and so on) are arranged on three floors at one end of the building.

Architecture:
Wingårdh Arkitektkontor
Location:
Malmö, Sweden
Area:
16,145 square feet (1500 square meters)
Completion:
2016
Photography:
André Pihl, Wingårdhs

MALMÖ
SALUHALL

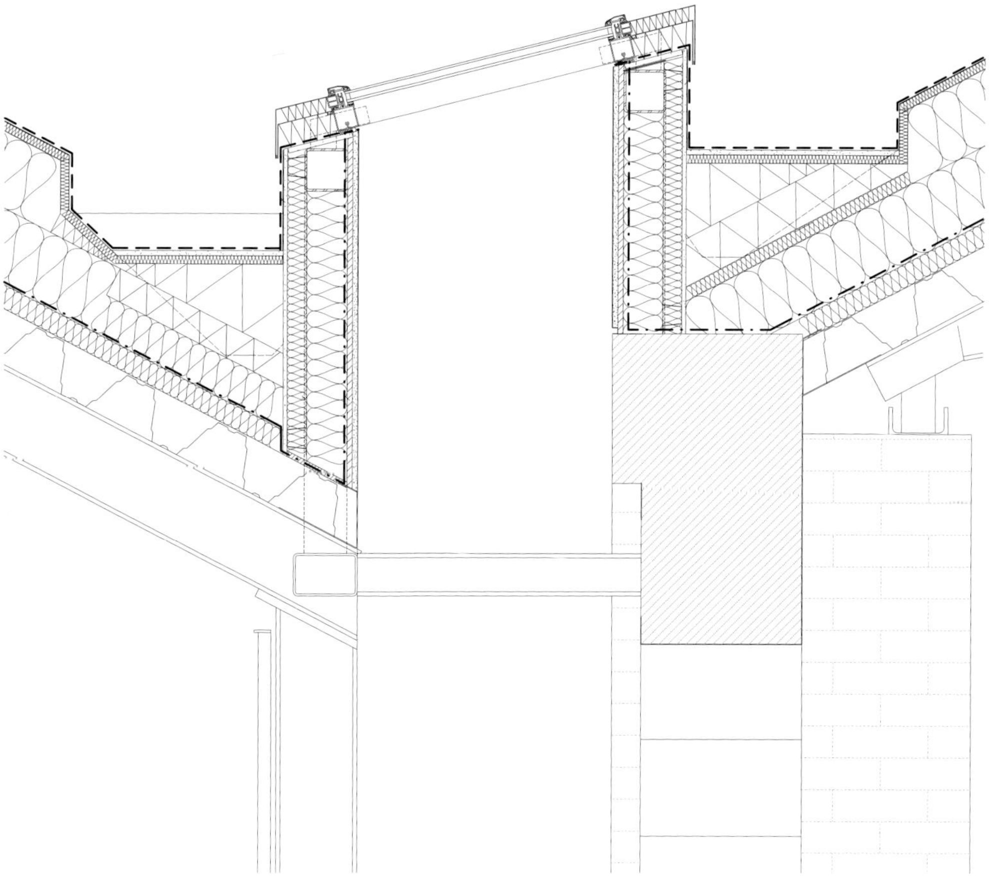

Detailed drawing

Elevations

FG HALLEN

LIMHAMNS KÖ
PAPI
RHS
13

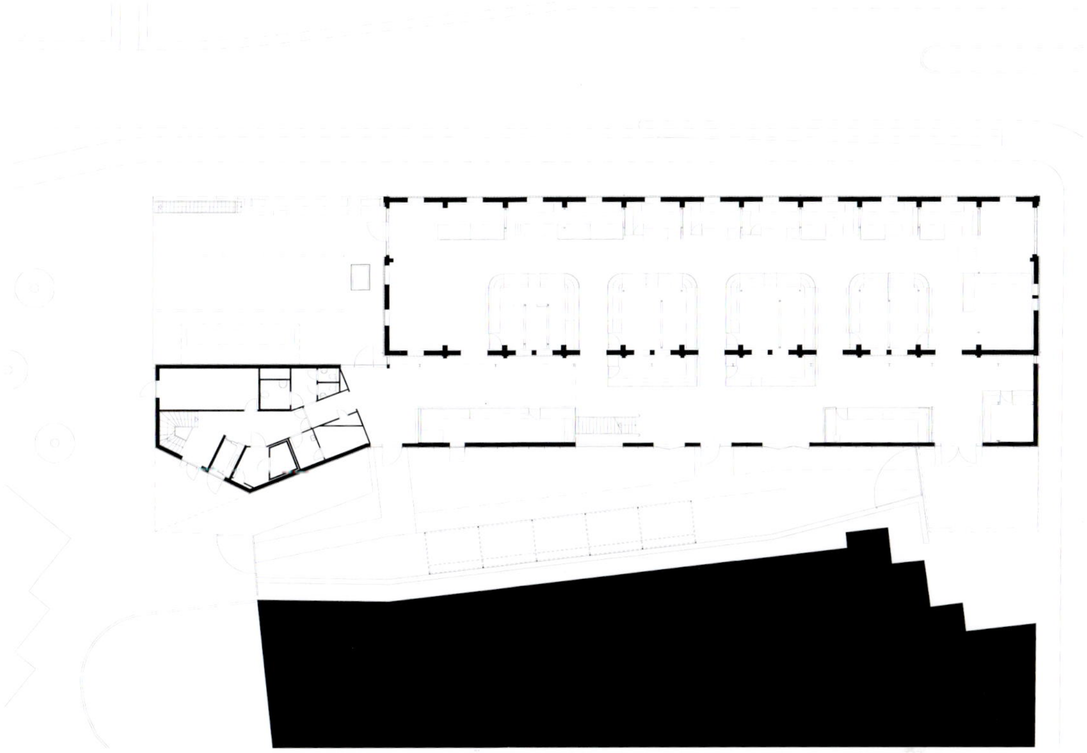

Floor plan

LYCÉE FRANÇAIS AND STUDIO MOLIÈRE

Architecture:
Dietmar Feichtinger Architectes
Location:
Vienna, Austria
Area:
38,653 square feet (3591 square meters)
Completion:
2016
Photography:
Hertha Hurnaus

This new intervention translates the language of the old by being positioned a short distance away from it. The new building mirrors and abstracts the proportions of the older building's openings and the heights of its floors and eaves.

The extension of Lycée Français and renovation of Studio Molière included the construction of a new building and the design of open spaces that allowed the architecture team to play with the contrast of materials, lights, and shadows.

The attempt in the nineteenth century to open up the old riding school is reflected in the new school building. The use of contrasts—technologies, construction methods, and materials—is expressed by reflecting the old building in the glass façade of the new school. This effect is reversed as it gets dark, when the new building illuminates the old studio.

The entrance, reception, and bookstore are located on the Liechtensteinstraße side of the site. The new reception area is set back from the alignment of the buildings and inserted into the building volume to provide an initial view into the covered space. By removing the two existing ceilings, this space acquires a generosity that reflects its importance. The lobby space is also opened up to just under the roof, and the large, pointed-arch windows flood the lobby with daylight, especially in the afternoon and evening, before performances commence. This space doubles as a passage that provides access to the new school building.

The new school building is located to the southwest of Studio Molière, with a new outside space between them. The glass façade of the new building reflects the façade of the original building. This is emphasized by the building's orientation, by the reduced detail of the façade, and by its luminosity, which is especially evident during sunset. The main entrance is located directly in

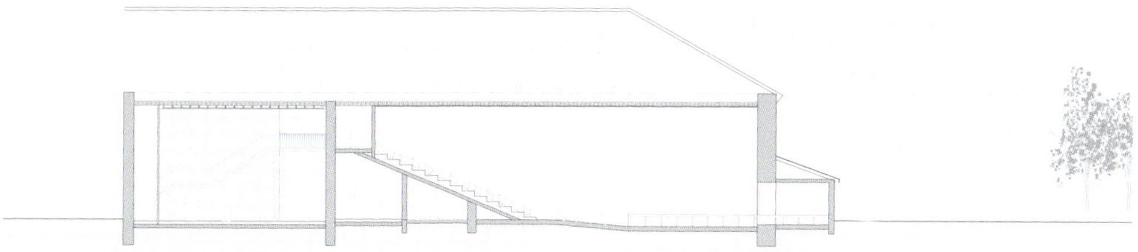

Section A-A

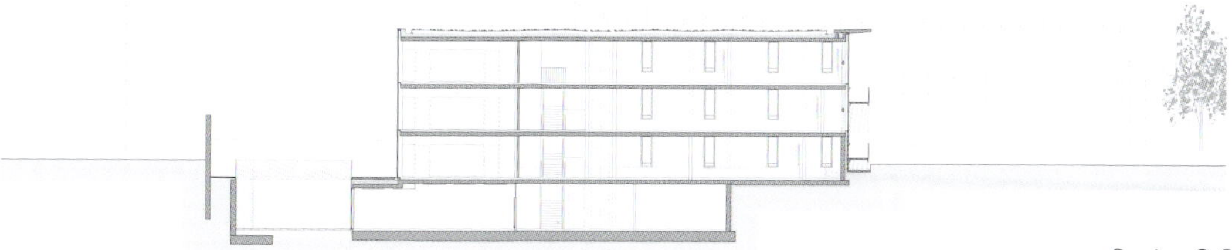

Section C-C

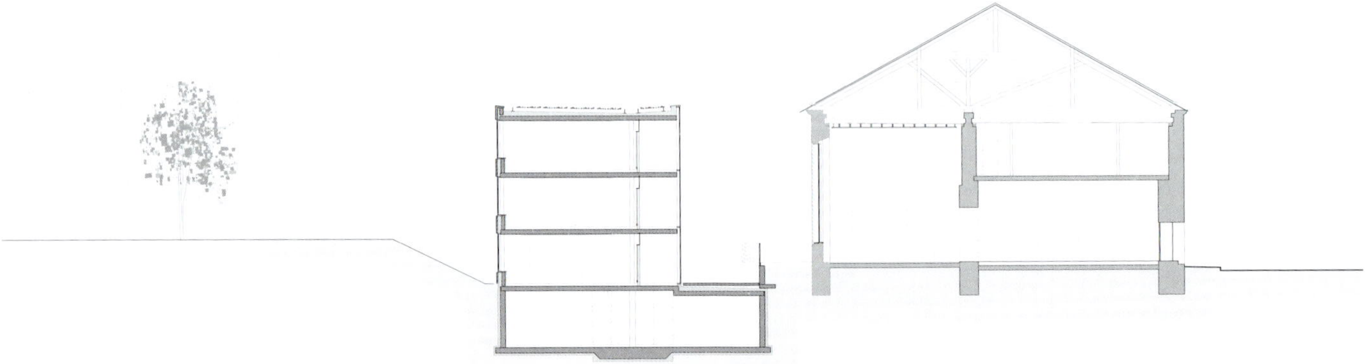

Section D-D

front of the existing Studio Molière exit, and the access to classrooms faces the Studio Molière building.

Structural adjustments made to the existing building included changing the log ceiling into a timber and reinforced-concrete ceiling, and replacing the existing attic trusses with steel frames. The windows were mostly restored, and new double glazing added where required.

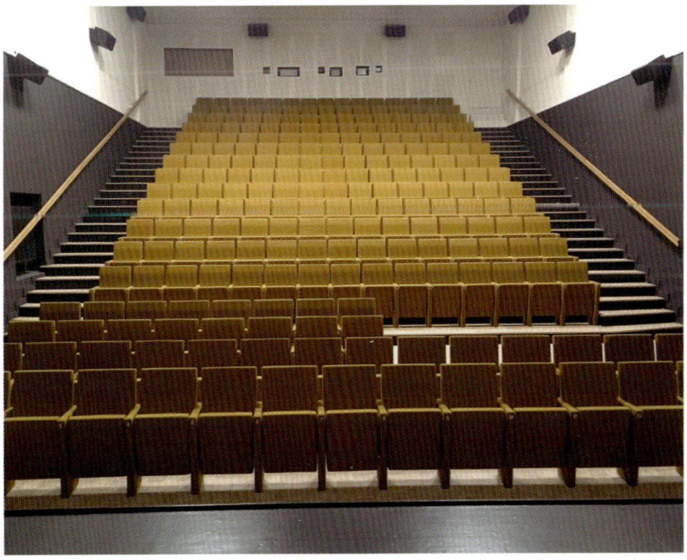

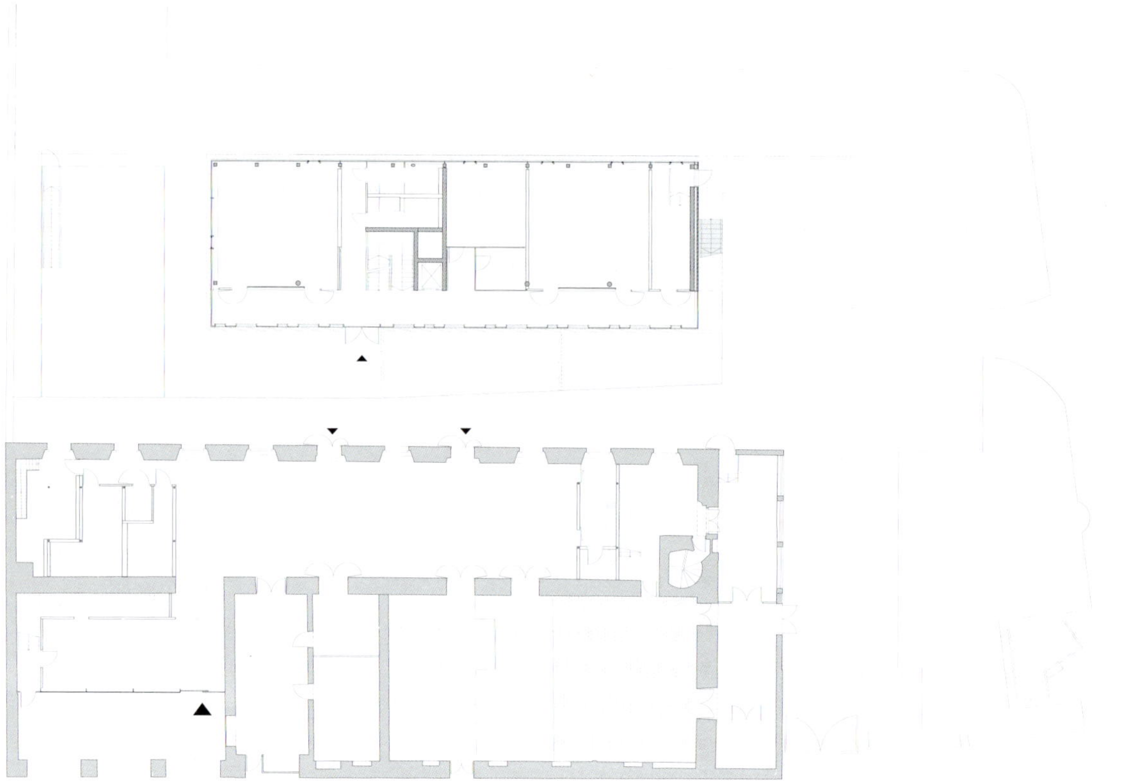

First-floor plan

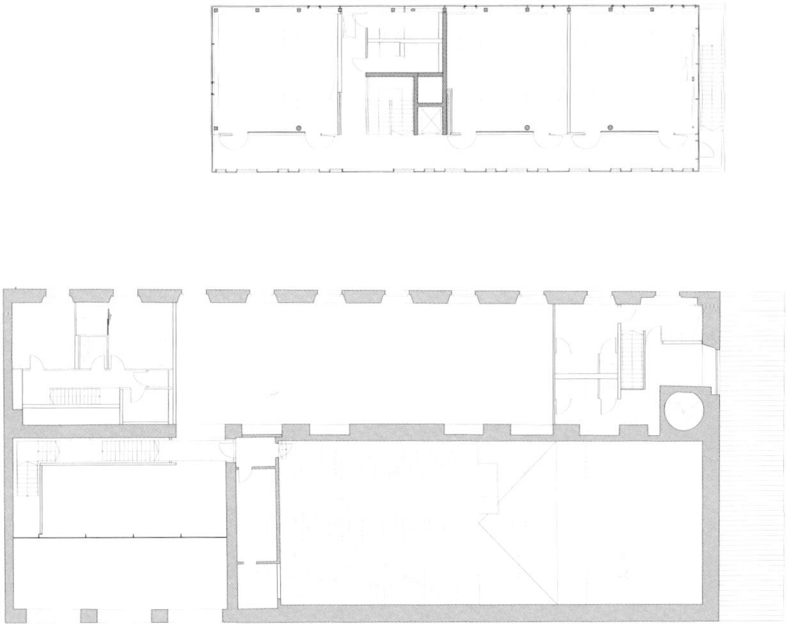

Third-floor plan

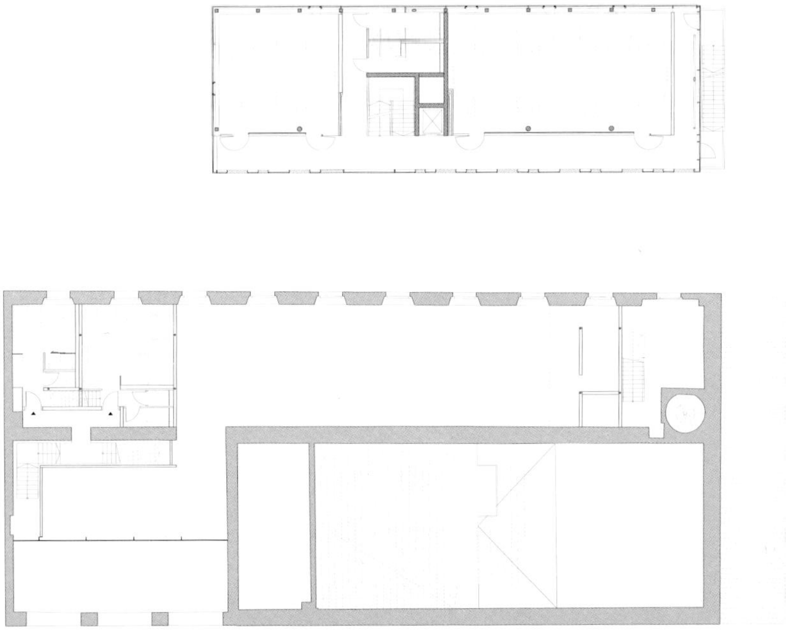

Second-floor plan

GUCCI HUB

The towering intervention establishes a formal and color contrast against the existing red brick warehouses, and picks up on their structural rhythm through a black ribbed façade that also provides sun control.

The renovation and redevelopment of the old Caproni aeronautical factory has transformed this building into Gucci's new Milan office. Built in 1915, the former factory was used for designing, assembling, and testing airplanes and is distinctive for its warehouses with shed-style rooms, large hangar, and internal corridors. The large complex now accommodates offices, showrooms, design and photography studios, spaces for hosting fashion shows, a canteen, and restaurant.

The renovation of the industrial site focused on enhancing the stylistic features of the original architecture. This has resulted in a contemporary office complex that meets modern-day needs and requirements while respecting the building's historical legacy.

The industrial warehouses are set out in a regular pattern across the site. They have exposed-brick façades and modular structural bays, and a new shed-style roof lets natural light into the interiors. The large hangar, with steel roof, has been transformed into space for hosting events and fashion shows. A central pedestrian path connects the axis along Via Mecenate, and section of warehouses were removed to create an internal plaza with landscaping.

A new six-story tower contrasts with the industrial nature of the old buildings. The tower, located to one side of the site, has a glass façade and external sunscreen devices. The tall and dark modern building breaks down the symmetry of the site and sets up powerful chromatic relations with the red-colored exposed bricks of the low-level warehouses.

Architecture:
Piuarch
Location:
Milan, Italy
Area:
326,700 square feet (30,000 square meters)
Completion:
2016
Photography:
Giovanni Hänninen

79

79

Site plan

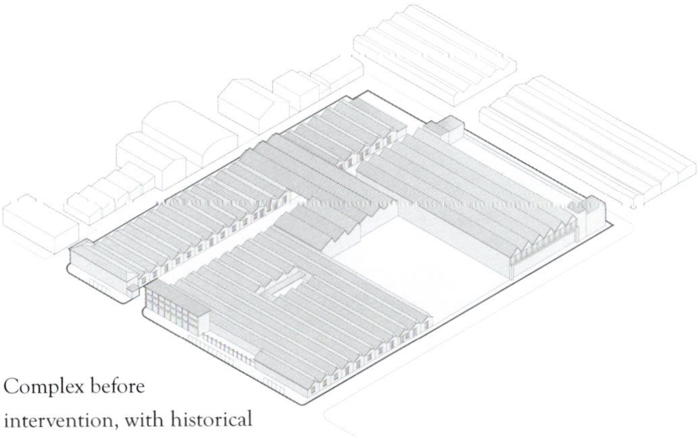

Complex before intervention, with historical buildings and elements added over the years

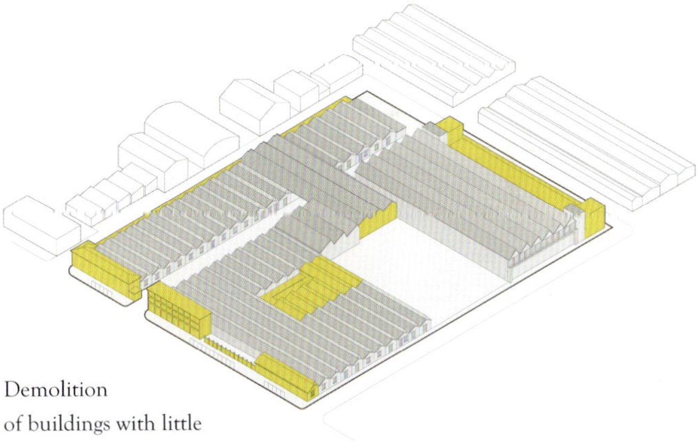

Demolition of buildings with little architectural value

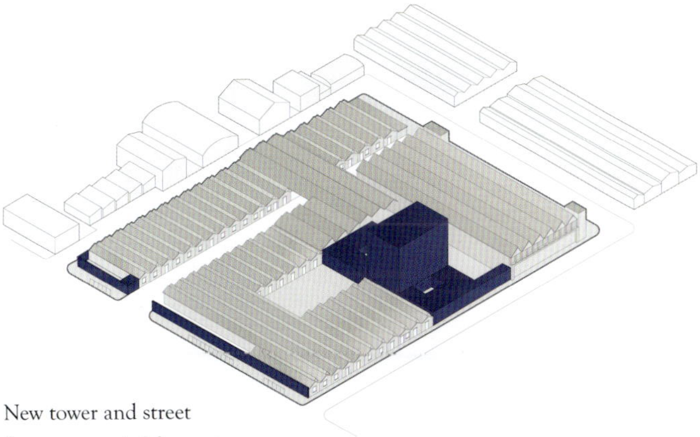

New tower and street frontage on via Mecenate

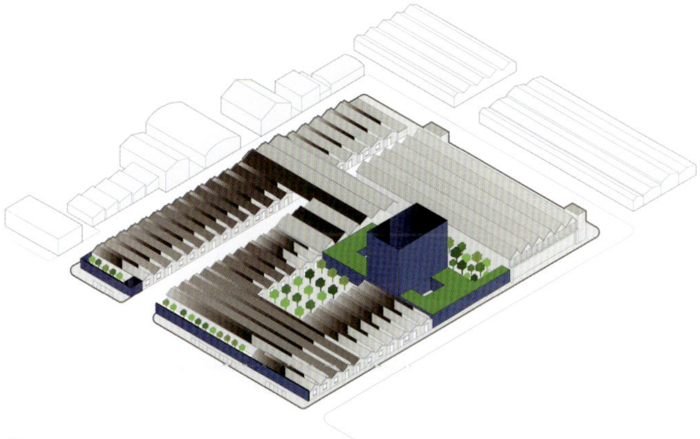

Green areas

B30

This juxtaposed intervention maintains formal continuity with the existing heritage building through an abstracted borrowing of the existing forms. Contrast with the austerity of the existing is achieved through transparency and visual connections between levels and the gardens beyond.

B30 is an imposing structure with a strong, distinct architectural character. The Grade 1-listed building was designed in 1917 by the chief government architect Daniel E.C. Knuttel for the Dutch Ministry of Agriculture, Industry and Trade in The Hague. Professor Hans Ruijssenaars renovated the building in 1994.

The B30 office block is located in The Hague city center, alongside the Haagse Bos green space. It stands on Bezuidenhoutseweg, an historical arterial route connecting the Huis ten Bosch royal palace and Het Binnenhof parliamentary building. The renovation creates a modern working environment that gives space to contemporary ideas regarding government transparency. The design has clear architectural volumes and layout that transform the enclosed, hierarchical building into an open, transparent, and inviting setting.

The architecture team mapped the essential qualities of the original design to create an inspired framework. As such, the historic building is seen not as a dead museum piece, but a vital and sustainable component of the total design.

Anchored in its urban setting, broader landscape, and historic environment, B30 features an accessible and transparent public first floor with a restaurant, café, library, meeting rooms, and seminar rooms. All passageways are aligned to create long sightlines through the building, enhance contact with the external environment, and simplify orientation and wayfinding.

Architecture:
KAAN Architecten
Location:
The Hague, Netherlands
Area:
226,042 square feet (21,000 square meters)
Completion:
2015
Photography:
Karin Borghouts, Sebastian van Damme

Northeast elevation

A large central atrium is the quiet heart of B30. Dutch artist Rob Birza designed a mosaic floor pattern with a garden abstraction that gives life to an internal landscape, visually connecting with the city forest and the new side gardens.

Knuttel's original design has been expanded on both sides. The Seminar Foyer features meeting rooms, seminar rooms, and a sunken auditorium running through the glazed space. The Work Foyer is characterized by lounge and working areas, an espresso bar, and a library. The foyers' partitions feature large pivoting glass doors encased with high-gloss aluminum frames opening to the gardens.

The atrium and the foyers have a series of daylight shafts that borrow from the ubiquitous original coffered ceilings, and manipulate the square base to be capped with triangular-shaped glass. These elements are positioned for optimal dispersion of sunlight, while preventing overheating by solar radiation.

The monumental staircase provides access to the magnificent former Minister's Room on the second floor. The atrium visually connects the four upper floors, which accommodate the workplaces of various institutions. A new level of offices is situated over the central part of the building and extends out to the roof. The ceiling height has been reduced from 98 feet (30 meters) to 65 feet (20 meters) to create a proportionate scale to the inner courtyard.

The façades of the new additions consist of sandblasted concrete frames filled with stone and a coloring agent that matches the tones of the original building. The change in hierarchical relations and the importance of the first floor has been expressed in the façade by enlarging the windows. The openings have been taken down to the stone plinth of the building, lowering the window sills and lengthening the jambs.

Longitudinal section

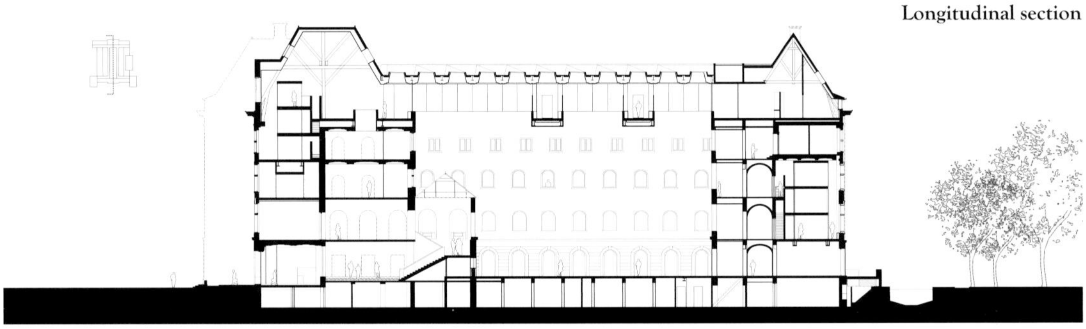

Cross section

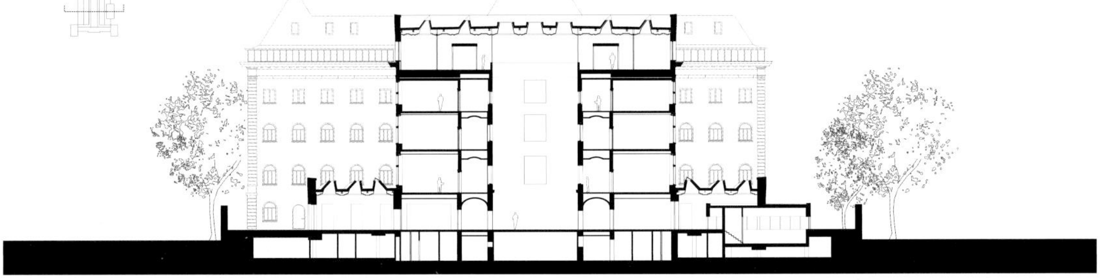

Detail of entrance sliding door

1. Air curtain column, aluminum coated RAL 8022, connected via basement
2. Clear glass, insulated monument glass
3. Columns, aluminum extrusions, coated RAL 8022
4. Girder, steel with aluminum sheets, coated RAL 8022
5. Sliding door/fixed glass, aluminum extrusions coated RAL 8022, clear glass
6. Monumental entrance door, existing, steel
7. Ceiling, profiled GRG and sheetrock, integrated lighting
8. Limestone ramon gray, honed
9. Limestone cenia, burned

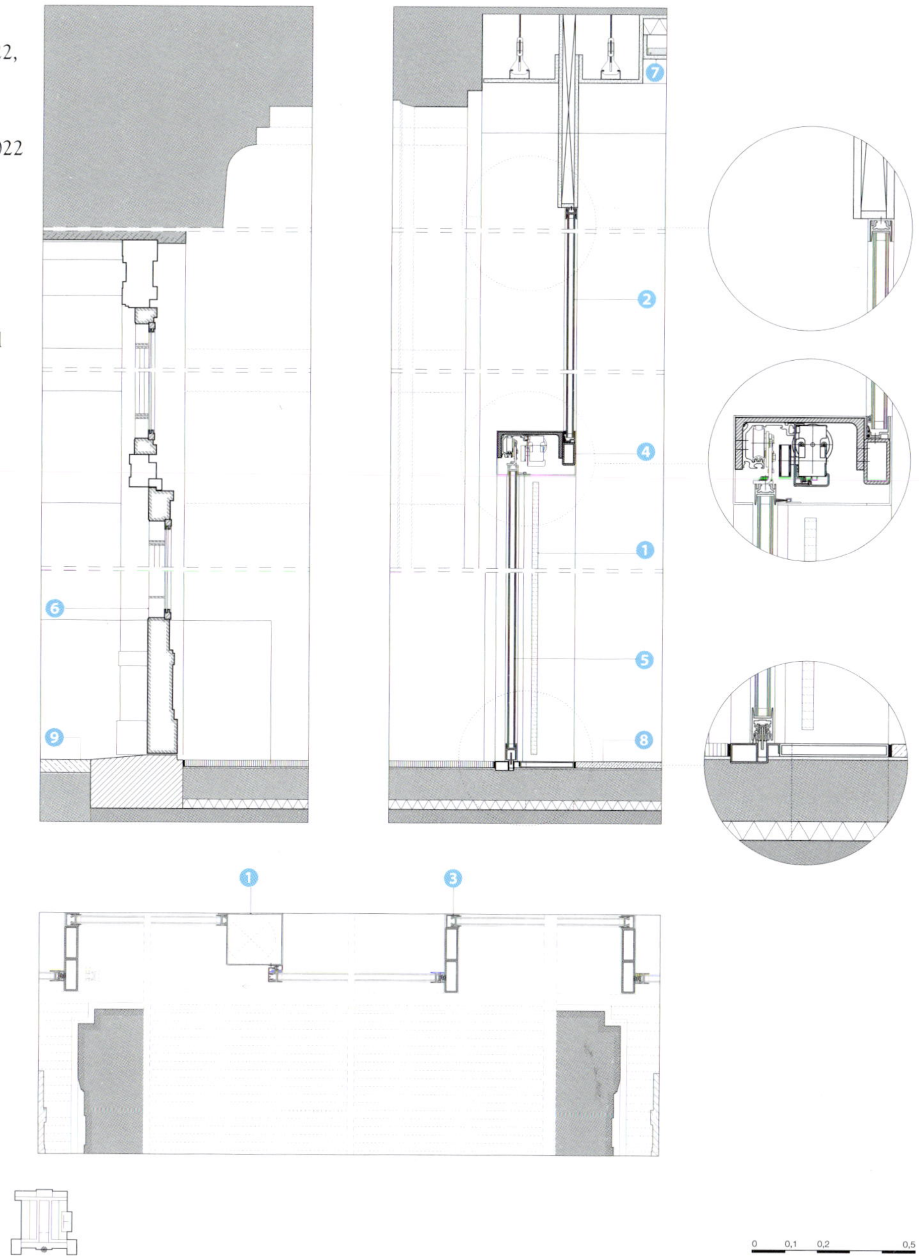

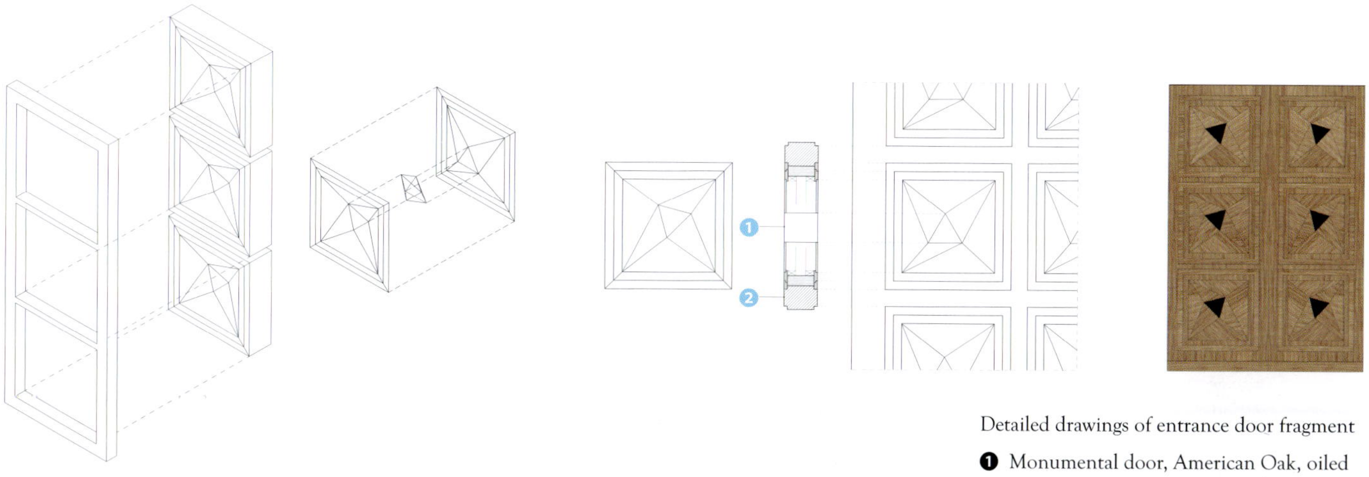

Detailed drawings of entrance door fragment

1. Monumental door, American Oak, oiled
2. Glass prisms

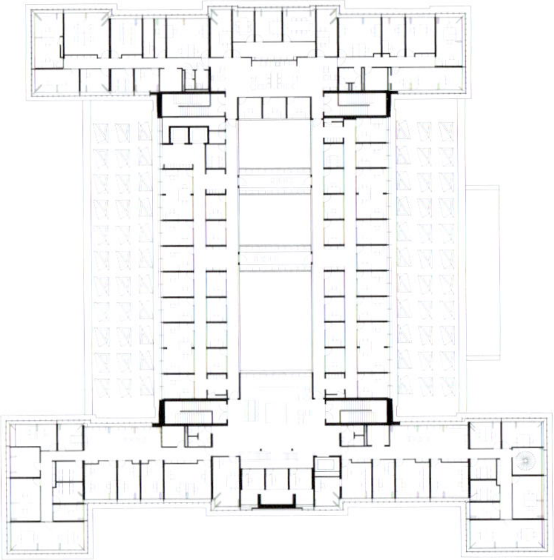

Fifth-floor plan

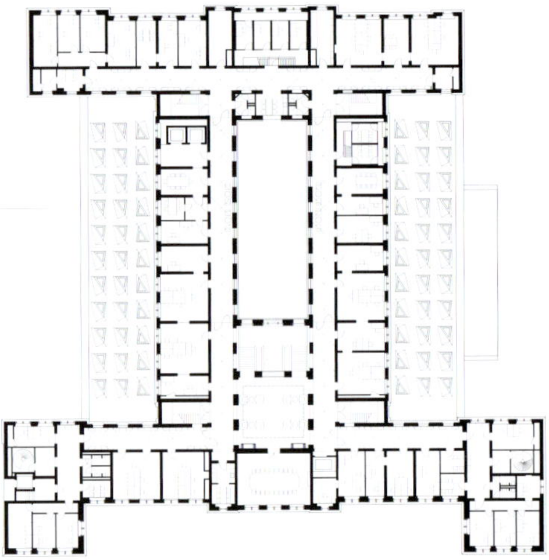

Second-floor plan

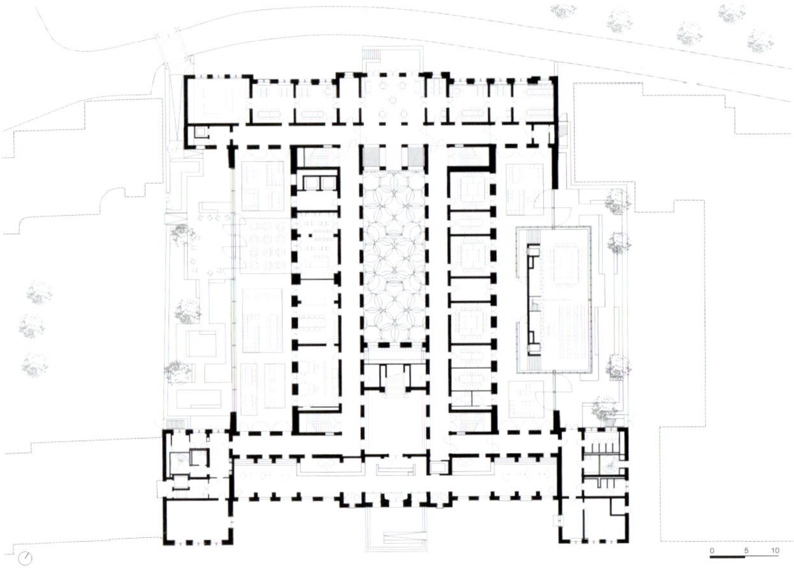

First-floor plan

1. Lightscoops, prefabricated sandwich elements, skylights with steel frames and HR++ clear glass
2. Shaped ceiling GRG (Glafiber Reinforced Gypsum), seamless
3. Wall-facing and top-cover limestone ramon gray, honed
4. Curtain wall, aluminum, anodized and gloss polished, corner glued glass
5. Limestone ramon gray floor, honed
6. Wall-facing American oak, veneer, min. 6 mm, oiled, integrated ventilation scoops
7. Acoustic base, cognac color
8. Limestone ramon gray steps, honed
9. Prefabricated concrete elements, profiled, san/marble surcharge, top acetified
10. Terrace/garden
11. Pivoting door, American Oak
12. Division wall, cladd with American Oak veneer, oiled
13. Connection curtain wall, pivoting door

Seminar room elevation

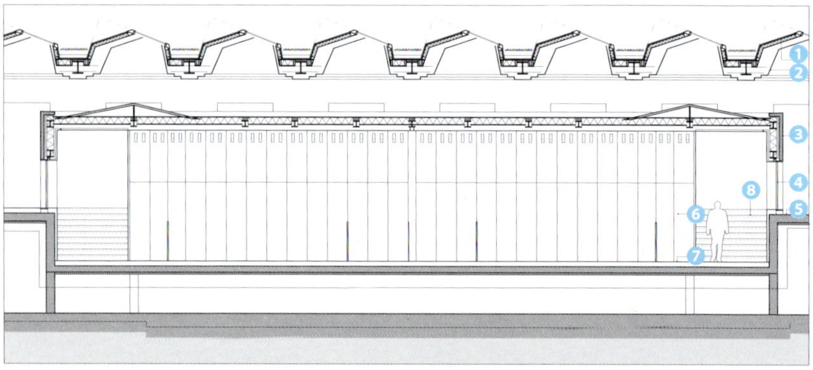

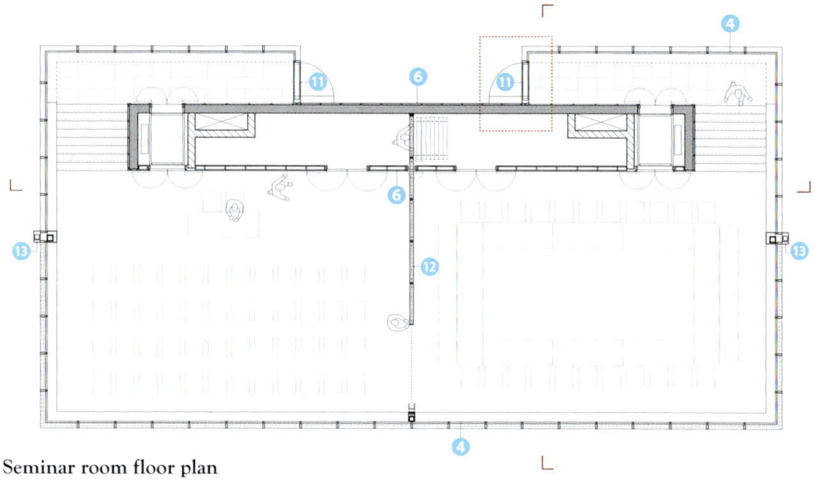

Seminar room floor plan

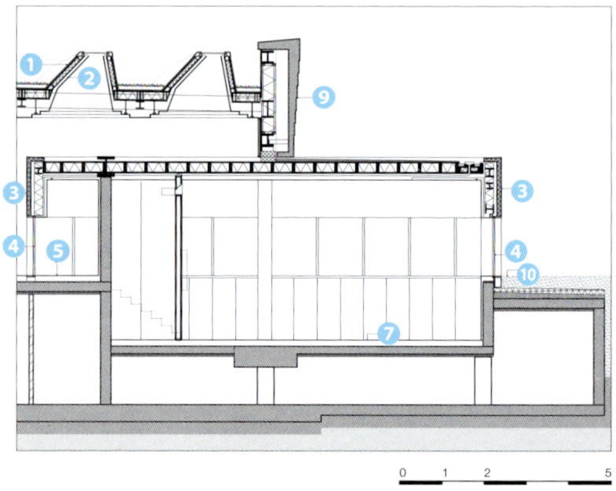

Seminar room section

LAYERING COURTYARD

This reconstruction project expands inward into its existing central courtyard, setting up a series of new courtyards and new spatial relationships that mediate between public and private spaces that are flooded with light.

Layering Courtyard is hidden in a traditional commercial block near Qianmen in Beijing. The original structure has the characteristics of a house from the Republican period, which are bigger and higher when compared with common residential houses. This particular building has a quadrangle courtyard, a row of arched doors and windows on the south-facing street side, and two-story houses on the northern side.

The housing structure had previously been completely rebuilt prior to the renovation. There were no doors, windows, or walls in the courtyard, but a structure made out of rough, exposed timber beams. It is said that it was a brothel in the Republican period, transformed into a bakery after the foundation of China, and later left unused after the reconstruction. The building will be a complex for public activities and living in the future.

The design was inspired by the "multi-layered courtyard" in traditional spaces, and the former inner courtyard has been changed into a "three-layered courtyard" to create a transition from public to private spaces. This layered structure creates a quiet, natural, and poetic scene in a noisy *hutong* neighborhood.

A portion of the building's roof on the southern side has been demolished to create the first layer between the street and interior space. A pitched-roof building has been added in the center, and two parallel bamboo gardens separate it from the houses on the northern and southern sides. This layered approach provides interior spaces with sunlight and a bamboo backdrop. The spaces are separate but penetrate each other. The glass

Architecture:
ARCHSTUDIO
Location:
Beijing, China
Area:
5705 square feet (530 square meters)
Completion:
2018
Photography:
CreatAR Images, Jin Weiqi

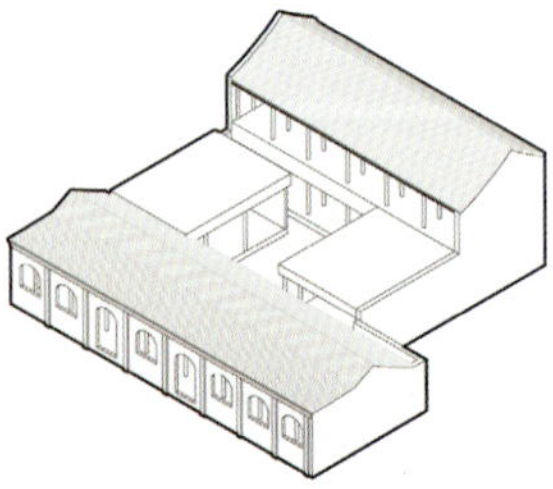

1. Original courtyard

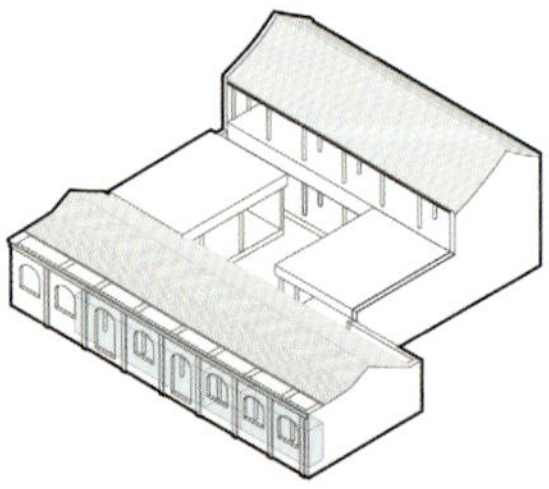

2. Southern room roof removed, forming the first layer courtyard

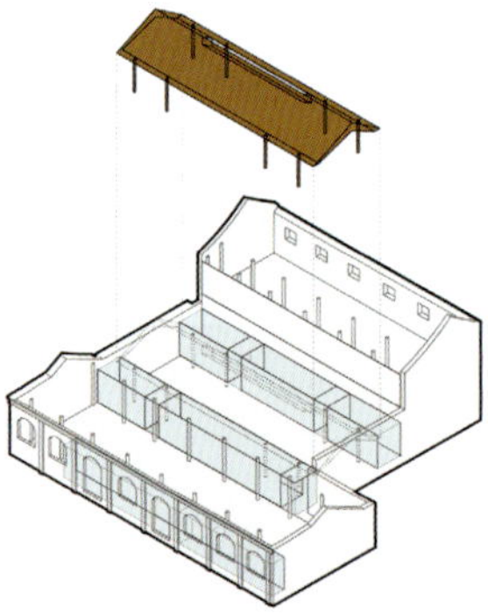

3. New roof structure added, forming the second and third layer courtyard

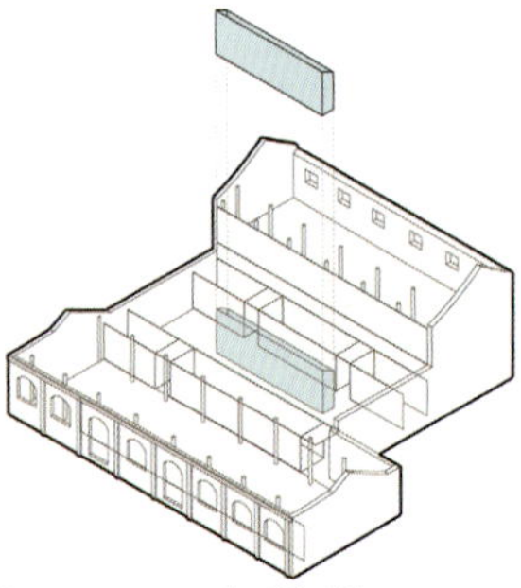

4. Water courtyard added between the buildings

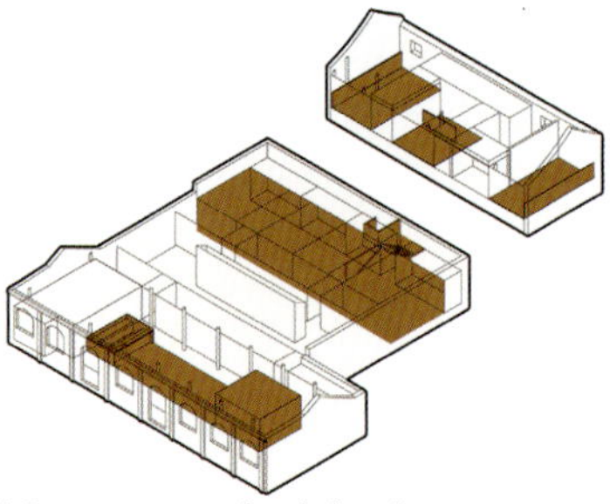

5. Interior space divided with wooden box structure

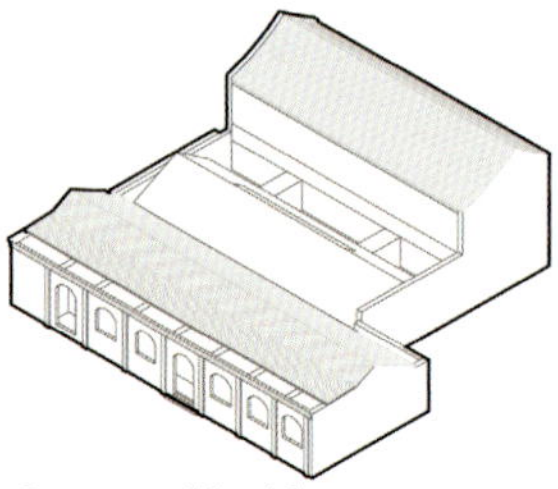

6. Renovated building

walls have frosted patterns, which reinforce the sense of translucency, thus achieving the layered juxtaposition of different scenes and living situations from outside to inside.

The usage patterns of the house follow the natural transition from openness to enclosure. The southern house is a place for public gathering activities, with an arrangement of reception space, dining room, bar, kitchen, office, warehouse, and so on. The original wooden beam and column structure was preserved as much as possible, and two new wooden service boxes placed inside to divide spaces of different scales.

Through the first layering courtyard, the window openings of the original building and the painted doors form the effect of a shadow wall, and outline a real and colorful scene of *hutong* life in the setting of a bamboo forest. The central building serves as a flexible multifunctional space, which can be used in conjunction with the front restaurant, as an independent exhibition hall, or integrated with the guest room area to become a rest place. There is a harmonious relationship between the new building and the two old buildings in terms of scale, lighting, and placement.

The inner spaces are built around a linear waterscape garden. Transparent, translucent, and reflective materials and furniture diminish the sense of solidity and create a light, floating atmosphere that contrasts with the old building and makes the spaces allusive.

The house on the northern side contains private spaces. The first floor is divided into four rooms by the original structure. The rest area and bathroom are distinct from each other by the change of materials. Each guest room has a bamboo courtyard, and the interior and exterior are connected. The second floor is divided into three rooms of different sizes. A floor-to-ceiling glass curtain wall provides views of the layered gray tile roofs, green trees, and blue sky.

Section

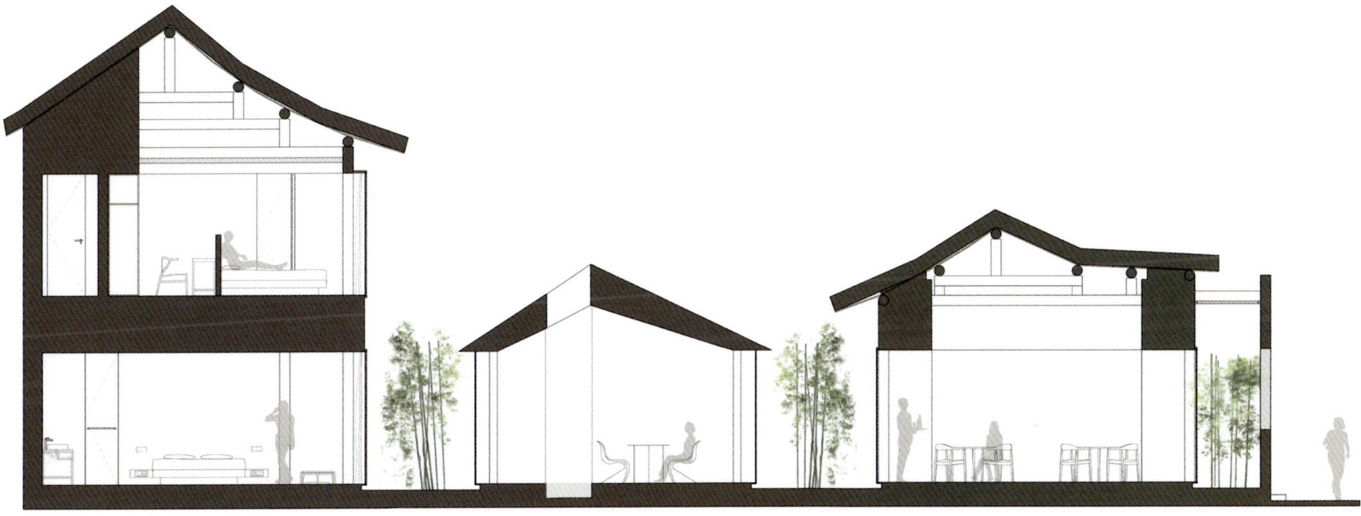

Floor plan

1. Main entrance
2. Secondary entrance
3. Dining room
4. VIP room
5. Reception
6. Bar
7. Kitchen
8. Courtyard
9. Restroom
10. Office
11. Equipment room
12. Multifunctional area
13. Water courtyard
14. Guest room
15. Linen room
16. Staircase

ANTWERP PORT HOUSE

This elevated intervention emerges as a diamond above the existing building and captures and reflects the sky through a form that contrasts sharply against the old. The new form references the surrounding context of the port, while creating an undeniably strong juxtaposition with the existing building below.

Antwerp Port House repurposes a derelict fire station as a new headquarters for the district. The project brings together the port's 500 staff that previously worked in separate buildings around the city. The architecture takes the form of an elevated extension that floats above the existing building. Shaped like the bow of a ship, the new structure points towards the Scheldt river, with a faceted glazed façade that reflects the changing tones and colors of the sky.

Following the construction of a new fire station, the old facility became redundant and relied on a change of use to ensure its preservation. Consequently, the disused fire house had to be integrated into the new project. The Flemish Government State Architecture Office, together with the city and port authorities, organized an architectural competition for the new headquarters. The design is informed by historical research and analysis of both the site and the existing building. Rather than concealing the existing façades, the design team built upwards—a particularly appropriate solution considering the existing building was originally intended to be a tower. Surrounded by water, the new façade is a glazed surface with triangular facets that allow the apparently smooth curves at either end of the building to be formed with flat sheets of glass.

While most of the triangular facets are transparent, some are opaque. This combination allowed the architecture team to control the amount of sunlight entering the building. Simultaneously, the alternation of transparent and opaque panels breaks down the volume of the new extension, giving panoramic views of the Scheldt, city, and port. The building's appearance

Architecture:
Zaha Hadid Architects
Location:
Antwerp, Belgium
Area:
41,995 square feet (12,800 square meters)
Completion:
2016
Photography:
Hufton+Crow, Tim Fischer

reinterprets Antwerp's reputation as the diamond capital of the world with a carefully cut form that has a changing appearance throughout the day.

The central courtyard has been enclosed with a glass roof, providing access to the historic public reading room and library within the restored and preserved fire truck hall. Panoramic lifts provide direct access to the new extension, and an external bridge between the existing building and new structure offers views of the city and port. The brief called for an activity-based office with related areas such as the restaurant, meeting rooms, and auditorium located at the center of the upper levels of the existing building and the lower floors of the extension. The remaining stories, more remote from the center, comprise open-plan offices.

The waterside site offered significant sustainable construction benefits, allowing materials and building components to be transported by water—an important requirement to meet the port's ecological targets. A borehole energy system pumps water to a depth of 80 meters below grade in more than 100 locations around the building to provide heating and cooling. Waterless lavatory fittings and motion detectors minimize water consumption while building automation and optimal daylight controls minimize artificial lighting.

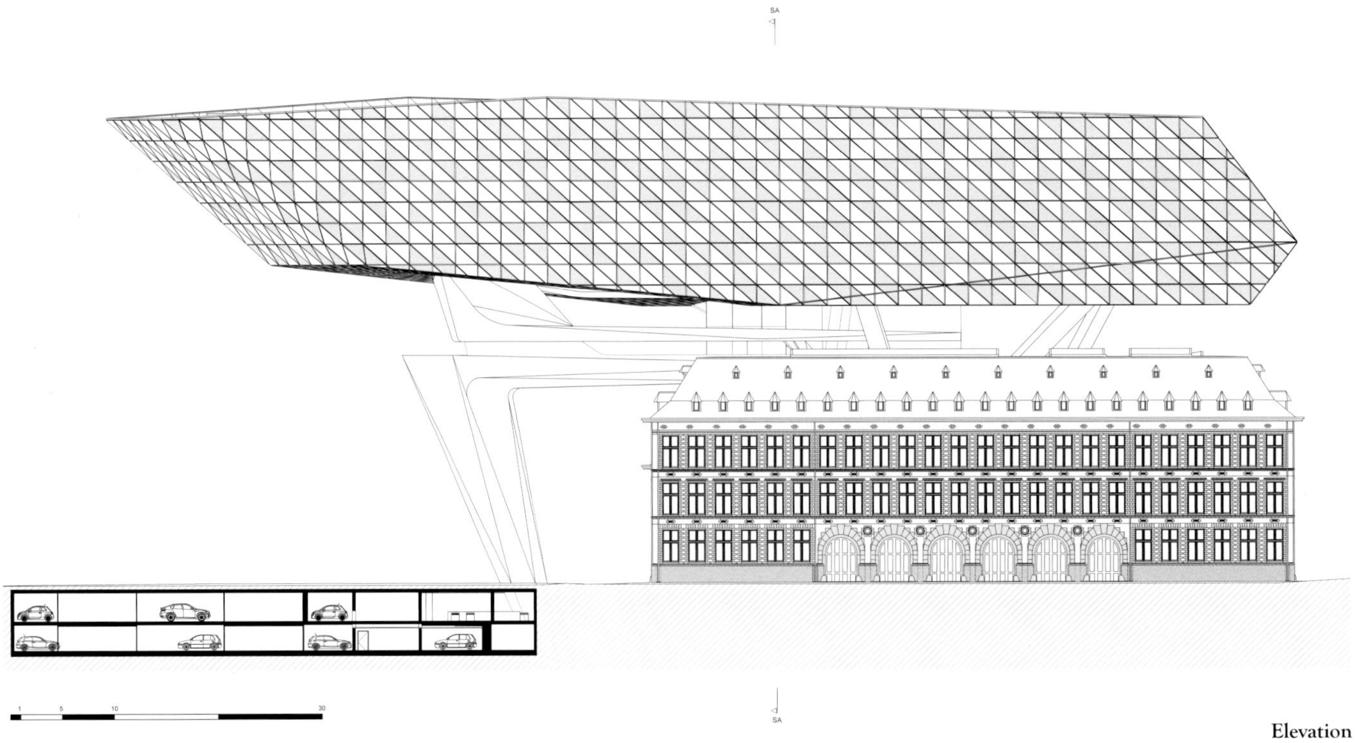

Elevation

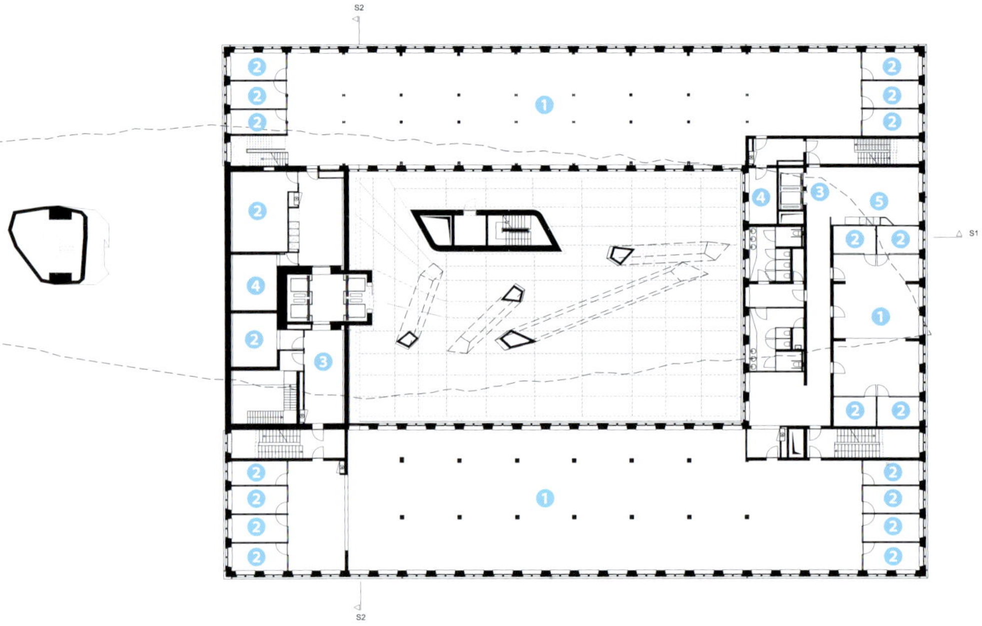

Third-floor plan

1. Offices
2. Meeting rooms
3. Lift lobby
4. Ups/data/local
5. Coffee corner

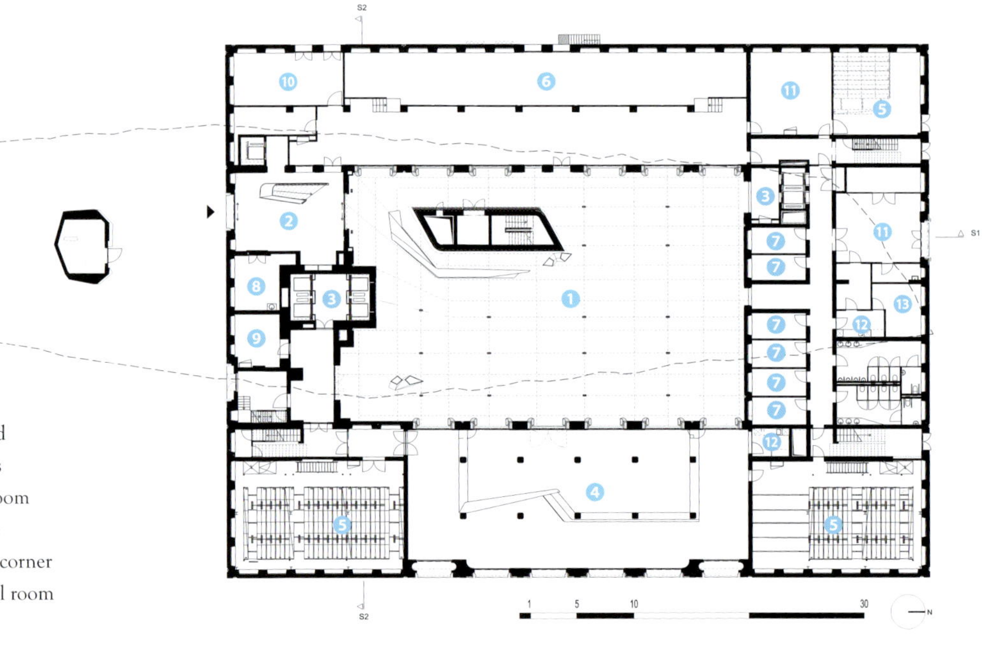

First-floor plan

1. Courtyard
2. Main entrance hall
3. Lift lobby
4. Library
5. Archive
6. Offices
7. Meeting room
8. First aid
9. Lockers
10. Print room
11. Storage
12. Coffee corner
13. Control room

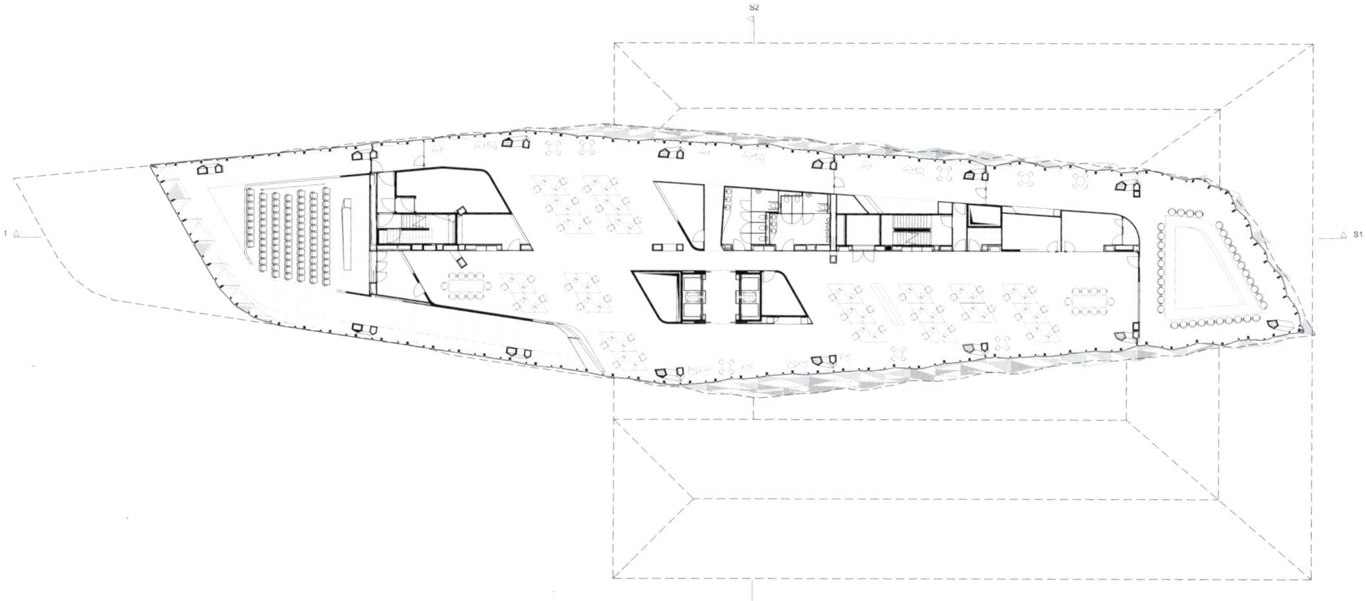

Eighth-floor plan

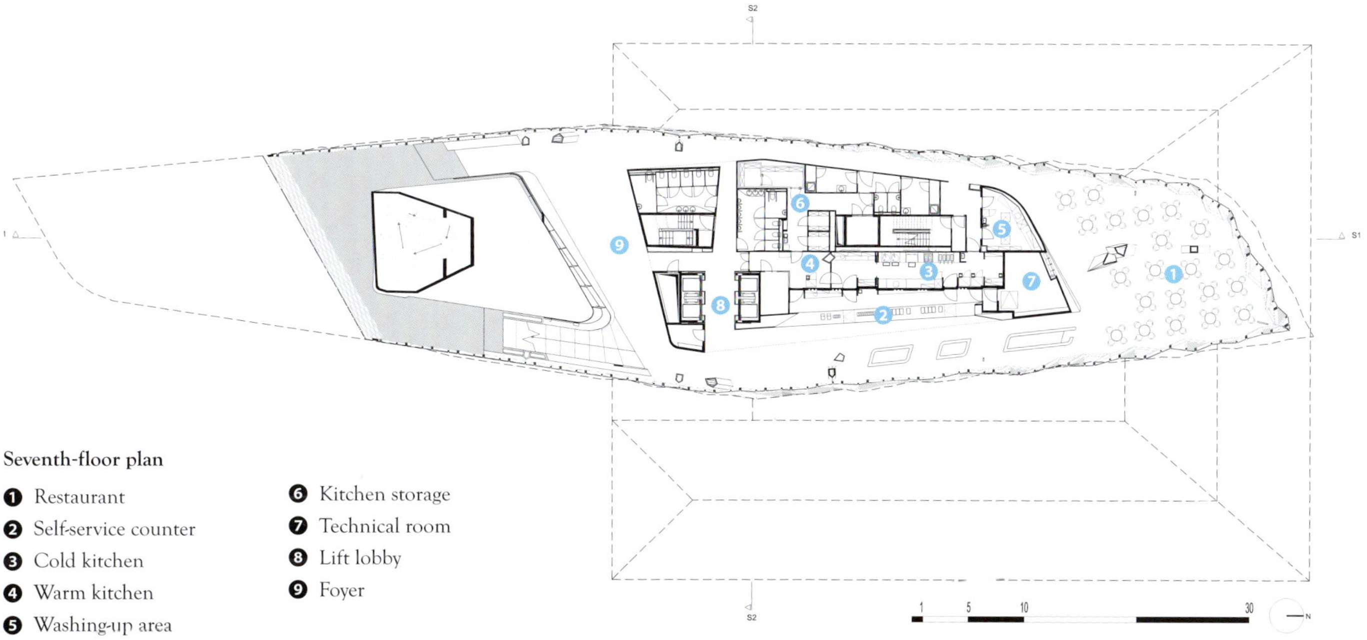

Seventh-floor plan

1. Restaurant
2. Self-service counter
3. Cold kitchen
4. Warm kitchen
5. Washing-up area
6. Kitchen storage
7. Technical room
8. Lift lobby
9. Foyer

STRATEGY 5

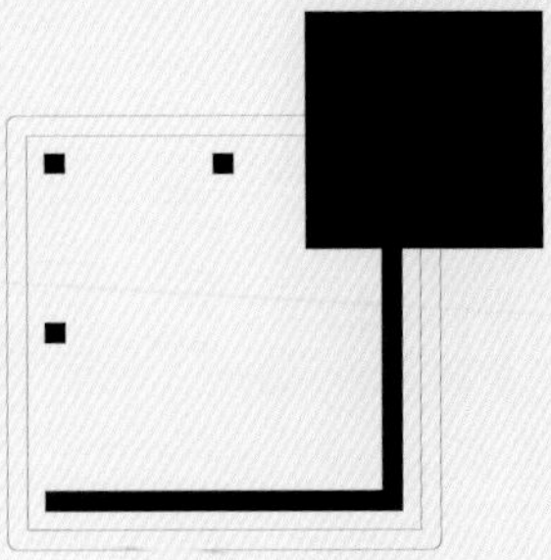

RECONSTRUCTION AND EXPANSION

The strategy of reconstruction and expansion is more comprehensive than the previous strategies, and it may impact the interior, exterior, and/or structure of an existing building. The new interior extends outwards and may reveal itself at varying scales. But however intensive the intervention, characteristics of the existing are nevertheless retained, even if selectively.

A building is reconstructed and expanded typically where the existing building is valued for selected aspects and not in its entirety. It is an approach that becomes necessary when the new function does fit comfortably in the existing and/or if the existing structure is not safe enough to be left as is. In this radical approach, the designer must weigh up what is valued against the new program demands, including the intention to ensure the existing building is useful in the present and future to safeguard its survival, even if considerably modified. Some of these modifications are more evident than others. In other words, they may modify the character of the existing, as is the case with "renovation and insertion," or they may discreetly enhance the services and the structural stability, as is often the case with "structural modification," in a way that may or may not be evident on the surface. The modifications may be structural, spatial, aesthetic, or a combination of these.

Typically, a reconstruction is necessary when the existing building has been structurally and/or spatially damaged or compromised, either through neglect over time or by a disaster, such as an earthquake or fire. It may however also need reconstruction to accommodate a new function. A new function will also necessitate expansion or partial demolition if the existing envelope does not provide the required volumes for the new program. In the case of this strategy, it is of utmost importance for the designer to be clear about the values placed on the host building given that aspects of the old may need to be sacrificed and replaced by the intervention to facilitate the new program.

What is considered sacred and nonnegotiable in the old building will depend on the primary importance placed on the building and the reasons for preserving it. If the existing architecture has significant heritage value, then the reconstruction and expansion will tend to be as discreet as possible so as not to detract from the original aesthetic. Interventions may include the careful and selective removal of later additions that have diminished the integrity of the original building, as was the case with Rijksmuseum, while extensions will tend to contrast so as not to be confused with the original.

While retaining the long-standing public thoroughfare through the museum building, the Rijksmuseum intervention transformed the entrance into a generous internal forecourt, providing large visitor crowds with access to information, orientation, stores, and refreshments. This was achieved through reconstruction by removing recent additions in the courtyards not considered to have heritage value. The basement below the thoroughfare was opened up to connect the two courtyards. This intervention may be considered a "renovation and insertion" in that the new material fuses with the existing building, although only at the base. However, the intervention does not only expand the existing museum within the confines of its footprint, it also expands outwards through the introduction of small pavilions on the approach that serve to announce a contemporary presence in this historical museum complex. The reconstruction intervention can be identified by its distinctive use of limestone that does not contrast with the language of the original building, but provides it with a solid and unifying base, complementing and supporting the heritage building structurally and aesthetically. The smaller interventions outside of the museum—the extensions—are identified through the use of the same limestone, which in this case contrasts against the original red brick. These smaller interventions may also be interpreted as "architecture as furniture" or "external juxtapositions" in that they can be seen as removable.

It is often the case that an urban environment is valued over and above individual buildings that collectively contribute to it. In this instance, the building's façade takes priority and if the structural or spatial qualities of the rest of the building are not able to satisfy the needs of the new intended functions, a reconstruction becomes necessary. A building may serve an important function as part of a set of buildings in an urban setting, as in House Lendenmann and Hotel Restaurant Krone, or it may be an icon that serves as a landmark, such as Co-op Oulun Tervahovin Siilot. Both will contribute to the overall character of a neighborhood, and more is negotiable for change beyond the valued façade that preserves the urban scale.

The town authorities identified the north-facing street façades of House Lendenmann as important to the adjoining public space, while the remaining part of the house was considered negligible. These façades were therefore carefully preserved to retain their original architectural character, with the reconstruction behind providing support for the structurally compromised front façades and opening up the rear to sun and views. The reconstruction is entirely new, with a new architectural language and spatial configuration that fits inside the envelope of the original, structurally fragile building. In this particular instance, the reconstruction borrowed its language from the traditional crafts of the village and has been wrapped in timber cladding. This approach provided the opportunity to accommodate three modern apartments with panoramic views towards the south. This partial preservation was the result of a need to retain the historical building and to accommodate a modern lifestyle.

In Rijksmuseum and House Lendenmann it was possible to conserve heritage through the preservation of material and the architectural language derived from that material. However, this is not always possible where the material has either been destroyed or is not structurally sound, as in Hotel Restaurant Krone and Co-op Oulun Tervahovin Siilot, but the building holds sufficient importance to necessitate a reconstruction

Destroyed in a fire, the façade of Hotel Restaurant Krone required reconstruction to preserve the historical role of the building marking the entrance to the old town. In this reconstruction, the valued qualities of the lost façade have been translated in a way that remained predominantly loyal to the language of the original, while at the same time offering a modern experience, with panoramic views and abundant light. This was achieved through several design strategies: The new construction retained the volume of the original building; fragments of stone walls and timber, not destroyed by the fire, were retained and juxtaposed against new materials; a similar but not identical arrangement of openings was introduced; and limestone concrete replaced the traditional limestone and lime-plastered walls. Unlike House Lendenmann, the preservation of Hotel Restaurant Krone, as opposed to the historical material, permitted a degree of translation while preserving its urban function.

When an iconic building becomes redundant and structurally unsound, the need to demolish raises questions about the loss of a building that provides cultural meaning beyond its footprint. An example of an approach to overcome this dilemma may be the one taken at Zeitz MOCAA described in "structural modification," where the structure was reinforced at great expense to preserve its cultural value. Alternatively, it can be rebuilt anew, as was the case of Co-op Oulun Tervahovin Siilot, which provides an opportunity to accommodate the new required functions without compromise and without losing the icon. This is a radical approach that does not value the material of the old, but favors only the building's ongoing historical value. However, in the reconstruction, some references have been made in memory of the material qualities of the building that was demolished. The volume of the reconstructed icon is made more evident through contrast of color and geometry. The portion extending beyond the original envelope is rectilinear and black, which allows the white, silo-like forms to stand out and be visible at a distance. Like a historical novel that blends history and fiction, this building is a contemporary retelling where some elements remain truthful to the original while others are new.

It is clear that the tension between heritage values and new programmatic demands has often dictated and determined the character of reconstruction and expansion projects. Programmatic demands may be technological, which in themselves demand reconstruction and expansion. In Office 3.0, the visible architectural intervention in the interior could be described within the design principles set out in "renovation and insertion" where the new transforms and modifies the character of the host building through the opening up of the plan, new minimalist surface treatment, the insertion of a stair, and insertion of a skylight to provide better quality of light. The reconstruction at Office 3.0, however, is technological, and therefore intangible. It entails the use of an app to control temperature, lighting, and the smart use of space. For this reconstruction to be made visible, the design necessitated an expansion that would serve as a demonstration of this new working environment facilitated through technology. This was achieved through pushing out the façade at street level and locating the social program in a steel-framed glass box. In this way, what would have remained an invisible reconstruction becomes visible and public.

While historical buildings are often valued for their architectural language or design, some may be valued because of the social histories they embody. The reconstruction of Daxi Tea Factory reflects the juxtaposition of its two functional programs: the pleasures of drinking tea and the tough environment of its production. The existing shed, where tea has been processed historically, is repurposed and expanded to embed spaces for visitors within the production process. The materials of the existing shed are presented in their rawness. Spatial qualities to enhance the visitor experience are achieved through the juxtaposition of the raw skeletal nature of the existing shed with moments of luxury, including views into a calm water-filled courtyard offered by the discrete extension.

On the other extreme of heritage is the material value of a building. In many instances, the location and its proximity of the building to a city center, notable landscape, or view may be more valued than its architectural character. Even if an existing building has no significant heritage value it may be worth preserving for its material and structural potential and its embodied energy. Rock Creek House serves as a counterpoint in this collection. It is probably the most extreme example of minimum preservation of the existing where the intervention pushes the boundary and dominates the dialogue of new and old. It is only the footprint and the brick shell that are preserved in this reconstruction, while the language of the existing has been entirely transformed into an abstracted modern aesthetic. Greater value is placed on the existing material of the brick envelope and on the location that provides accessibility to the city center and potential connection to the surrounding landscape. Old and new are seamlessly stitched together erasing traces of the old character of the structure while making full use of what it has to offer. While a large number of window openings have been retained, these no longer reinforce the symmetry and order that belonged to the original design language. Instead they now fit into a new ordering system and form part of a façade composition that connects the experience of the occupant with the landscape beyond in a variety of ways. The garden façade to the south, where connection to the landscape was most crucial, received the more radical reconstruction, which entailed additional structural reinforcement to the exterior brick walls. The reconstruction also rationalizes the layout of the interior, which is no longer stratified with hidden serving spaces. Instead the intervention expands the family spaces within the existing shell by modifying the basement and attic to provide more livable rooms for the occupants. The expansion also connects the previously stratified floors through a new staircase and double volumes.

In reconstruction and expansion, the new function being introduced to the existing building plays a key role in the dialogue between old and new. In this strategy, a tension emerges between the most valued attributes of the old, be they historical or social, material, or iconic, and the demands of the new program, be they spatial, structural, or technological.

RIJKSMUSEUM

The original courtyard spaces are recovered to fit the scale of the museum. Small extensions introduce a contrasting modern language through the abstract use of a new yet traditional material. The strategic link established below the pedestrian thoroughfare reconnects formerly separate parts of the building.

Rijksmuseum in Amsterdam was designed in the late-nineteenth century by Dutch architect Pierre Cuypers. The function of the building was twofold: One part serves as the national museum, and the other is the gateway to the south of Amsterdam.

The museum's use has been challenging due its urban role as a connecting element between what was then the existing city to the north and the newer developments towards the south. A walkway—virtually a street—runs through the building from north to south, dividing it in two parts. This necessitates two entrances, both towards the north, and two main staircases. The eastern and western parts of the building are therefore only joined on the second floor, with the first floor and basement divided by the walkway.

The building has undergone many interventions over the last century, and the need for exhibition space has led to building within the courtyards, resulting in a lack of natural light. As these courtyards and gallery spaces lost their original size and shape, it resulted in a kind of labyrinth with a lack of wayfinding for visitors. The main hall was also unable to accommodate high numbers of visitors and lacked essential services such as information areas, shops, cafés, and auditoriums.

The intervention reinstates the original dimensions of the courtyards and exhibition spaces, and provides an impressive central hall by linking the east and west courtyards of the building. The hall houses all essential services for visitors, and offers a suitable space on the scale that the grandeur of the building deserves.

Architecture:
Cruz y Ortiz Arquitectos
Location:
Amsterdam, Netherlands
Area:
322,917 square feet (3000 square meters)
Completion:
2013
Photography:
Pedro Pegenaute, Myra May, Rijksmuseum, Duccio Malagamba

South elevation

Transversal section

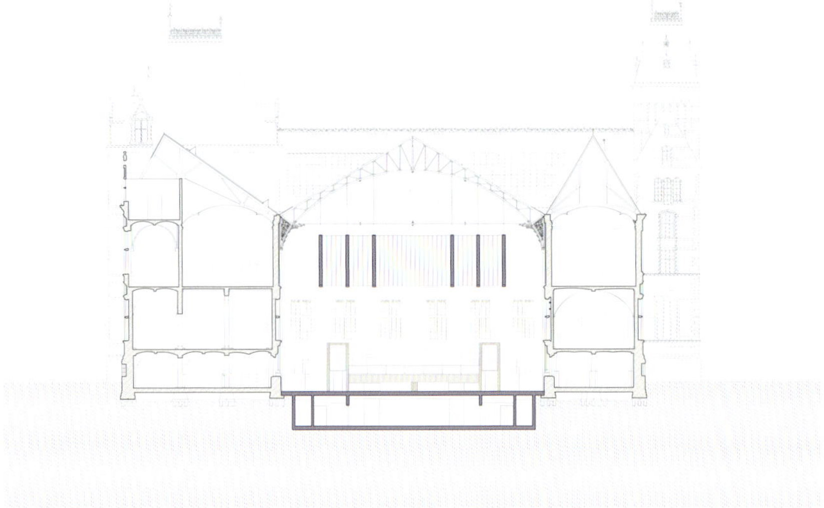

The renovation uses natural limestone, which is not present in other areas of the building, but unites the old and new without complacency in the juxtaposition or contrast. This same material was used in the two new small interventions.

Longitudinal section

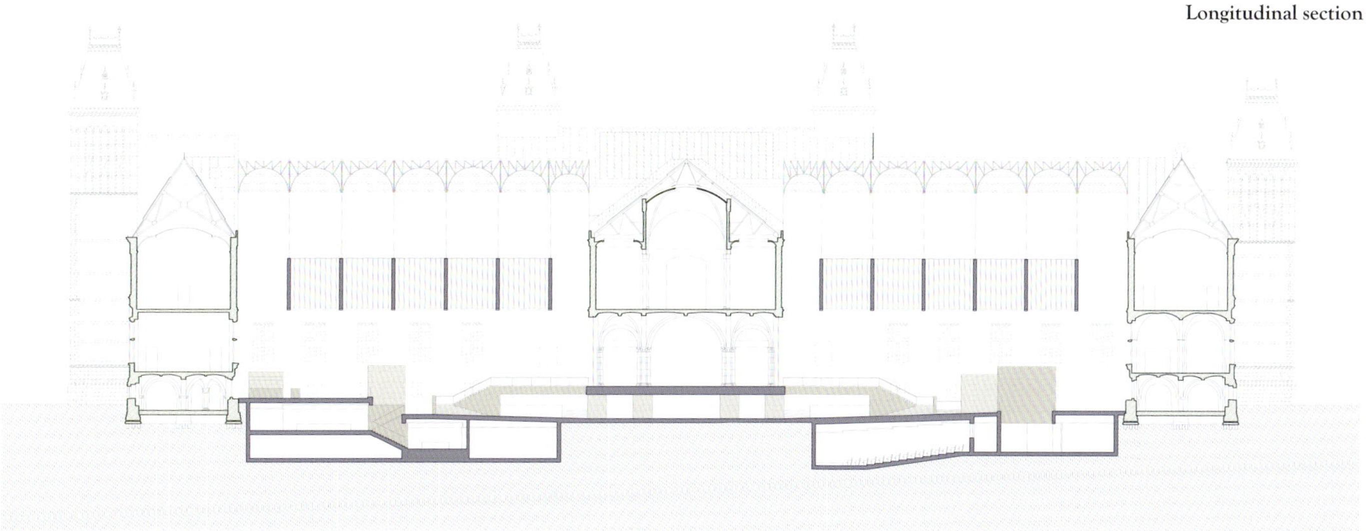

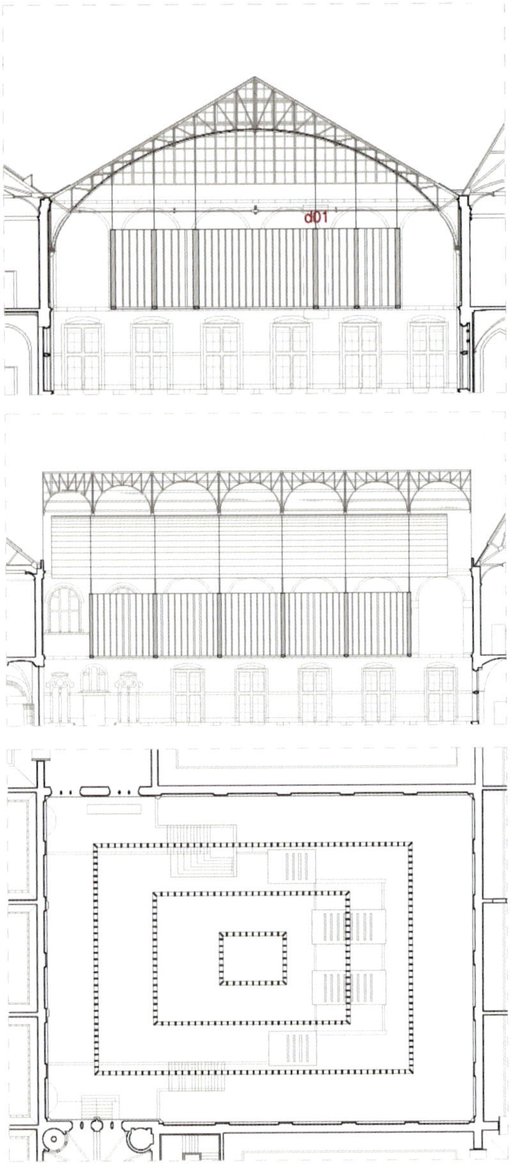

Detail of chandelier

Cruz y Ortiz Arquitectos

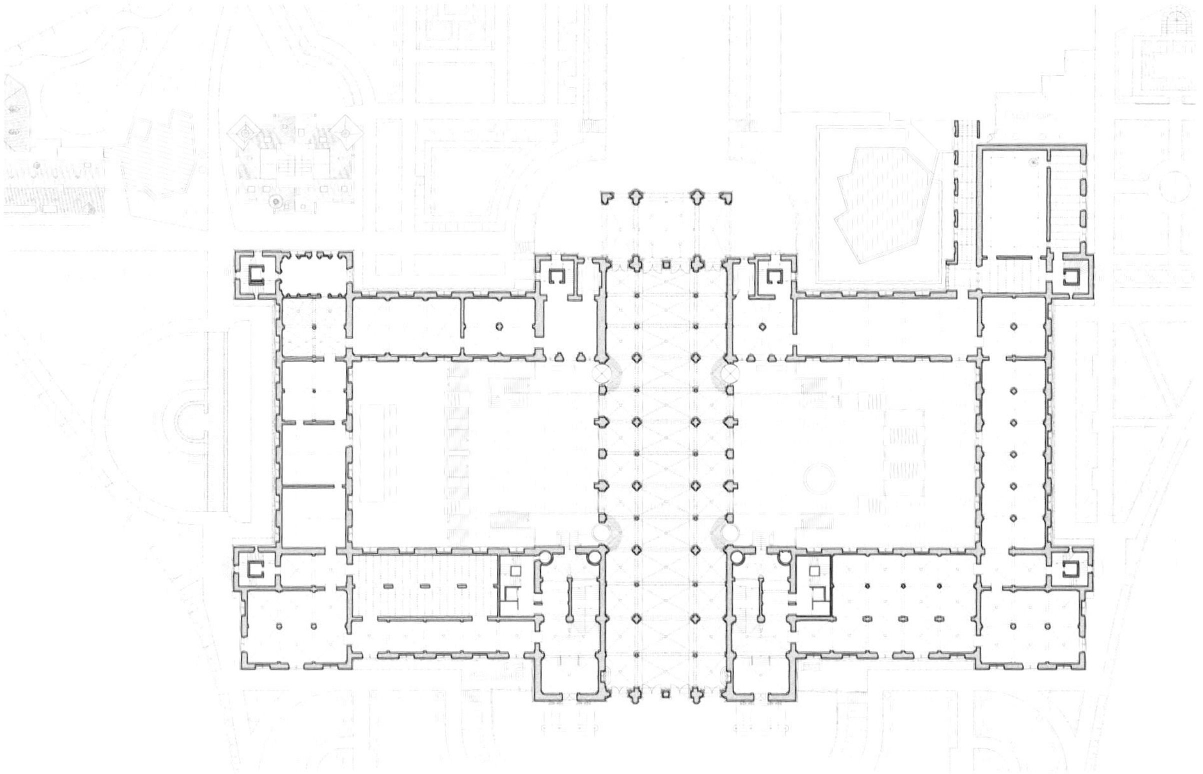

Second-floor plan

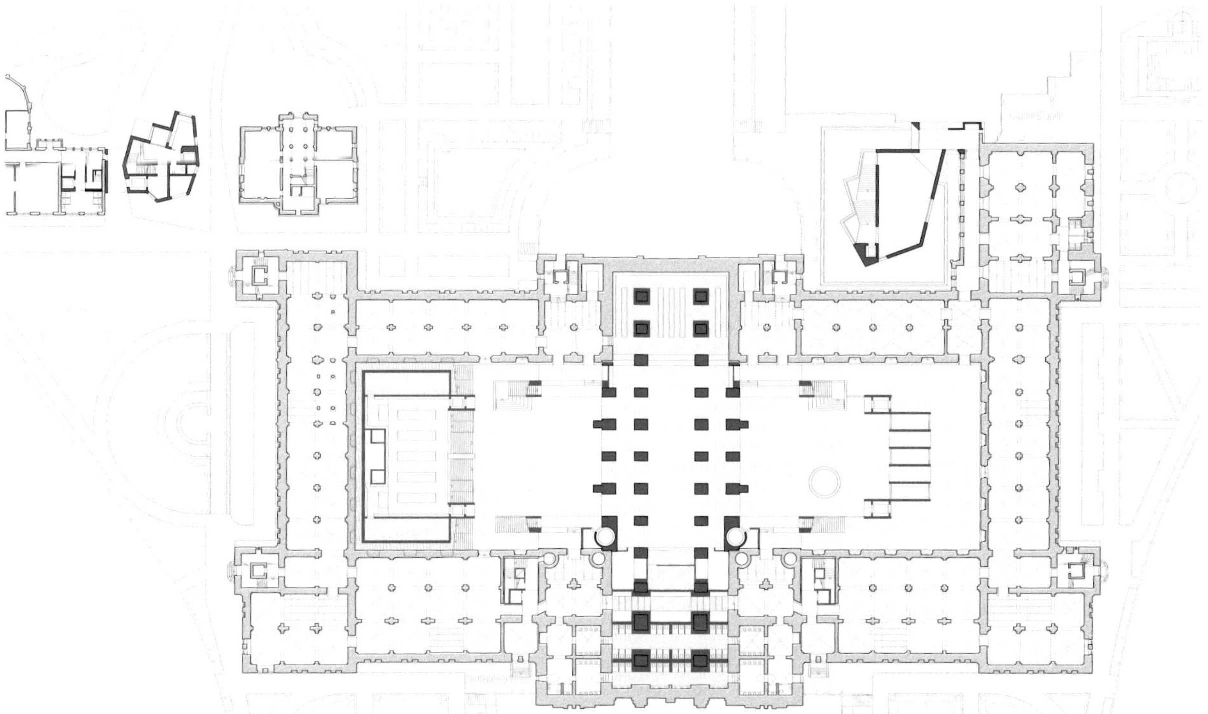

First-floor plan

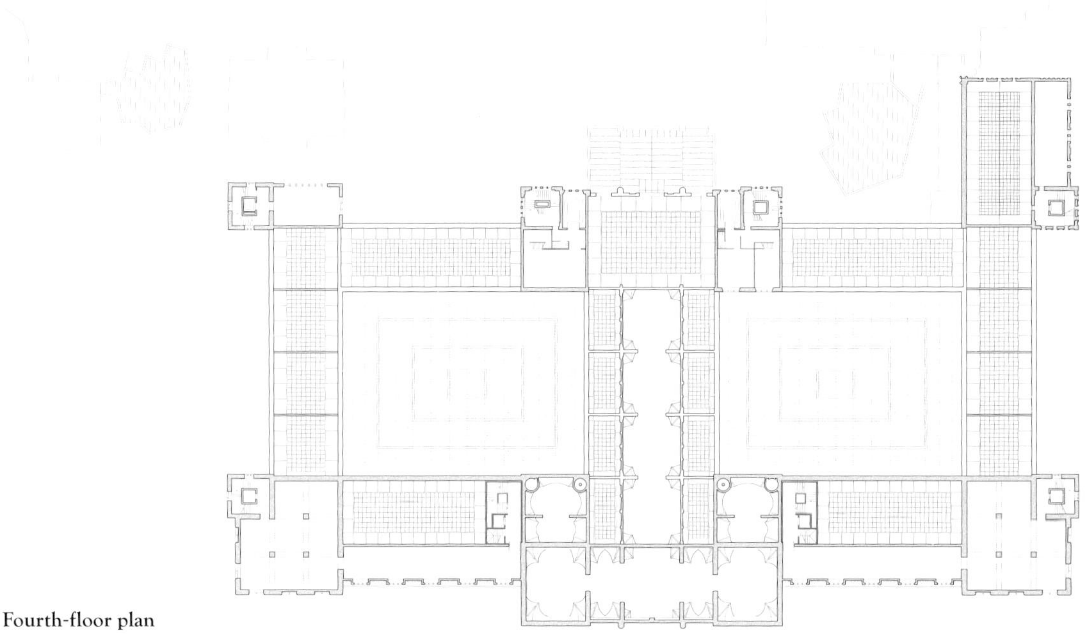

Fourth-floor plan

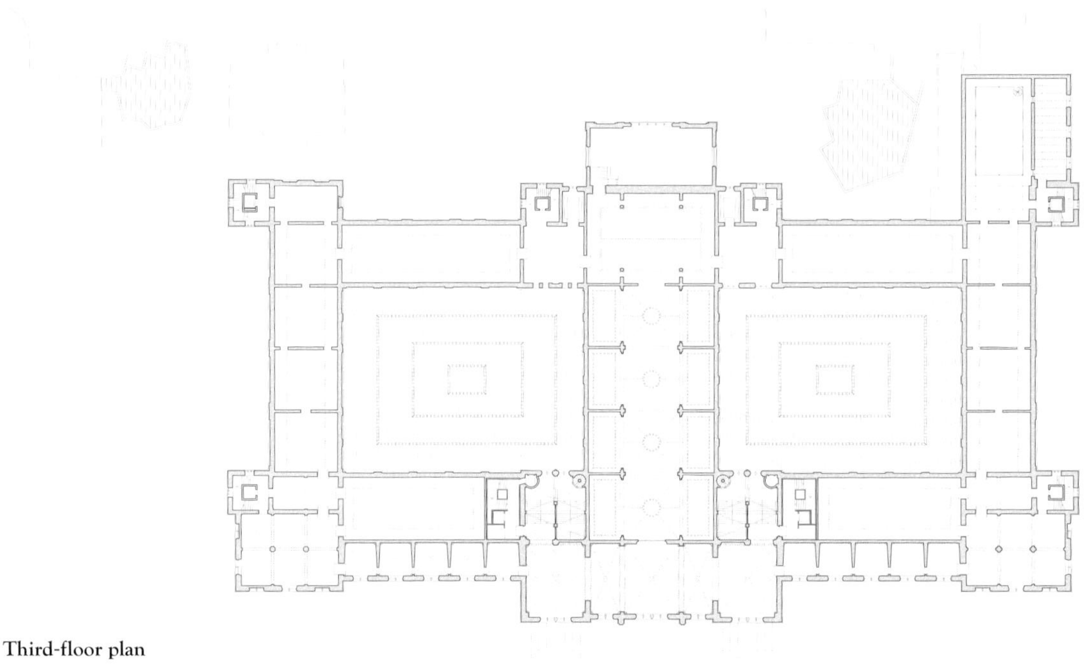

Third-floor plan

HOUSE LENDENMANN

A new structure supports the fragile street façade, preserving the historic streetscape. The new insertion accommodates three modern, light-filled apartments within the envelope of the original volume.

The medieval town of Regensberg has a unique location, history, and urban clarity. The historic town center consists of the Oberburg and Unterberg roads and the town's castle, which dates back to the foundation of Regensberg in 1244. Its location on the eastern foothills of the Jura Mountains offers spectacular views of the Zürich lowlands and the Alps.

House Lendenmann, a two-story half-timbered building located on the southern slope of Unterberg, is one of many historical jewels found in Regensberg. The poor state of the building, due to structural damage and improper repairs, meant a simple renovation was no longer possible. In close cooperation with the municipality and the townscape protection committee, the architecture team decided to partially demolish and rebuild the house in its original volume. Two front half-timbered façades and a vaulted cellar have been preserved, and three sculptural, modern, multi-family houses have been constructed behind the historical façade of the building.

The three apartments were created between the distinctive façades of the original building. The north façade with filigree truss and muntin window faces the town and is a valuable component of the historic township. The generous south side has an additional floor due to the slope of the site and provides a breathtaking view over the Swiss landscape. The contrast between the opposing façades made it possible to develop a dynamic interplay of proportion, light, and materiality.

Small, wooden-paneled chambers create a peaceful and safe atmosphere, while also providing a link to the history of the area. Large white spaces

Architecture:
L3P Architekten
Location:
Regensberg, Switzerland
Area:
5048 square feet (469 square meters)
Completion:
2015
Photography:
Sabrina Scheja

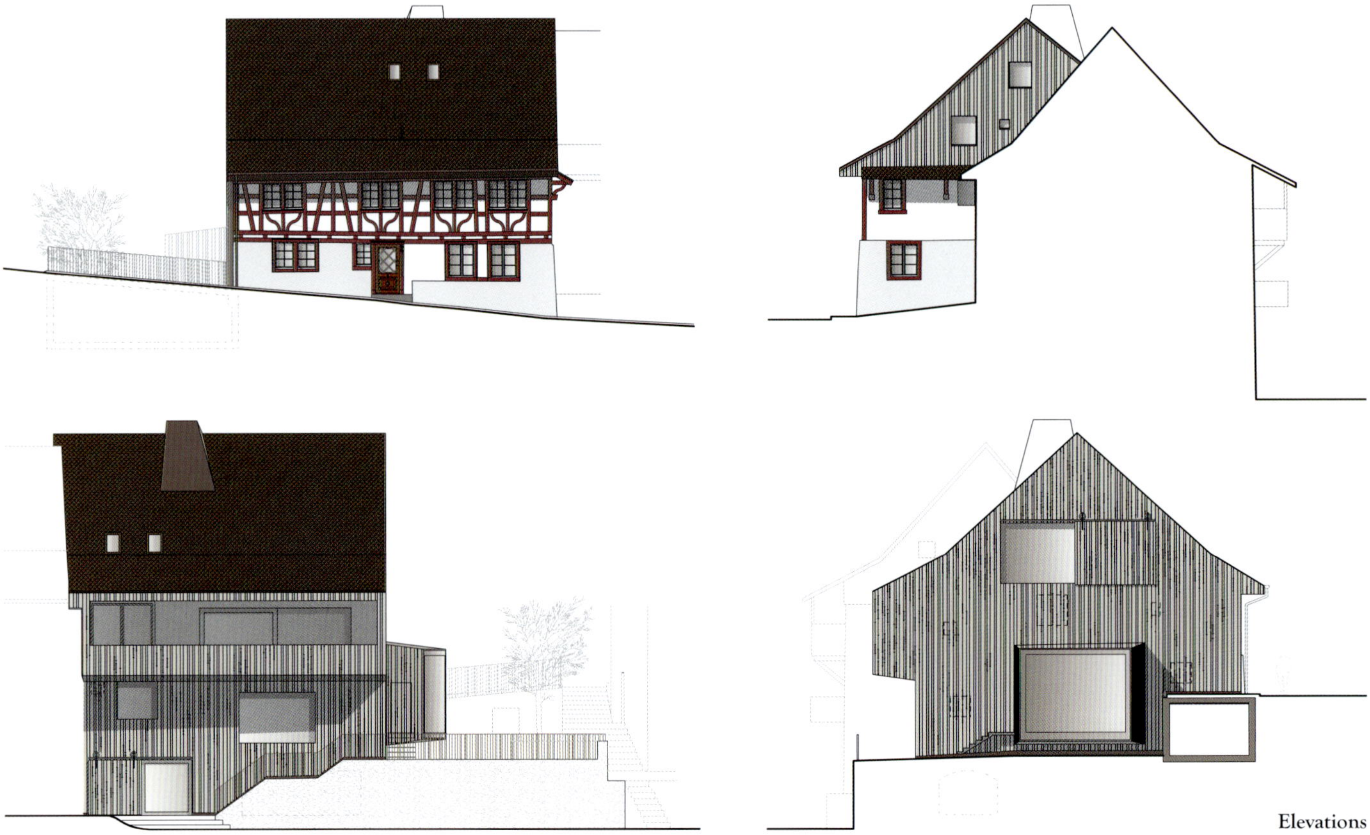

Elevations

encircling the chambers have generous openings for panoramic views. Alternating levels and ceiling heights transform the perspective of the rooms into a three-dimensional journey with ever-changing views and light conditions.

The contrast between old and new is clearly demonstrated in the façade. The new gray-spruce façade wraps around the new build, incorporating the preserved façade and reshaping the original volume. A light-guiding fireplace in the attic, a cantilevered bay window, and sliding doors incorporate vernacular elements and restructure the outer skin. The semitransparent timber cladding has irregular patterning, still prevalent in the rural construction culture. The new façade dissolves into a delicate envelope, providing the exterior and interior with an interplay between light and shadows.

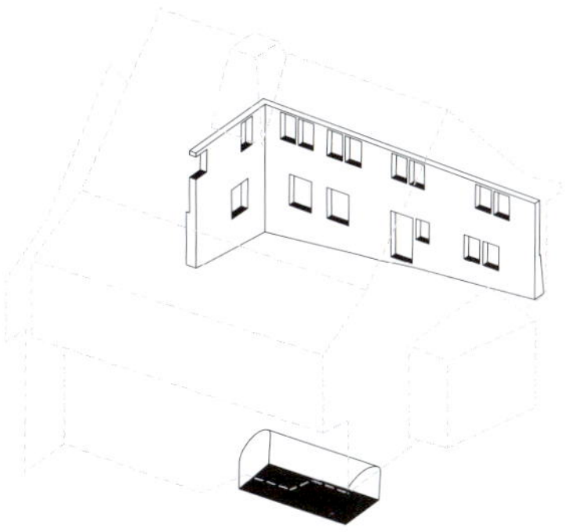

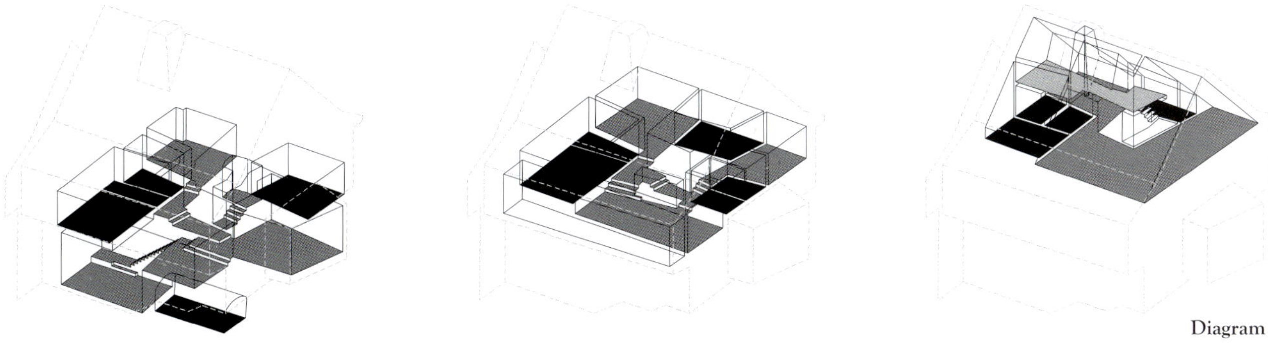

Diagram of interior

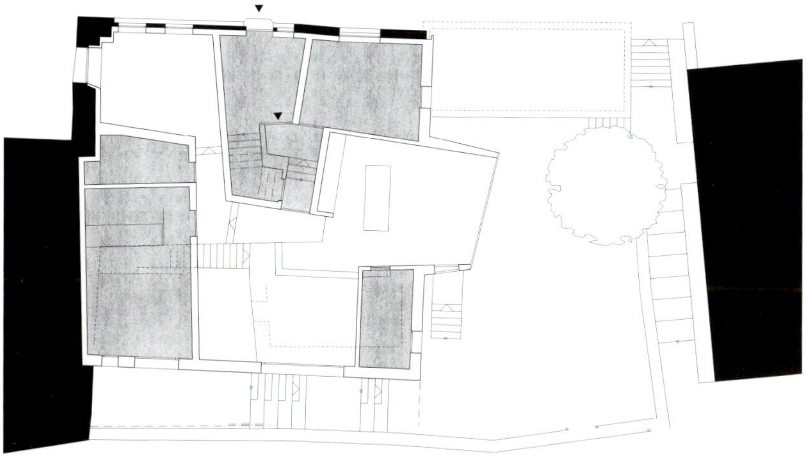

First-floor plan

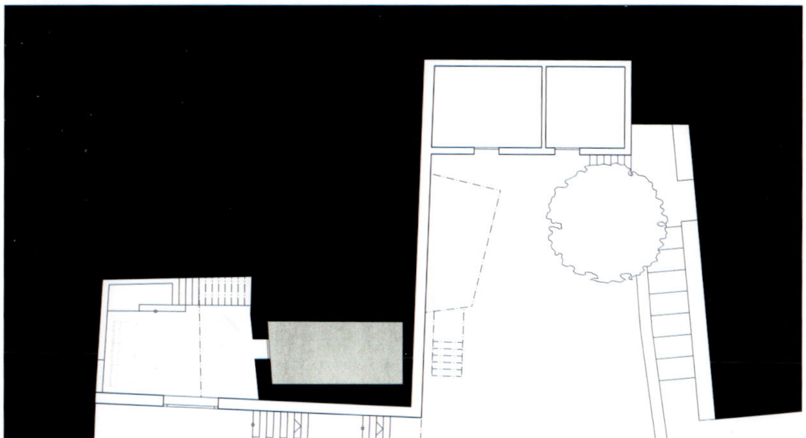

Basement floor plan

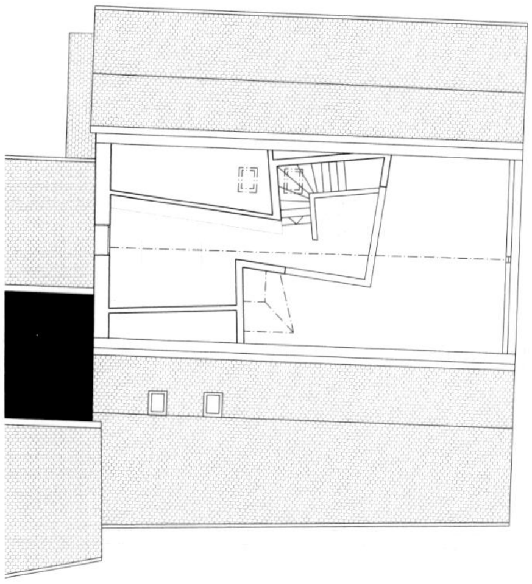

Gallery floor plan

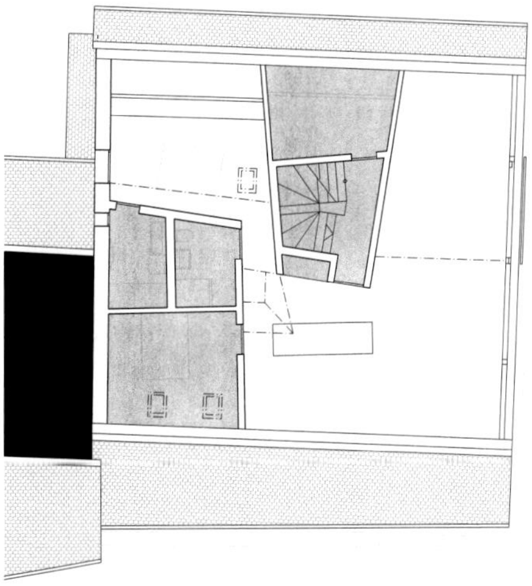

Third-floor plan

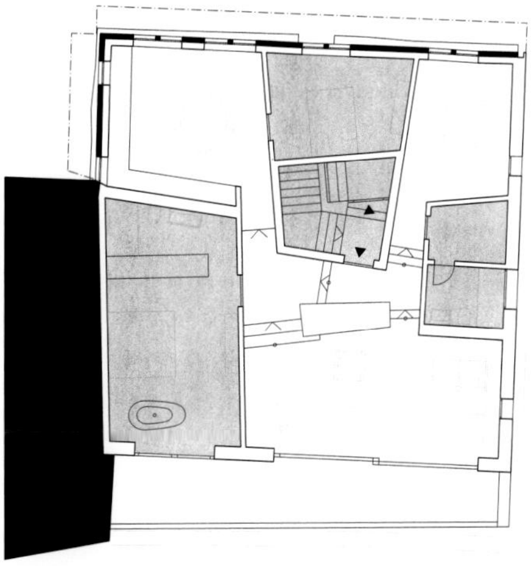

Second-floor plan

HOTEL RESTAURANT KRONE

This fire-damaged building is reconstructed within its preexisting envelope to retain its historic form. New exterior finishes mimic older ones to allow the revitalised building to fit harmoniously into its historic setting.

The former Gasthaus zur Krone Regensberg was a traditional tavern that had accrued a lot of history over several centuries. The inn was closed in 1997 and converted into a house with two residences, until a major fire destroyed up to 85 percent of the property in 2011. Krone forms the entrance to Oberburg, the historic castle ring, and is still today the only public access to the old town. This gateway location required a sensitive reconstruction of the house.

The house has been adaptively reused as a hotel and restaurant again. The volume and roof shape had to remain unchanged so as not disrupt the city ring. However, the architecture team wanted to clearly show contemporary building culture formally, technically, and materially. As most of the town was constructed with limestone, new portions of the façade have been built with limestone concrete to reference this basic material. The fine mesh of the lime-plastered walls and the modern concrete façades create an exciting interplay. Window reveals and perforated sheeting are burnished brass, and panoramic windows—up to 23-feet (7-meters) long—are interrupted by the delicate perforated sheets, which filter daylight through the interior.

The tension between existing and new buildings is also an essential feature of the interior. While the part of the building spared by the fire has natural stone walls and wood that is reminiscent of a stable, the new public spaces and the main entrance through the house are formally modern and flooded with light. This bright monolithic central space has lime-plastered walls and provides access to the guest rooms, which, in contrast, have sleek, modern materials.

Architecture:
L3P Architekten
Location:
Regensberg, Switzerland
Area:
5381 square feet (500 square meters)
Completion:
2015
Photography:
Sabrina Scheja

Elevation

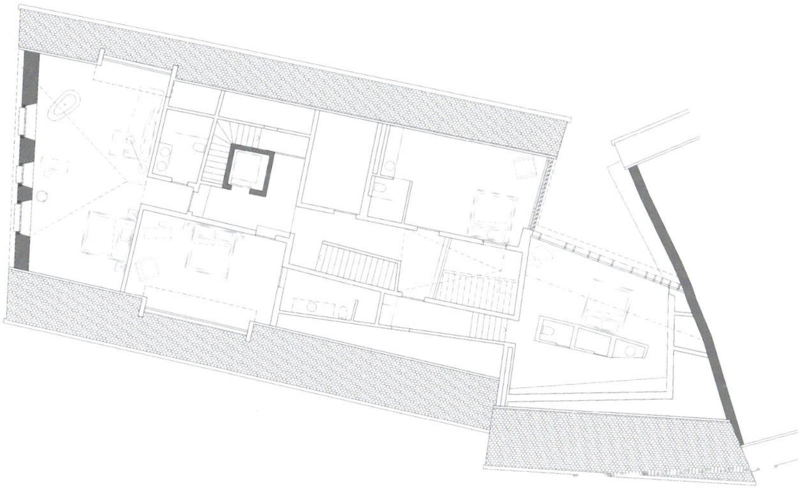

Attic floor plan

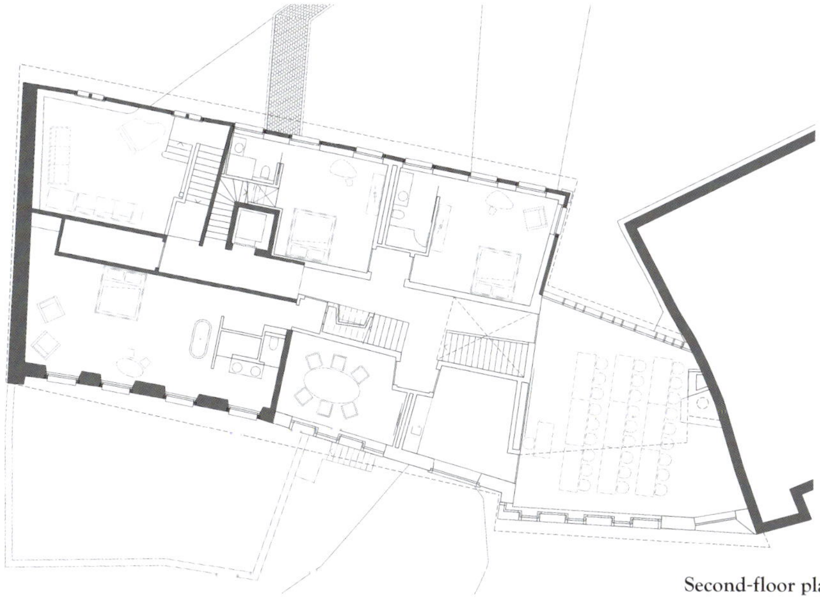

Second-floor plan

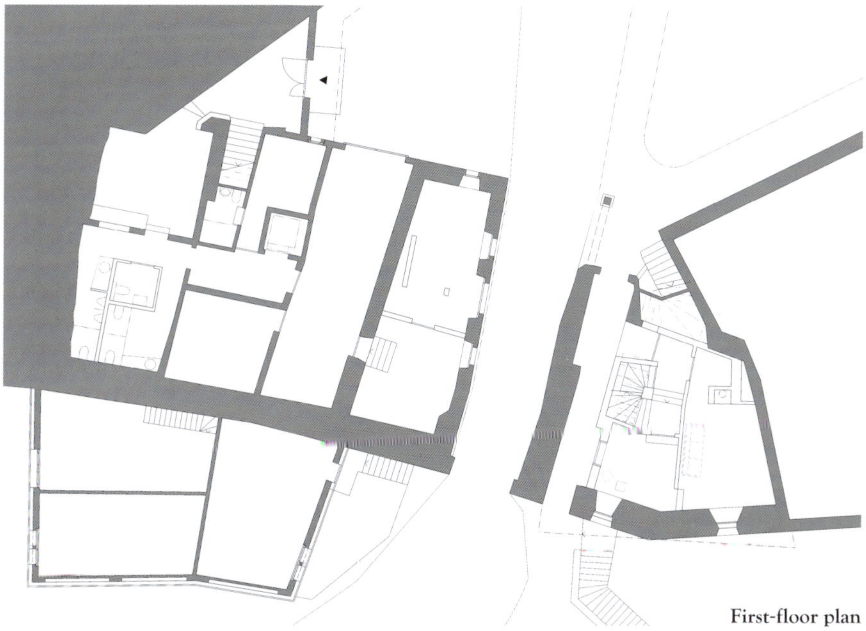

First-floor plan

CO-OP OULUN TERVAHOVIN SIILOT

The reconstruction of these former silos improves their structural stability to allow for a flexibility of use. A necessary extension contrasts in color and geometry to the cylindrical forms and highlights their iconic nature.

Transforming the mid-century cylindrical grain silos into a contemporary residential building has given new life to Toppilansalmi in Oulu, Finland. The nature of the project changed early on as most of the old landmark structures had to be dismantled due to their poor condition. As stipulated by the town plan, as much as possible of the original outer silo aesthetic was recreated. This reimagining allowed for a vast variety of layouts for the 95 apartments.

The round silo structures were utilized as balconies. The balcony openings are enhanced with metal trelliswork that maintains the round shape of the silos while providing sufficient privacy. The trelliswork blocks part of the direct sunlight yet is still sparse enough to let light pass and allow views through to the landscape.

A rectangular building expands the silo structure. The contemporary façade has reflective black and gray glass with colored jetties relating to the elements of the courtyard. The courtyard offers intriguing views inside the structure and its colorful fire escape and refined, contrasting materials create a memorable space. Here, the dialogue of the building masses representative of three different eras is in full display.

The first two floors consist of loft apartments with galleries, with 16-foot-high (5-meter-high) open living spaces. This allowed the top seven floor apartments to have a ceiling height of 10.5 feet (3.2 meters). Large full-height windows allow light into the apartments. The windows and glazed surfaces were designed in close cooperation with a manufacturer to

Architecture:
PAVE Architects
Location:
Oulu, Finland
Area:
82,882 square feet (7700 square meters)
Completion:
2014
Photography:
Arno de la Chapelle

create something new and unique, allowing for unobstructed views and practicality throughout.

The raw, in-situ-cast concrete surfaces are in keeping with the original industrial atmosphere of the area. The industrial design of the corridors, combined with contemporary solutions and materials, creates a unique, hotel-like feel. The possibility of purchasing an apartment in a semi-finished state gave owners greater freedom in defining the final layout, fixtures, and finishes of their new home.

Sections

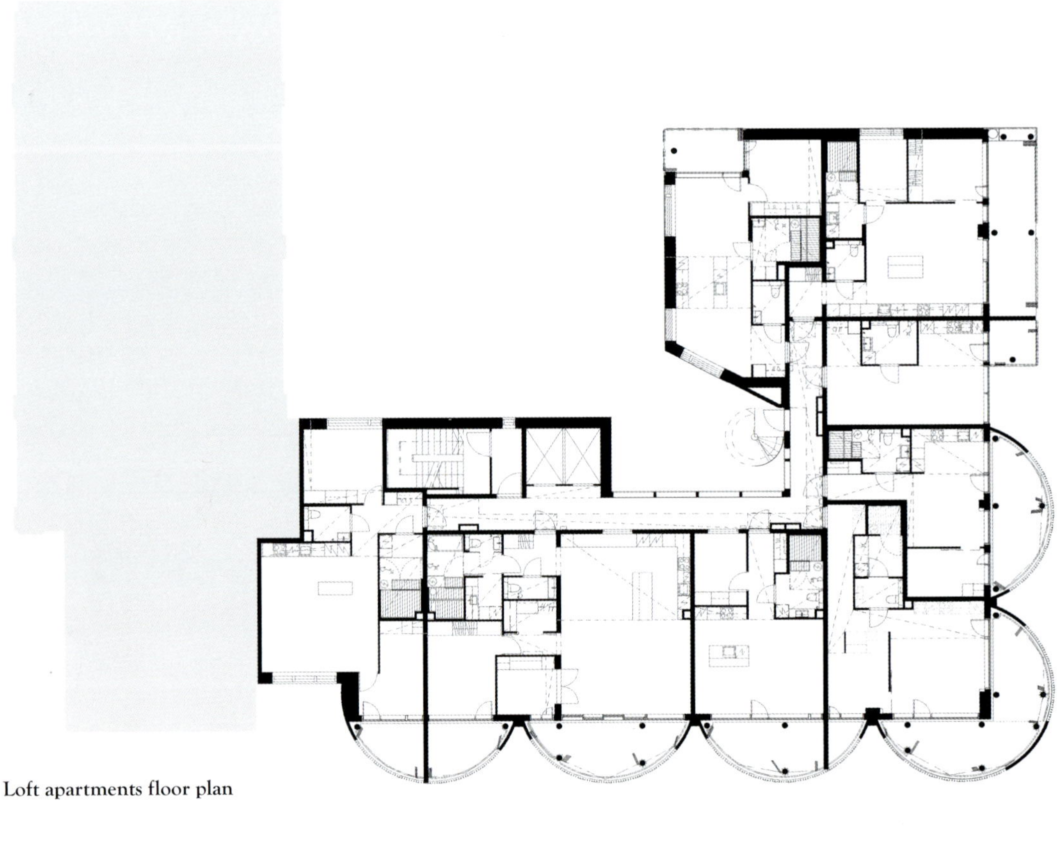

Loft apartments floor plan

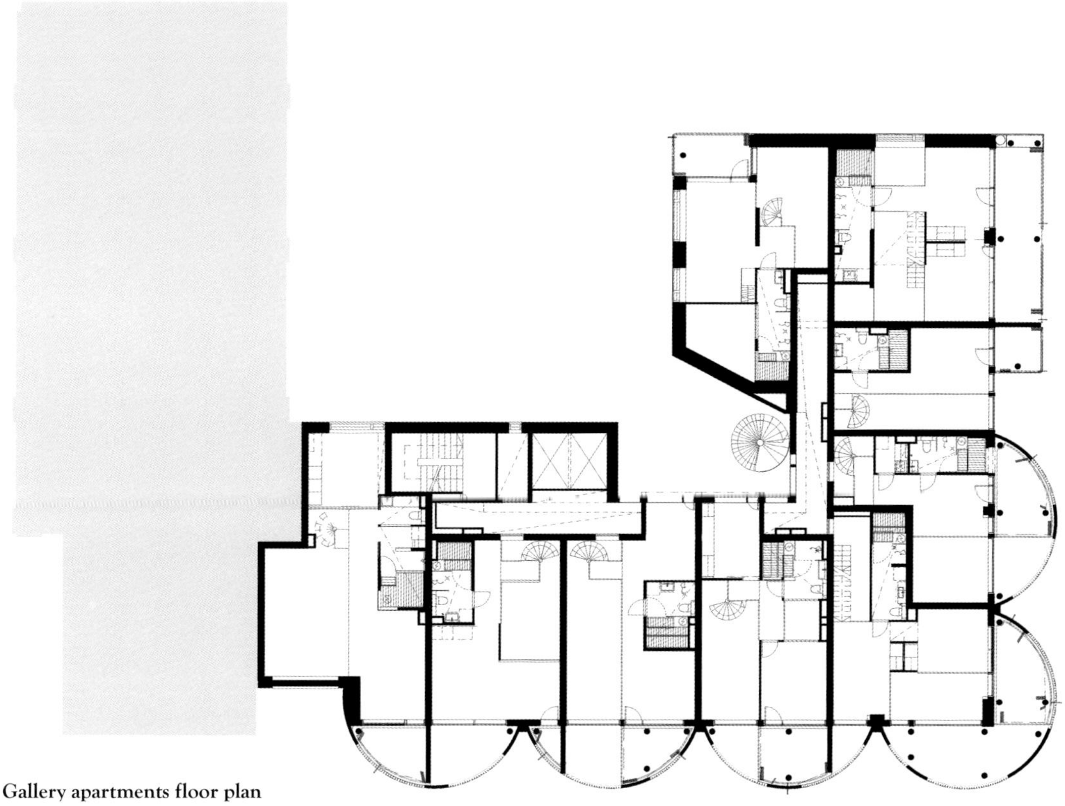

Gallery apartments floor plan

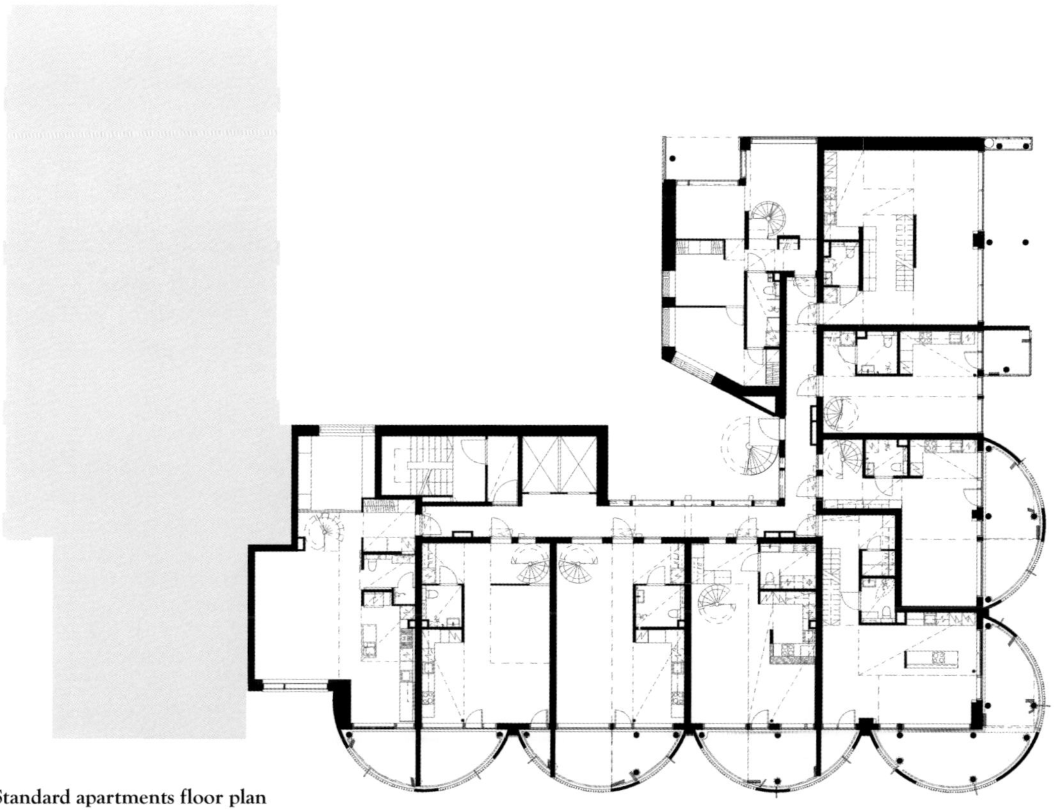

Standard apartments floor plan

OFFICE 3.0

The highly technological reconstruction of this building's interior presents itself to the public through a glass extension that visibly displays working life, which is climatically moderated through modern technology.

Architecture:
Carlo Ratti Associati
Location:
Turin, Italy
Area:
32,291 square feet (3000 square meters)
Completion:
2017
Photography:
Beppe Giardino

The renovation of the Agnelli Foundation's landmark twentieth-century building in Turin has transformed it into Office 3.0, an advanced, app-controlled environment that offers a glimpse of the workplace of the future. The new Agnelli Foundation headquarters, organized around a 32,291-square-foot (3000-square-meter) co-working space, pioneers a new technology for personalized heating and cooling—an "environmental bubble" that follows workers from room to room and allows for better thermal comfort and reduces energy waste.

Internet-of-Things sensors permeate the building and allow the monitoring of different sets of data, including occupancy levels, lighting, carbon dioxide concentration, and the status of meeting rooms. Based on this information, the building management system (BMS) responds dynamically, adjusting lighting, heating, and room booking in real-time. Real-time occupancy information also promotes human encounters: By seamlessly integrating digital technologies within the physical space, the design can forge better relationships between people and the building they inhabit, fostering interaction and creativity.

In addition to controlling heating, cooling, and lighting, the app also allows users to book spaces and facilities within the building, such as meeting rooms and shared desk space. Because the app knows its users' locations, workspaces can be suggested on the basis of both proximity and availability.

For the rest of the fit out, the architecture team opened up the office space into the city. A protruding glass volume floats over the shurbs and provides

space for a café. It lends an inclusive character to the building, serving as an inviting element for passersby. This theme continues inside the building, with new connections between spaces. An expansive skylight illuminates the staircase, which is dominated by a kaleidoscopic installation, *La Congiuntura del Tempo*, by Olafur Eliasson.

Section

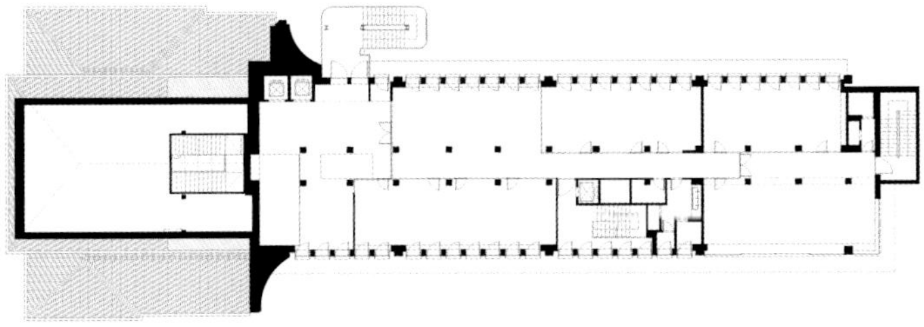

Fourth-floor plan

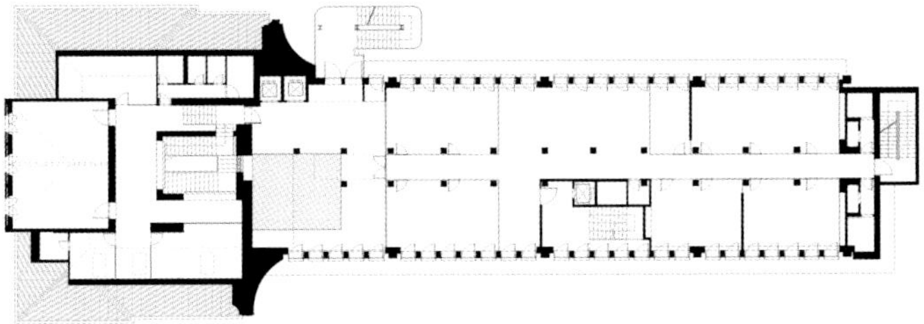

Third-floor plan

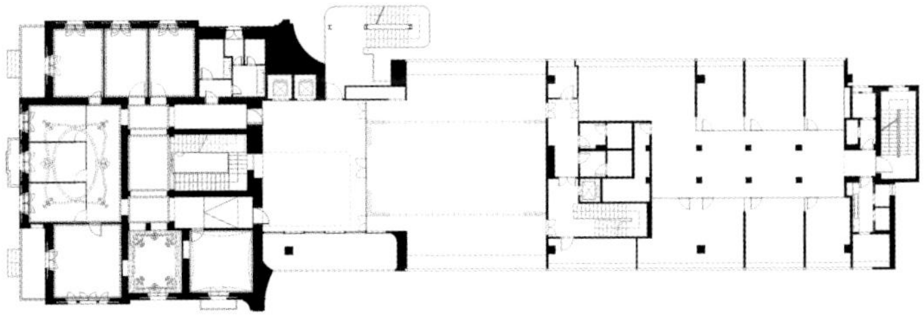

Second-floor plan

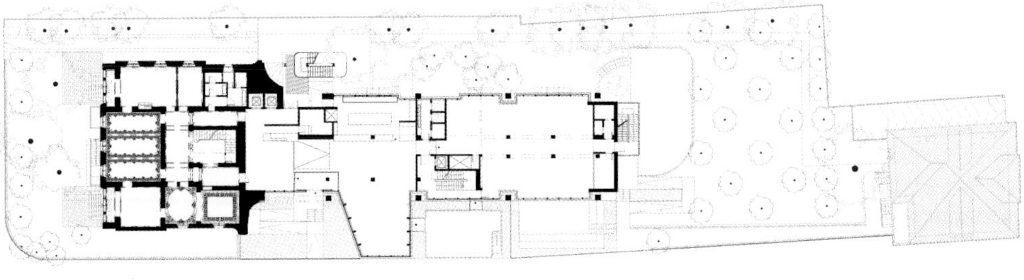

First-floor plan

DAXI TEA FACTORY

The experience of drinking tea is recontextualized in this factory in response to the continually evolving practice of appreciating tea. The building's factory aesthetic is combined with traditional references to create a modern blend of industry and tranquility.

Daxi Tea Factory is nestled on a mountain near Tzuhu, Taiwan. The brick structure with cypress-wood roof trusses was built in 1926, during the Japanese occupation when a large amount of tea was exported. A fire in 1956 almost completely destroyed the factory, and it was rebuilt following a decree from Chiang Kai-shek, leader of the Republic of China.

Tea trade declined as the international economy moved through peaks and troughs. Because of this, the factory was abandoned for a period of time until it was revived in 2010. The renovated space includes a tea-making room, restaurant, retail store, tea library, and multimedia room, and it has been transformed into a conceptual complex that combines the ideas of natural farming with tourism opportunities.

The differentiation between the old and new structure allowed for the merging of old and new thinking. The architecture team was also faced with a series of challenges and opportunities, such as the trees and vines. They cling to the wall and destroy the waterproofing fabric, but create a sense of wilderness that nourishes the soul, and they help to slowly but deliberately activate the space.

The factory space possesses a large number of agricultural products and highly practical tea-making facilities. The retail store collects a large number of works from Asian craftspeople and artists as well as works about tea art, such as paintings, plant-fiber products, recycled ironwork, and furniture from Java, creating an exhibition space in its own right.

Architecture:
Divooe Zein Architects
Location:
Taiwan, China
Area:
129,166 sqaure feet (12,000 square meters)
Completion:
2013
Photography:
Jetso Yu

The building focuses on functionality and achieves the combination of tradition and modernity. The factory space is designed for a modern and robust way of drinking tea, while still allowing this substance to settle the soul, and to provide comfort and pleasure.

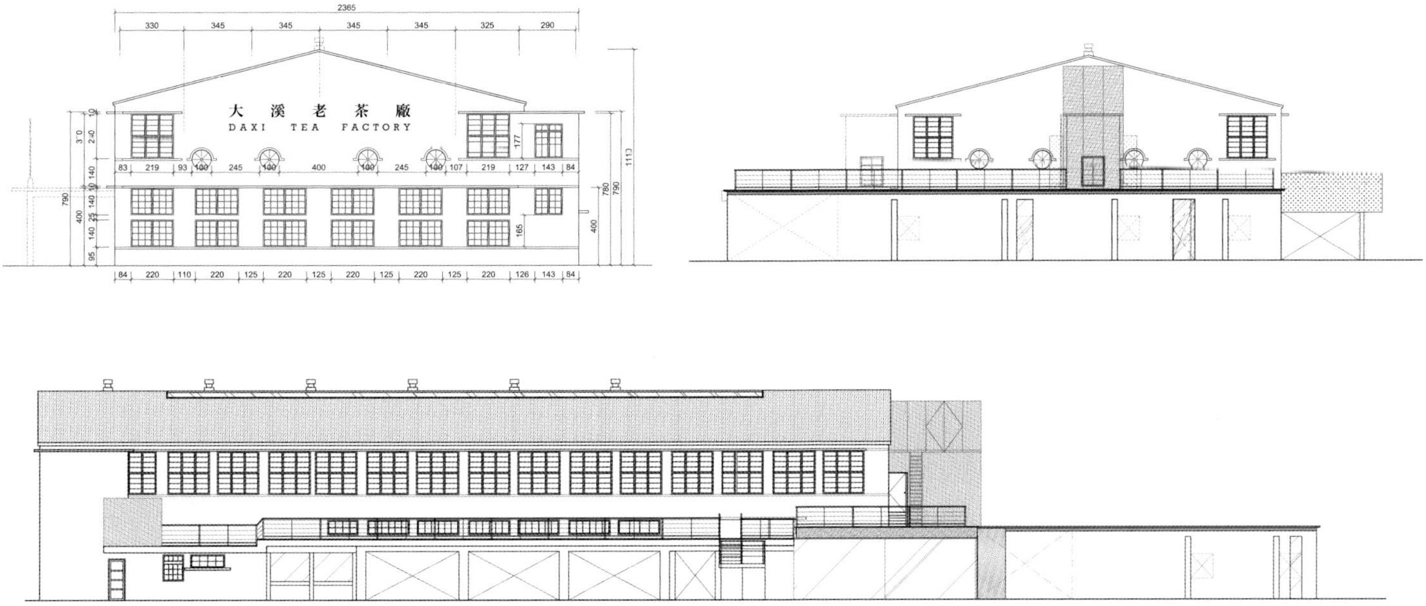

Elevations

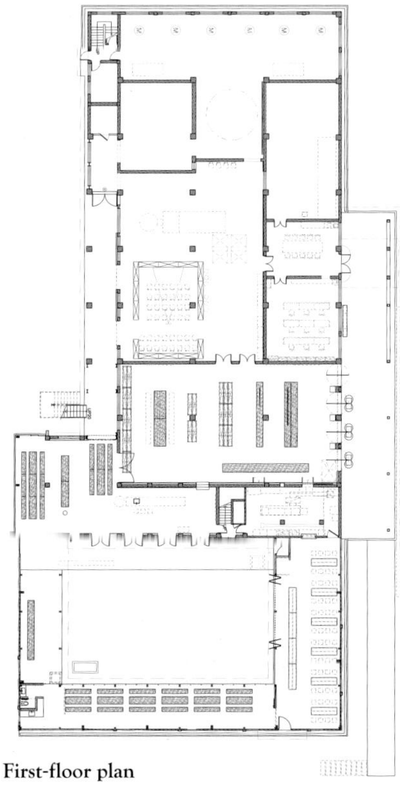

First-floor plan

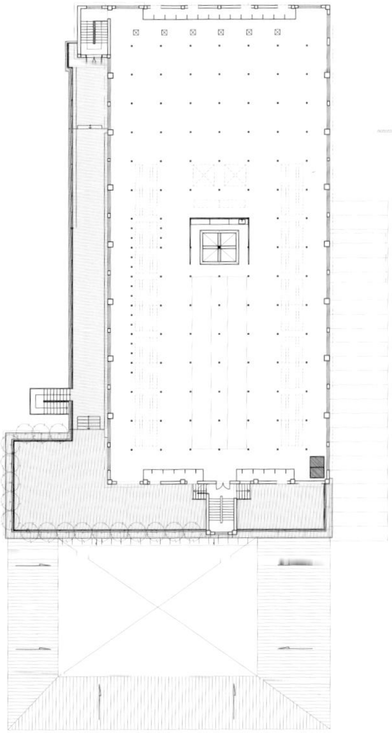

Second-floor plan

ROCK CREEK HOUSE

A new staircase provides a fluid connection to all four levels of this family home in which the basement and attic have been transformed into living space and bedrooms. Double-height volumes and large new openings create a link to natural light and the surrounding landscape.

Rock Creek House is the adaptive reuse of a 1920 brick structure. It was originally composed of two floors, plus an attic and mechanical basement, which is at the garden level. The renovation and adaptation leveraged the connection with the landscape and the robustness of the existing structure, modifying the attic and basement to double the size of the house for a family of five and two or three staff members.

The most salient spatial intervention was the introduction of a new staircase at the center of the house, as well as two multi-height spaces. One double-height space at the entry connects the garden with a new living room that extends to the south. The second connects the north-facing entry to the former attic, which is now a research and play loft for the kids, and is capped with a skylight. These two interventions interconnect and seamlessly intertwine the once stratified storage, bedrooms, work areas, and living areas.

The north-facing façade to the street remains relatively intact, while the south-facing façade is more generously exposed and extended into the garden. By expanding the glazing on the south, and establishing a more precise relationship between rooms and their apertures, a new architectural order is established on the south that is more informal, open, and in dialogue with nature. This very simple strategy had one of the most radical impacts on the structure of the building. Expanding the square footage of glass on the southern face altered the load-bearing function of the brick wall to become a curtain wall, with a steel structure providing both compressive and lateral stability.

Architecture:
NADAAA
Location:
Washington, D.C., United States
Area:
10,193 square feet (947 square meters)
Completion:
2016
Photography:
John Horner

Economical in its spatial organization, the project leverages the existing composition of the house to maximize its architectural and programmatic impact without the need for demolition or an entire new construction. Perimeter walls and two internal north-south walls are brick load-bearing walls, and the southern wall is reinforced steel with brick infill. All framing is with wood—existing and new—and plaster and millwork interiors have a lighter character.

New mechanical systems have been placed as split systems so that different spaces can be activated separately as required. Radiant heat within the subfloor warms the house, and new well-insulated windows provide a solid weather barrier while encouraging cross ventilation.

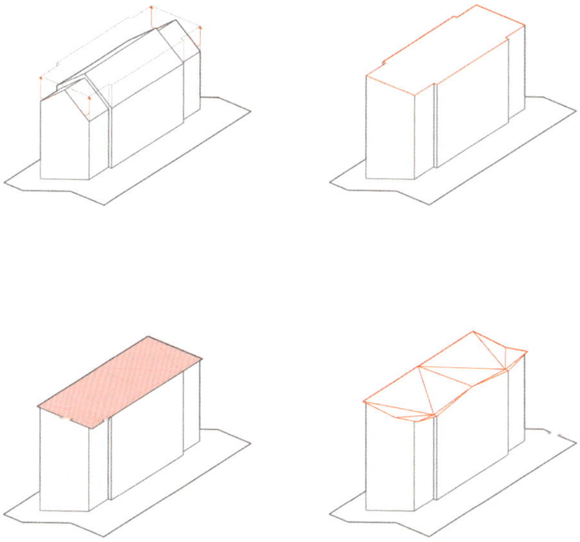

Diagrams of roof

Axonometric drawing

Cross-section through spiral stair

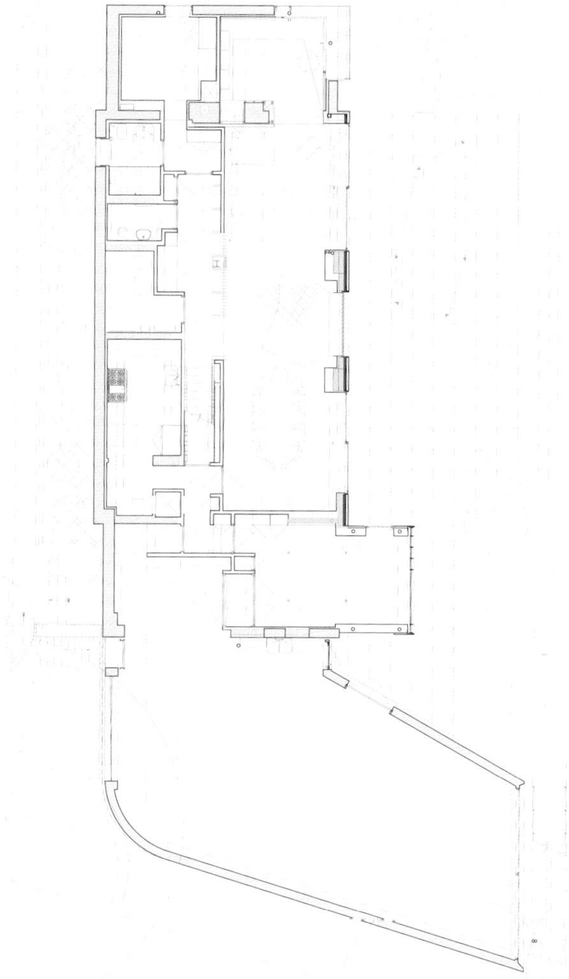

First-floor plan

Exterior wall section

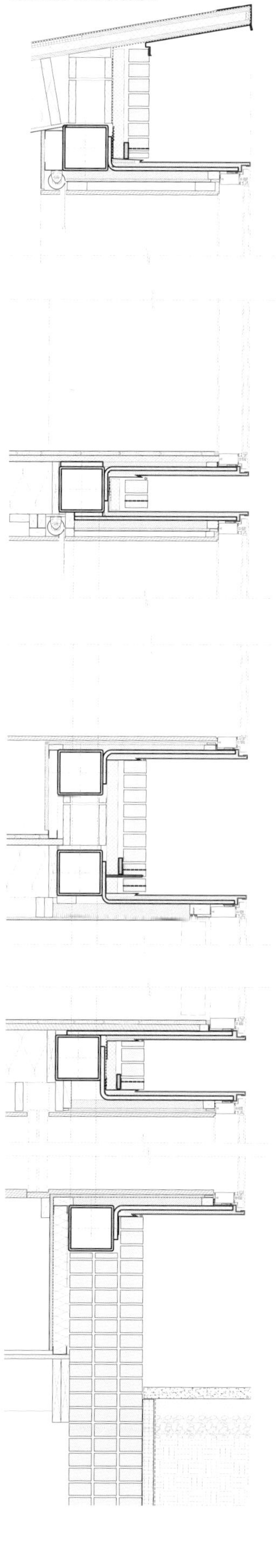

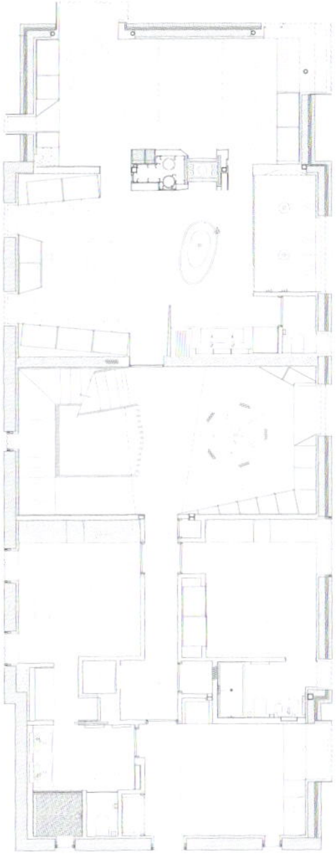

Third-floor plan

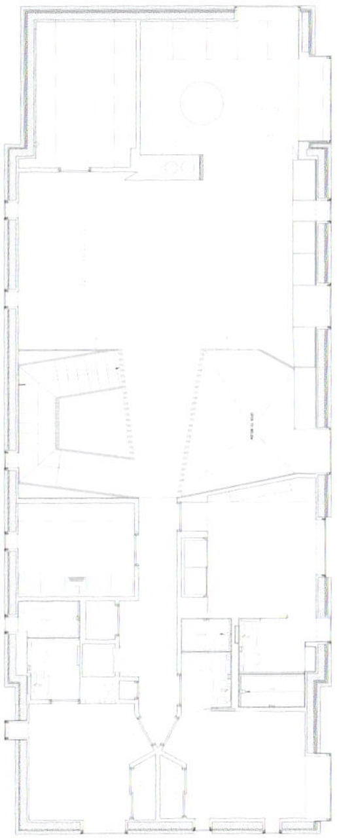

Fourth-floor plan

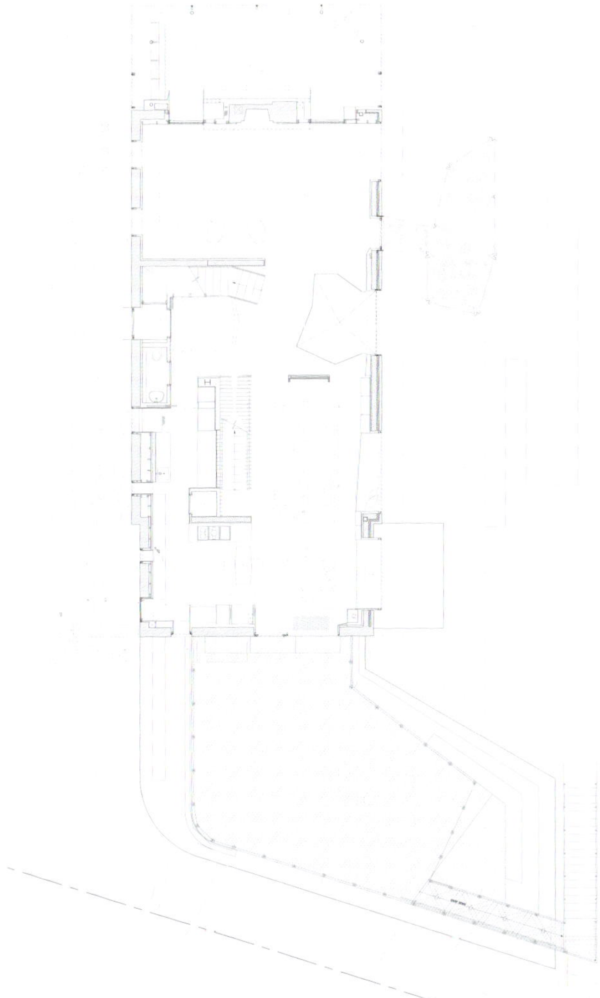

Second-floor plan

EPILOGUE

Heritage and development are often regarded in a dualistic fashion as being mutually exclusive. This tension between old and new can sometimes result in a conservationist approach that does not sufficiently allow for growth, urbanization, and densification. Or it can cause a condition where the past is completely overwritten in the name of progress. This diverse collection of projects of different scales highlights the possibilities of a hybrid approach that can simultaneously preserve valued aspects of the past while allowing for imaginative transformation and adaptation for the future.

Evident in all of these case studies is that both the old and the new are valued. The old can be valued because of its tangible nature in terms of its form, age, aesthetic, craftsmanship, or contribution to an urban setting. It may have high economic value or embodied energy. It can also be valued because of its intangible qualities related to its social meaning, cultural importance, or because it was designed by a famous practitioner. A specific value often provides a generative impulse for imaginative adaptation or transformation, which in turn can ensure the continued existence of the old. This unlocking of latent potential is inherently an important aspect of the new, but the new can be valued for its contemporary aesthetic appeal, usefulness, innovation, or iconic nature. In the same way that the existing condition can be a catalyst for adaptation or transformation, the reimagined building can be a catalyst for its surrounding context.

The determination of value and latent potential emerges out of a rigorous and engaged reading of an existing building and its physical, economic, and social context. The old has to be thoroughly understood and documented before a new intervention can be inserted or attached in order to create a meaningful dialogue with the old. In many cases, the old has been adapted a number of times prior to the latest intervention and sometimes all of these intermediate layers are valued sufficiently to be incorporated into the latest adaptation. In other cases, the intermediate layers are removed or overwritten to create a two-sided engagement between the original layer and the latest intervention. The dialogue between old and new can be conversational or it can be confrontational. It can be respectful or it can punctuate difference through opposition. Regardless of the nature of the engagement, in these collected case studies neither the old nor the new is subservient to the other, and this equally-weighted layering of past and present gives these projects a temporal depth that is difficult, if not impossible, to achieve with newly built works.

While the identified strategies are a way of categorizing the case studies, they also offer a way of understanding the different methods of building transformation and adaptive reuse. Approaches are seldom singular in nature and projects often incorporate a range of strategies, but there is usually one primary driver for the new intervention. Being explicit about what this primary design driver is can enable one to have a more focused approach to the new intervention, which in turn will allow for a clearer reading of a transformed or adapted building.

The cases presented are testimony to the opportunities offered by existing buildings. On the one hand, architects have a duty towards old buildings as heritage, whether their value lies in material fabric or memories and associations. On the other hand, there is the responsibility of acknowledging the embodied energy in buildings already built and the importance of limiting, if not mitigating, the carbon footprint of development. However, working with the old offers a more exciting opportunity for architects, which is to imagine a new life overlaid onto an existing one, in a palimpsest of meaningful dialogues, to produce exceptional design.

Working with existing buildings can be challenging and it can often be more difficult than designing something entirely new. The architect has to engage directly with the work of another architect, which requires an imaginative design-based approach that can generate a conversation between the existing building and the new intervention: a dialogue between old and new.

Michael Louw and Stella Papanicolaou

INDEX

Gus Wüstemann Architects P128

www.guswustemann.com
architects@guswustemann.com

Heatherwick Studio P136

www.heatherwick.com
communications@heatherwick.com

KAAN Architecten P186

www.kaanarchitecten.com
press@mintlist.info

Klaarchitectuur P48

www.klaarchitectuur.be
info@klaarchitectuur.be

L3P Architekten P228

www.l3p.ch
info@l3p.ch

Martínez Lapeña – Torres Arquitectos P58

www.jamlet.net
jamlet@coac.net

Mei architects and planners P98

www.mei-arch.eu
PR@mei-arch.eu

NADAAA P272

www.nadaaa.com
nada@nadaaa.com

Piuarch P180

www.piuarch.it
STUDIO@PIUARCH.IT

PAVE Architects P250

www.pavearkkitehdit.fi
office@pavearkkitehdit.fi

PRESENT Architecture P68

www.presentarchitecture.com
info@presentarchitecture.com

Tiago do Vale Architects P90

www.tiagodovale.com
info@tiagodovale.com

Váncza Művek Studio P82

www.vanczamuvek.hu
vm@vanczamuvek.hu

Wingårdh Arkitektkontor P166

www.wingardhs.se
wingardh@wingardhs.se

Zaha Hadid Architects P206

www.zaha-hadid.com
mail@zaha-hadid.com

Published in Australia in 2019 by
The Images Publishing Group Pty Ltd
ABN 89 059 734 431

Offices
Australia
6 Bastow Place
Mulgrave, Victoria 3170
Australia
Tel: +61 3 9561 5544

United States
6 West 18th Street 4B
New York, NY 10011
United States
Tel: +1 212 645 1111

Shanghai
6F, Building C, 838 Guangji Road
Hongkou District, Shanghai 200434
China
Tel: +86 021 31260822

books@imagespublishing.com
www.imagespublishing.com

Copyright © The Images Publishing Group Pty Ltd 2019
The Images Publishing Group Reference Number: 1524

All rights reserved. Apart from any fair dealing for the purposes of private study, research, criticism or review as permitted under the Copyright Act, no part of this publication may be reproduced, stored in a retrieval system or transmitted in any form by any means, electronic, mechanical, photocopying, recording or otherwise, without the written permission of the publisher.

NATIONAL LIBRARY OF AUSTRALIA

A catalogue record for this book is available from the National Library of Australia

Title: Buildings Reimagined: A Dialogue Between Old and New
Author: Michael Louw and Stella Papanicolaou (Introductory texts)
ISBN: 9781864708257

Printed by Everbest Printing Investment Limited, in Hong Kong/China

IMAGES has included on its website a page for special notices in relation to this and its other publications. Please visit www.imagespublishing.com

Every effort has been made to trace the original source of copyright material contained in this book. The publishers would be pleased to hear from copyright holders to rectify any errors or omissions.
The information and illustrations in this publication have been prepared and supplied by Michael Low, Stella Papanicolaou, and the contributors. While all reasonable efforts have been made to ensure accuracy, the publishers do not, under any circumstances, accept responsibility for errors, omissions and representations, express or implied.